SCRATCH

Writers, Money, and the Art of Making a Living

EDITED BY

MANJULA MARTIN

SIMON & SCHUSTER PAPERBACKS

New York   London   Toronto   Sydney   New Delhi

Simon & Schuster Paperbacks
An Imprint of Simon & Schuster, Inc.
1230 Avenue of the Americas
New York, NY 10020

First Simon & Schuster trade paperback edition January 2017

SIMON & SCHUSTER PAPERBACKS and colophon are registered
trademarks of Simon & Schuster, Inc.

For information about special discounts for bulk purchases,
please contact Simon & Schuster Special Sales at 1-866-506-1949 or
business@simonandschuster.com.

The Simon & Schuster Speakers Bureau can bring authors to your
live event. For more information or to book an event, contact the
Simon & Schuster Speakers Bureau at 1-866-248-3049 or
visit our website at www.simonspeakers.com.

Interior design by Ellen Sasahara

Manufactured in the United States of America

1 3 5 7 9 10 8 6 4 2

Library of Congress Cataloging-in-Publication Data
Names: Martin, Manjula, editor.
Title: Scratch : writers, money, and the art of making a living / edited by
Manjula Martin.
Other titles: Writers, money, and the art of making a living
Description: New York : Simon & Schuster, 2017.
Identifiers: LCCN 2016024580 | ISBN 9781501134579 (paperback)
Subjects: LCSH: Authorship. | Authors and publishers. |
Authorship—Marketing. | Authorship—Vocational guidance. |
Arts—Economic
aspects. | Authors, American—21st century—Biography—Anecdotes. |
Work—Psychological aspects. | Self-realization. | BISAC: LITERARY
COLLECTIONS / Essays. | LANGUAGE ARTS & DISCIPLINES /
Publishing. |
BIOGRAPHY & AUTOBIOGRAPHY / Literary.
Classification: LCC PN101.S33 2017 | DDC 808.02023—dc23 LC record
available at https://lccn.loc.gov/2016024580

ISBN 978-1-5011-3457-9
ISBN 978-1-5011-3459-3 (ebook)

Copyright credits continued on pages 279–286.

Dedicated to our teachers, librarians, and booksellers, with gratitude for your labor and love

CONTENTS

Contents

THE DAILY GRIND

SOMEDAY

INTRODUCTION

Manjula Martin

scratch

/skraCH/

verb
1. To scrape the surface of something.
2. To assemble a desired result through hard work and perseverance.
"scratch out a living"
3. To make something out of whatever is at hand.
"made from scratch"
"a scratch crew"

noun
Writing that is extemporaneous or hurried, usually by hand.
"she wrote so passionately that it was difficult to read the resulting chicken scratch"

informal
Slang for "money."

True or false: Writers should be paid for everything they write. Writers should just pay their dues and count themselves lucky to be published. You should never quit your day job. You'll know you're successful when you can quit your day job. Writing is an art, not a business. Writers should be entrepreneurs. Digital technology has destroyed the market for writing. The Internet will set us all free.

Sound familiar?

Introduction

In every stage of their careers, working writers are in a constant state of negotiation: work and life, art and commerce, writing and publishing. In the public eye and within our communities, authors are said to practice a calling, an art form, a passion—but rarely a job. We are often told by more successful writers to "do it for the love," but we are rarely told how to turn love into a living.

That's where this book comes in.

Scratch magazine was initially developed out of a need for greater transparency in the discussion about work and money within the community of writers. This book deepens that discussion. The interviews and essays that make up this edition come from some of today's most prominent and promising voices, offering candid and informative stories about their experiences at different stages in their careers. In newspapers and on social media, through blogs and informal networks, writers are just now starting to break the silence about what it's really like to be *working* writers. *New York Times* cultural critic A. O. Scott writes, "Nobody would argue against the idea that art has a social value, and yet almost nobody will assert that society therefore has an obligation to protect that value by acknowledging, and compensating, the labor of the people who produce it." In *Salon*, an author's confession that she is "sponsored" by her husband unleashed a torrent of think pieces. On Medium, online lightning rod Emily Gould published a frequently shared essay describing how she spent most of a $200,000 advance (spoiler alert: unwisely). And in the *New Yorker*—which itself is perhaps the reigning symbol of opacity in publishing—Junot Díaz wrote a scathing takedown of racism in MFA programs and barriers to inclusive access in the publishing business. In my own experience as the founder of *Scratch* and *Who Pays Writers?*, a crowdsourced database of freelance writing rates, I've heard time and again from writers who are yearning for any scrap of information they can find about how their own profession functions economically. These heated discussions speak to a need for more openness about how, exactly, literature and the people who make it are valued.

There are stories of artistic and economic struggle in this collection, sure, but more so these are stories of inspiration, empathy, and perseverance. And a few are even pretty damn funny. Taken as a whole, this book is by and for writers who are building careers that deftly encompass all we are: a little bit artist, a little bit hawker, and a whole lot of love. We don't deny that the dream—the drive and ambition and imagination that make a person decide to do a ridiculous thing like be a writer—is important. The love is real. But so is real life. We all need to make a living, whether we "make it" or not.

If I've learned one thing while working with these amazing authors on this difficult topic, it's that the art of making a living is always evolving; the economics of literature are diverse. Some writers choose to freelance—journalism, copywriting, editing. Some teach and fit in their creative work around their class schedules. Some do a combination of both. Many writers have means of income that have nothing to do with the publishing world—paramedic, law clerk, carpenter. What the authors in *Scratch* have in common is that they are creative professionals navigating and expanding the relationship between art and commerce every day.

Within this spectrum of authors are those who haven't always taken the usual paths to a writing career. It's particularly easy for people with economic and social privileges to say, "Do what you love and the money will follow." But it's not always so simple for the rest—the people without prestigious degrees or parents standing ready to help with a loan. *Scratch*'s vision of a thriving literary community includes authors writing from the margins, people who may have additional obstacles to crafting careers that enable their artistic work but also pay the rent.

When preparing this book for publication, I was often asked

by potential writers and readers alike, "So, which side are you on: commerce or literature?" But to be honest, if this is a contest, I don't much care who wins; I'm more interested in how we all got here, and where we'll go next. Literature and commerce will always be (and have always been) somewhat at odds with each other, uneasy bedfellows—an odd couple. For authors, the path to success is not always one of hardship. Nor is it always a direct route.

The authors in *Scratch* are looking beyond binaries to seek greater truths about writing, work, money, and publishing. In the business and art of literature there are no rules, no surefire steps to success, no amount of "tips" or lists that can guarantee you will increase your income or readership. Ultimately, for each and every writer, the answer to the question "how do you sell a thing like love?" has to be found within their own practice, within the context of their life and work, their resources and desires.

What if each writer could learn to navigate the balance between art and commerce for themselves, making choices according to their means and temperament and finding the best way to put their work—their own, specific, beautiful work—into the marketplace? What if, instead of parachuting into whatever flame war about publishing and pay is happening at the moment and then forgetting we were ever there, those who make literature and those who buy and fund literature sat down and listened to each other's stories?

I realize that "it's complicated" may not be what you wanted to hear when you picked up a book about how writers make a living. I realize it's hard when we're all thirsty for answers. But, as you'll see in the more than two dozen perspectives represented here, there really are no easy answers. There is experience and example and wisdom and luck, and it's up to each writer to put them all together into something shaped like a career, to develop a balance between art and commerce that leaves them nurtured enough to keep writing. Besides, we wouldn't be true to our profession if we went for the quick fix, would we? Show me a writer who goes for easy answers and I'll show you a person who is uncurious, uninteresting, too thirsty to make it to the next shimmering oasis. The authors in the following pages are right there in the weeds along with readers, navigating the complex relationships among art, life, and work at different stages in their careers—and revealing the heart of American literature in the process.

Care to join us?

EARLY DAYS

OWNING THIS

Julia Fierro

M y family moved when I was in fourth grade, into a ramshackle home on a desirable woodsy island off Long Island Sound. The location and school district seemed a steal despite the house's decrepitude—moldy ceilings, termite-infested walls, and a well that pumped metallic-tasting water—and my father, a Southern Italian immigrant born into poverty and pestilence, also a survivor of WWII, performed miracles with jars of spackle and the discontinued paint he'd bought half off at some faraway hardware store he frequented for its sales. We loved our new home, and delighted in calling it "our mansion," despite the way it seemed to sag under its sad history. *Abandoned by the previous owners*, the pert Realtor explained, *a family with three sons*. She had sped through the summary—*teenage boys turned delinquent, drugs and alcohol, a messy divorce*, etc., etc. Years later, we'd hear the full story. The mother of the wild boys had tried to kill herself, twice. First, by stabbing herself in the kitchen where we'd sing "Happy Birthday" and hold Christmas family dinners. Second, and this time successfully, by jumping out the window in the room that would become my bedroom.

What mattered most to me as a child growing up in that house wasn't the story of that lost family but what they left behind. Books. Shelves upon shelves of books that covered two walls in the musty, cavernous basement. Some hardcovers, but mostly dog-eared paperbacks and pocket-sized mass-market editions, almost all novels. From *Madame Bovary* to *The Clan of the Cave Bear* to *The Rise and Fall of the Third Reich*. My parents did not care about the books (or, I suspect, consider their genre, their quality, or their suitability for a young reader like myself). Through their immigrant and working class–bred eyes, books were books—to be admired, collected, and displayed in the hope that their sophisticated light would reflect back on you. I imagine this practice of imbuing objects with transformative power is common in people with immigrant and blue-collar roots. Isn't it a pillar of the American Dream? Money, spent in the right way, can allow you to reinvent your identity. Rewrite your story—past, present, and future drafts.

It wasn't as if I'd never had books. My father, for whom reading in English is still a challenge but whose yearning to learn never stopped him from trying, drove me to the public library every Saturday morning. But the books in the basement were my own—I could read them while eating, take them on hikes in the woods, even flip through their pages while soaking in the bathtub. I could do with them as I pleased. They made me giddy with power.

Today, I own approximately three thousand books. I have gone into debt buying books and made poor financial choices, again and again, for the love of books—buying a stack of glossy-covered novels instead of paying off bills, binge-ordering a dozen buzzed-about novels online instead of putting money aside for my children's college fund. When my annual credit card report arrives each year, and when I prepare my annual taxes, I wince at the hefty number under Books, and wonder, naively, if there was a computing mistake. Why can't I borrow those books from the library? Why must I own them?

§

I arrived at the Iowa Writers' Workshop a few weeks before my twenty-third birthday, my car towing a U-Haul filled mostly with books that my then boyfriend, whom I would marry shortly after graduation, had helped me pack and carry. I had focused on Early American and Russian literature as an undergraduate, and I thought of those books' authors as my family, a mostly white, dead, and bearded male family (except for matriarch Edith Wharton). Like most families, it wasn't one I'd chosen myself. These were the books I'd been assigned in high school and college, almost all part of the established literary canon.

I knew little about contemporary authors; the few collections of short stories I'd read left me feeling hollow and longing for the grand ideas and hyperbolic emotions of Dostoyevsky and Hawthorne. It wasn't until my first graduate program party in Iowa City, where I spent the night talking to a group of poets (i.e., the most well-read people on the planet) that I realized I was in over my head. They chattered endlessly about authors I'd never heard of—David Foster Wallace, Tobias Wolff, Lorrie Moore, and countless other living writers. If the *poets* had read these fiction writers, then, surely, I should have.

The next morning, I cashed my loan check and rushed to the famous Iowa City bookstore, Prairie Lights. I hurried back home, as fast as I could, carrying heavy bags full of contemporary short story collections. What if another student in the writing program saw me? They'd know I was a fraud. I returned to that bookstore, and every other bookstore in town. Soon my apartment's bookshelves overflowed with new and used books. I hoped they would help make me look, and sound, like a legitimate writer.

I made friends with another MFA student who, like me, had grown up in a working-class family composed of nonreaders. Compared to the rest of the students in our program, it seemed as if my friend and I had, at birth, by some miracle of chance, been tapped on the head by a magical book fairy—a blessing and a curse, for it made us so unlike those we grew up among. In my friend's apartment, autographed first edition hardcovers sat gleaming in plastic wrap behind glass-enclosed bookshelves. We sat on his threadbare sofa and he showed me his books. I held them as delicately as if they were newborns.

I, too, began to collect first edition hardcovers with the hope that one of those revered contemporary authors would visit our program, which they often did, and I could have them sign the spotless title page, wrap the book in plastic, and place it on the highest bookshelf for safekeeping. First edition hardcovers are hard to come by, and I began searching for and buying books online through collectors. My loan money moved from my bank account to my bookshelf, and not once did I stop myself, look around my apartment at the stacks of unread books—several lifetimes' worth— and think of Jay Gatsby and his library of pristine uncut books. My fear was too loud. Fear that I was inauthentic, undeserving of a place among my mostly Ivy League–educated classmates who, it seemed, were more well-read than even the gray-haired authors who were our professors. My books were a barricade I built between that fear and myself.

§

After I graduated, my soon-to-be-husband once again packed and carried boxes of my books—ten times what we'd arrived with only two years earlier—and we drove a U-Haul from Iowa City to New York City. We performed what had by then become our ritual— carrying my thousands of books up five flights of stairs, followed by my obsessive organizing of the bookshelves according to genre. It was the fall of 2002 and our future felt invincibly bright—I had signed with a literary agent at a big agency, who was certain my first novel would be a hit, and photocopies of said novel were landing on the desks of editors throughout the city. I was interviewing for teaching positions at universities, and my husband had a lead on several jobs. The dreamy writer's life I had envisioned in graduate school, crafted by borrowing my more experienced classmates' lofty expectations as well as my tuition funds, seemed inevitable.

Six months later, my novel had been rejected by what seemed like every editor in New York City, I was being paid less than ten thousand dollars a year as an adjunct professor, and my husband had secured, and lost, several jobs. We stopped paying our bills so we could scrape rent together each month. I rarely left the apartment except to teach, avoided literary events, and, for the first time, stopped visiting bookstores. I wasn't writing. The slow and continuous rejection of my novel had destroyed the borrowed confidence I'd had at Iowa. What shocked me most was that I couldn't read. My treasured books were now a reminder that I had failed. They sat undisturbed on my shelves, dusty reminders that, perhaps, after all, I shouldn't have tried to rise above my station.

I am still amazed that I found the confidence to post an ad on Craigslist—"Iowa grad teaching fiction workshop in Brooklyn"— and I know that it was the need to talk about books, about how they thrill and comfort and save us, that lifted me from my pathetic self-pity and allowed me to hold the very first writing class, in my dimly lit Brooklyn kitchen, that would grow into the Sackett Street Writers' Workshop, today home to over three thousand writers. With each class of motivated and enthusiastic students, many so talented and hardworking I considered them my peers, my faith in myself, and others, regrew—this time as sturdy and deep as the roots of a tree.

I began to sell my collection of books, one at a time, and I started with those I treasured most—the first editions signed by my favorite novelists. I sold them online and made back only a quarter of what I'd spent buying them but, slowly, we paid off our debts.

As the shelves grew bare, my kitchen filled night after night with living, breathing writers, and it was through these writers—mostly unpublished and unpolished, but all mad for books—that I found the courage to return to writing.

I continue to buy books and I've replaced some of those favorites I sold years ago. I continue to feel little guilt for the thousands of dollars I spend on books each year. I have my excuses—I'm supporting writers, many friends and colleagues. I'm supporting publishing, independent bookstores, literature with a capital *L*. But really I buy too many books because books were, and always will be, my redemption.

WITH COMPLIMENTS

Nina MacLaughlin

T he mornings, at first, were long and leisurely. Soft boiled eggs on buttered toast, coffee, unrushed, relaxed chatter; the small orange kitchen felt especially warm as winter wrapped itself around Cambridge. It was the start of a welcome annual shift. As the year moved into winter, the carpentry work I do, and had been doing for three years at that point, slowed, as it always did in the lead-up to Thanksgiving, and I shifted into writing mode. Instead of waking up and racing off to build bookshelves or slam hickory floorboards with a mallet or hang cabinets or frame a deck or swear over installing crown molding, I eased into the days and worked on freelance projects, book reviews, profiles. I liked the rhythm of the year: the cold months at my computer, mid-November through mid-January, the rest spent building, the balance of bodywork and brainwork, the approach and retreat from putting words together.

Except this winter, the carpentry work didn't pick back up. January ended and no calls had come from my boss, an unflappable carpenter whom I'd been learning from since quitting my journalism job in 2008. I left messages: *What's the word?*, *What's cooking?*, *When's the next project start?* She did not call back. Fine at first; I savored the short days, content to read and write and walk in the snow. January dissolved into February and the days began to feel a little emptier. I'd quit my newspaper job because I was soul-weary of sitting in front of a computer; carpentry proved an ideal antidote. But not if there were no jobs. From the darker, more nervous pockets of my brain came whispers as the snow kept coming and work did not pick up: *You made a mistake.* Fears accumulated, the question pressed: *What now?* I'd made this leap, started a new career, and the thought of having to start fresh again—it was daunting, exhausting, too much.

Mid-February, March, the days were getting longer, I was dipping into my savings, waiting for a call that wouldn't come. Things weren't working out. I wasn't making enough to pay the rent. With nothing but time, tasks that should've taken a couple of hours I allowed to occupy days.

Time pressed and question marks hovered like hummingbirds gone desperate and mean. *Failure,* my brain told me. *Failure.*

During these months I wrote a book review for Jessa Crispin at *Bookslut.* I wrote about Philip Connors's book *Fire Season,* a wise and beautiful memoir about how he left his job at the *Wall Street Journal* in the aftermath of the September 11 warmongering to work as a fire lookout in New Mexico. I admire Connors's writing, loved the book, and was pleased to be able to bring a little bit of attention to it. *Bookslut* was likewise a site I admired, and Crispin a writer and editor who it always felt an honor and treat to write for.

I wrote the review for free.

And did I feel guilty for it? For the hours spent reading the book, the time spent reading Connors's essays printed elsewhere, the hours spent writing the review? Knowing my time and efforts would not be compensated, knowing I needed money actively and urgently? Did I feel angry about it? I did not. I justified it easily: it was purpose, focus, work. It meant fewer of my hours would be occupied by staring dead-eyed into the dark maw of the Internet. It was keeping my writing muscles flexed. Writing for free looked like work. It felt like work. But it was the illusion of work, a fun house mirror reflection. One crucial aspect was missing. Still, maybe the illusion was enough.

Some days later, in came an e-mail from Connors's editor at Ecco Press, praising the review. I've written a lot of book reviews; this had never happened. I was delighted. I needed the boost, a little gust of wind in my flaccid sails. Amazing how a dose now and then of *attagirl* can lift a person, help them on their way.

I gushed to my boyfriend. "Listen to this!"

He listened. And I looked up from reading the editor's e-mail, waiting to hear, "That's great, nice job, well done."

Instead, he looked at me, steely eyed. "Too bad compliments don't pay the rent."

Compliments do not pay the rent. It was true what he said, and it felt like a punch. Here was the illusion dismantled, like a stone thrown through the glass, shards on the floor, edges sharp and threatening. A review for free isn't work and compliments are not dollars. They can help you put one foot in front of the other, remind you that maybe yes you are on the right track, keep going, keep pushing. But they will not buy you groceries. I needed both—the illusion and the truth, the small boost (you're on the right track) and the blunt dose of reality, the bludgeon of fact. In that moment though, I was crushed, furious with my boyfriend—couldn't he see that I'd needed a pat on the back during dark days? Some flash of good? I pushed out of my mind his experience of that time: He'd been shouldering the bills, watched me slump, witnessed my time disappearing. He was right, and his comment underlined my fears, the sense that I had taken a wrong turn and needed now to find my way out. It's easier to be angry.

I wrote the editor back with my thanks, grateful that he'd read the review, that he'd reached out with kind words about it. He wrote again to say he'd read some of what I'd written about my carpentry work; he wrote about his father building bookshelves; he wrote, "If you ever consider writing a book, please let me know."

A dream. Such good luck. Too good to be true. More than I ever would've allowed myself to hope for. The conversation continued from there. We had lunch in New York. He set up meetings for me with agents. I signed on with one and started working on a proposal. In the meantime, the carpentry work, after a fallow period of nearly five months, picked back up. I was back to both building and writing. Once the proposal was finished, we took it first to the editor who'd approached me, who was now at W. W. Norton, and gave him the first look. He wanted it. Norton wanted it. I signed a contract and got a handsome advance. Am I above a glowing, gloating feeling? A narrow-eyed sense of satisfaction that, right, yes, compliments don't pay the rent, but a book advance sure does, a book advance that came about from a book review written for free? I am not above that. Were those unpaid hours worth it? Yes, yes. I hold it in my head like a jewel. Maybe that makes me a small person.

And so there is the shimmery recommendation, within my rightful reach: Put yourself out there! Write widely! Write as much as you can for places you admire! Who cares if you don't get paid! It's always darkest before the dawn! Seek out good editors, good publications, and do your best work! With luck and effort who knows what will happen!

Wouldn't we all love that simple summing up? Do it well and put it out there and doors will open, eventually some fairy editor will descend, recognize something, lead you on exactly the path you've been wanting to travel down since you were a child writing stories about giants and talking chipmunks.

Sometimes it works out that way. Mostly it doesn't. And of course it matters to be paid. It matters a great deal. I have let myself believe the myth that the opportunity is payment, the practice and the audience forms of currency. And maybe at a certain stage, you need to believe it. But I am more and more struck with the sense that a great scam is afoot and writers are getting duped. I don't tile someone's kitchen floor for free. I don't dig four-foot holes in the ground for the framing of a deck unpaid. To spend a day chopping cedar boards to line a ceiling, load and unload stacks of lumber, to sand the surface of a table, to measure, mark, and cut—this is labor, and though I am glad to have the work, I am not a volunteer. Likewise with writing. Putting words together is a different pursuit from building rooms and stairs and shelves. But writing is work as well, and when we agree to volunteer, to have our time and effort go uncompensated, when we buy into the lie on the hope that maybe something, someday will come of this, we perpetuate a corrupt and broken system. I am guilty of it. In part because I understand the complications, the rewards, that compensation can sometimes take other forms than money, and that sometimes the act is enough.

I wrote a piece for free. It led to a book deal. It led to writing a book. This was a combination of events and an outcome that still, in moments, feels unreal, shimmery. I was able to do what I most wanted to do, and get paid for it. The book came out. And now I continue the rush and hustle. Sometimes I write for free; mostly I try not to. I continue to work with wood. I lay my trust in the building of decks, the making of tables, the assembling of words into sentences into thoughts into stories—craft, skill, art, work, all. People wonder when you're allowed to call yourself a writer. I think maybe the answer is when you recognize that it is work.

FAITH, HOPE, AND CREDIT

Cheryl Strayed

in conversation with Manjula Martin

Manjula Martin: Before this interview, we were talking a bit about how taboo it still is for writers to discuss income. You said that, even though you believe in talking openly about money, you were nervous about doing the interview. Why is it important to you to talk about the financial side of being a writer?

Cheryl Strayed: I feel strongly that we're only hurting ourselves as writers by being so secretive about money. There's no other job in the world where you get your master's degree in that field and you're like, *Well, I might make zero or I might make $5 million!* We don't have any standards in that way, and we probably never will. There will always be such a wide range of what writers are paid, but at least we could give each other information.

What was the financial experience like for you when you sold your first novel, *Torch*?
I was paid a $100,000 advance for *Torch*.

That sounds so huge to me.
Yes. It was November 2003, and I was at the Virginia Center for the Creative Arts at a residency, and I distinctly remember yelling—shrieking—into the phone to my husband, "A hundred thousand

14

dollars! A hundred thousand dollars!" And we were both just flipping out. We were like, *Our life is changed.*

And oh my god, I was so grateful. And I know how lucky I was to get that. I understand that I'm very fortunate. But I do think it's helpful to share information, so I want to talk about what that kind of advance really means.

Please do.

First of all, you don't just get a check for $100,000. You get four checks: one on signing, one on delivery—and that's not just when you finish the draft, but after the editing process, when it's going to the printer. I learned that lesson the hard way. And then you get another check on publication of the hardcover, and another check on publication of the paperback.

So, I sold *Torch* in 2003. I got that first $25,000. My agent took fifteen percent, and then I had around $21,000. But I didn't think about taxes. And if you're a writer who has, like, no money, and then you cash a check for $25,000, you're going to be taxed fully on that.

Did you put it in an IRA or anything like that?

I needed it to pay my rent. I had accrued $50,000 in credit card debt to write that book. The same thing happened later with *Wild*, only I was in deeper debt. So I got that check for *Torch*, and it was gone the next day. I actually paid my credit card bill. *Poof!*

Then I did revisions, and I had a baby, and the next check didn't come until 2005. I got my third check in February 2006, when it was published, and my final check when the paperback came out in 2007.

So I sold my book for $100,000, and what I received was a check for about $21,000 a year over the course of four years, and I paid a third of that to the IRS. Don't get me wrong, the book deal helped a lot—it was like getting a grant every year for four years. But it wasn't enough to live off. So, I guess it was a humbling lesson!

How did you live during those years?
I taught, did freelance journalism, wrote essays for magazines that pay—all the things I usually do for money. My husband is a documentary filmmaker, so he doesn't make any money either, but he would take work for money, too, and we scratched together a living. And all those years we qualified for food stamps. We never applied for them.

Why not?
I grew up poor, and I did get food stamps as a kid, so there was a sense of shame about it. And I also acknowledged that we were poor by choice. Here we were, two people with master's degrees, choosing to keep faith with our art, and because of that we were poor. That's different from being poor—really poor, actually poor. And I know that because I came from those people. And I just couldn't take in that way from our society.

At the end of the day, if I had really needed to get a job that paid the bills, I could have. And I always chose not to, because I wanted to write. So I didn't feel entitled to public assistance.

And you were in worse debt at the time that you sold *Wild*?
We almost lost our house before I sold *Wild*. I think we had about $85,000 in credit card debt by the time I sold that book. I can say that now because I don't have any debt, but I was so ashamed of that.

How did that debt stack up?
It was really interesting. By the time *Torch* was published, we had two kids under the age of two. So here I was, trying to write my second book with two babies, and we were just busting our asses. During those years we were spending more on childcare than I was making. And we would always be so broke and ashamed and putting things on the credit card. Really getting into trouble.

Here's another thing that's so interesting about money that people never talk about: there are all these invisible advantages and privileges people have. Parents who help out with a down payment, or a grandparent who takes the kids every Tuesday. Parents who pay for college. We didn't have any of that. I also had student loan debt from my undergraduate degree that I finally paid off on my forty-fourth birthday, thanks to *Wild*.

When I started to write *Wild*, I started to feel like I could sell this book. I just needed time to write it. So I was always fighting to try to find time to write the book—with the kids and earning a living and teaching and all those things. By the end of 2008, I had finished the first 130 pages or so.

How did you sell it? What was that process like?
In November 2008, I took *Wild* out to sell, and I had to take it to Houghton Mifflin because they published *Torch* and had right of first refusal. I was reluctant because my editor there had been let go—and I could have refused their offer, but I was so destitute. My agent called me and said, "They're working up an offer," and I said, "Oh my god! Whatever it is, I'll accept it, and please put a rush on the check because we need the money!"

But these were the darkest days of the publishing industry. I then got a call saying they couldn't make the offer, because as of that day there was a freeze on acquisitions at the company. It made the *New York Times*; it was a big deal. And I think I was one of the first authors to know about it because my book deal disappeared that day.

So by the time I took it out again in April 2009, my former editor, Janet Silver, had become an agent, and I decided to have her represent me. She took it out, and within a couple of days I was speaking to several editors who wanted the book, and I sold it to Knopf for $400,000. And that's when I was like, *Oh my god. Thank you. Thank you.*

Again, the great, funny irony about that was that I got my first check, and we spent it all on credit card bills.

Did you at least go out to dinner or something?
We went and had sushi. But our life didn't change. We only got out of credit card debt. But it changed in that way, trust me. As anyone who's been in severe credit card debt knows, it was a nightmare. All these financially minded people said we should apply for bankruptcy. But it was like the food stamps, you know?

And I finished the book within the year. Then it went through this long wait to be published—technically it was done a year before it was published. So I had to twiddle my thumbs for a year. And during that time, Dear Sugar stepped into the breach.

And Dear Sugar, your advice column, was for free?
Labor of love. But that's the thing about both *Wild* and *Torch*. They're no different from Dear Sugar. I would have written those books whether I was paid for them or not. They're all labors of love. Of course, that doesn't mean I'm not totally ambitious. I'm really ambitious.

Did you aspire to be a famous writer?
I want to be recognized for beautiful work, for good work, for real work. I really want to be recognized for that. Which is different from saying I want to be famous.

If you want to be famous, don't be a writer. When I was first thinking of myself as a writer back in my teens, the shorthand for that was fame. But then I started to really understand what writing was and who writers were. Who were the writers I valued the most as a young woman learning to write? They were people like Alice Munro, Raymond Carver, Richard Ford, Mary Gaitskill, and Toni Morrison.

Those people I just named are super-famous in *our* world, but most of the world doesn't know them. So pretty quickly, to me it wasn't about fame—it was about accomplishment. Once you let go of that fame thing, it's the first step in really being able to focus on doing good work. Because you can't fake it. That's the deal with writing. You can't fake it. You read an Alice Munro story—and it's there or it's not, you know? So I let that go pretty early on.

With fame, you have to get over it. You do. Because you will actually not succeed because of it.

An experience that's often paired with being famous is being rich. What has it been like for you to realize you are making money off your books? Did you have any idea beforehand that *Wild* would sell well? I mean, usually there are some signs that a book will be big.
It was like a train that was approaching and the roar kept getting louder. Because the publisher had sat on it for so long, booksellers and magazine editors—all the people who tell people what books to read—had a chance to read *Wild*. So I did have a sense that it was going to get a lot of coverage. But what makes a book successful is if readers actually buy it. We see lots of books get huge amounts of press and then disappear.

That first week that *Wild* debuted at number seven on the *New York Times* bestseller list, all I knew was that that was enough. I didn't even allow myself ever to dream that dream, and it came true. It was a beautiful moment. And then it stayed on the list.

What did that feel like? To see that this might become a long-term thing, being a best-selling author?
Having a book become a best seller was a more complicated process than most people would assume.

For example, in April 2012 the book had been out a month. I was on my book tour, and I was traveling around, and everyone was treating me like this big glorious best-selling author, and my husband texted me saying, *Our April rent check bounced. Why did it bounce?* And I replied, *Because we don't have any money in our checking account!*

And we laughed until we cried. Because we couldn't complain to anyone, and no one would believe us, but it was like, my book is on the *New York Times* bestseller list right now and we do not have any money in our checking account.

The first royalties I received for *Wild* were in January 2013. So it was almost a year before my life actually changed.

You were raised working class. Have you switched classes now?
You know when I switched classes? When I was eighteen and I went to college. I mean, I think you can go to college and stay working class, but I culture-hopped. After the experience of college, even though I was poor all those years, I occupied a different place in the culture than I had before. I had an education. I had a subscription to the *New Yorker*. I was friends with amazing people who were accomplished in all kinds of fields—essentially the elites of our world. And some of those people were poor and some were millionaires.

I haven't actually changed in that regard at all since *Wild*'s success. The difference is, now, in that same tribe I've been in since I was eighteen, I'm one of the people who has money instead of one of the people who doesn't.

The only thing that's changed is that I can pay my bills. I can afford to not be desperate anymore. I can buy boots not in thrift stores! But the culture and the community and the things I think about people and the world and the way I feel about myself and my family—none of that has changed one iota.

There's this narrative we have, that if you have success, you become a different person. You leave behind the little people. And it's like, *No, no, I don't even believe there are little people—how could I leave them behind? I am the little people.*

When *Wild* first came out, I recall some of the press and stories about your life and career seemed to imply you're a late bloomer. How do you feel about that phrase?

Well, I think it's hilarious. That's such a strange way to think of a writer. I wrote *Wild* when I was, like, forty. And my writing career has actually followed a very smooth trajectory: I knew passionately from a very young age I wanted to be a writer. I majored in English, and I spent my twenties apprenticing myself to the craft. I came out of my twenties knowing that I needed the shelter a fully funded graduate program would offer me. The MFA program at Syracuse allowed me three years, essentially, to have a grant and write. I wrote my first book there; a couple of years out of grad school, I sold it, and a few years later, I sold my next book. . . . I think there's nothing late about it!

So it's not like, *Oh, I'm just over here germinating like a little quiet seed, and then ta-da, I'm blooming!*

Once, on my Facebook page, somebody said I had come out of nowhere with *Wild*, and that made me mad. I wasn't mad for myself, I was mad for the community of writers I feel very much a part of, who all knew me before *Wild* was published. I'm talking about the community of people who go to AWP [the Association of Writers & Writing Programs annual conference], the people who are writers, poets, creative writing teachers, etc. Those people knew about me: I was publishing essays, a novel, I was teaching. And just because suddenly a whole bunch more people knew about my work, that doesn't negate the people who've known about me all along. So I hated that phrasing—*out of nowhere*. Because it implied that where I was was nowhere. Just because our culture doesn't recognize most of those twelve thousand people who gather at AWP every year doesn't mean those people aren't incredibly successful.

How do you define success?
The way I define and measure success, all through my life and still to this day, is, can I answer the questions: Have I done the work I needed to do? Did I do it as well as I could? Did I give it everything I had? If you can say, "Yes, I did," that's success. And then other stuff happens—your book is on the bestseller list, or Oprah calls—or maybe not. Maybe it gets trashed in the *New York Times*. Or maybe it's absolutely ignored by everyone, which happens. Those things are not about success. Those are about things that happen to you.

One thing I've tried to do as Sugar—and something all books do or should do—is encourage people to be able to hold many truths at once, because together they form a greater truth. So on one hand I'm apologetic that we're sitting here in this beautiful house that *Wild* bought. But I know I did the work; I know I earned it. I also know that thousands of other writers out there, working away as we speak, have worked equally hard. They earned it, too. And they didn't have that magic bunny come along and make their book a best seller, so they didn't get that thing. Both experiences are true.

Life ain't fair, as they say?
You have to take what you've been given and make the best of it and use it for good in the world. And that would be my belief whether I were applying for food stamps tomorrow or not.

ON STAYING HUNGRY

Rachael Maddux

There may be no advice given to young creative types more often than "Stay hungry." Hunger is encouraged by commencement speakers, noted as a requirement in job listings, looked back on fondly by one-time strivers now on the far side of their golden years. Hunger is everything because it's nothing—not yet—just raw promise, one lack that may eclipse others: talent, pedigree, luck. Like sharks, the hungry must always keep moving, hunting, killing, "killing it." We assure the hungry that they are poised to go far—over and beyond the bodies of the frightened and dull and easily sated. At the end of the day they will stand smiling, jaws bloodied, still wanting more.

When we talk about hunger this way—as shorthand for a certain noble stripe of ambition—we tend to obscure its root in our bodies, our biology. Even in this strange sliver of the world where food is ample to the point of threat, hunger remains a real, animal sensation. Every few hours our bodies rumble with discomfort and we are expected to soothe them, whether or not we understand or trust the nature of their want. Perhaps this hunger is honest, or perhaps it's just that you smelled the cookies baking or you got stood up or cut off or side-eyed or just happened to see the clock hit eleven thirty, a time you were hungry before. Hunger confuses the needs of our minds with the needs of our bellies. Hunger lies like a child.

But then, whether or not you give into your hunger, even if you give it nothing at all, it always slinks away; but then, it always returns. It is a fundamental condition. We seem to forget this when we talk about the appetites of the young. "Stay hungry," we tell them, as if they have been drafted into some cannibal army and must devour their own to have any hope of survival. "Stay hungry," we tell them, as if they have any choice at all.

§

The hungriest I've ever been was in the months and years right after college. When I was hired before graduation as an administrative assistant at the music magazine where I'd interned my senior year, I felt like some Dickensian urchin scooped up off the street and plopped down at a heaving banquet. It all seemed too fantastic to be trusted. This was 2007, 2008. Magazines were combusting all around us, the economy itself verging on implosion. I didn't know how much time I had left. And I was hungry. So I gorged myself.

Never mind the fact that, metaphors aside, my paychecks were barely enough to live on; never mind that I subsisted mostly on rice and beans and cereal and rare restaurant dinners halved to stretch into lunch the next day; never mind that I was skin and bones, skinnier than I'll ever be again. I was doing work I wanted desperately to be doing, and I was rewarded for doing it well with even more work. I was promoted to editorial assistant, then assistant editor, then associate editor; I wrote short profiles, then longer profiles, reviews and longer reviews, news stories for the website and live reviews and festival blogs and lists, then features, then a column of thousands of words every week. The work wasn't just falling into my lap, it was avalanching all around me. But who was I to complain? *You'd better clean your plate—starving children in Brooklyn would kill for that review!* When I held a copy of the issue bearing my first cover story, I expected to experience some sort of transcendent satisfaction, or at least some palpable sense of leveling up. Instead my stomach just grumbled, my appetite already recalibrating.

When the magazine finally met its fate and I was laid off, I expected my appetite to shrink in response to the work's diminished supply. Instead, it seemed to grow. If my staff job had felt like being one of Fagin's boys at a feast, freelancing felt like Dumpster diving and table-scrap swiping—less posh, but limitless in another way. I felt even less like I could say no. Even after I got another day job writing for a nonprofit, I was saying yes and yes and yes to freelance work, pitching and writing and pitching and writing on the train both ways to work, on my lunch breaks, at home every night, all through my weekends. To fill the gaps, I fired off blog posts and tweets about any half-formed thought that crossed my mind— terrified of silence, terrified of losing momentum, terrified of sitting still long enough to feel that old rumble in my belly.

I sustained myself with one thought: *This is what you wanted!* At first it was an honest reminder. Then it became wide smiling, manic. Then it came to seem like more of an admonition, as if from a babysitter standing baffled over a crying child: *This is what you wanted! You were hungry, now you're being fed, you're eating it up, why aren't you full yet? Why aren't you happy? What is the matter? How can you be so hungry? How can you still be so hungry?*

When I think of how I felt about my work then, I think of Mr. Creosote, the massively obese man in *Monty Python's The Meaning of Life*, who ravages a French restaurant with his vast appetite. He eats his way through the menu and beyond and has coated all surrounding patrons and waitstaff in his globulus vomit by the time he stops and sighs, apparently sated. The maître d' emerges, tentative, with a silver tray: "And finally, monsieur, a wafer-thin mint." Mr. Creosote urps, resists, finally relents. His arms are immobile under their own weight, so the mint is placed into his mouth like a com-

Rachael Maddux

munion wafer. Upon swallowing, Mr. Creosote promptly explodes, his guts splattering all over the dining room, his body rendered a hollowed-out carcass, his giant heart still beating at the back of his shattered rib cage. And then the maître d' returns. Punch line: "Thank you, sir. And now, here's ze check." We don't see how much it's for, but that's beside the point. You can stay hungry, but there's always a cost.

§

For a certain kind of hunger, the act of eating is its own reward, the matter of nutrition secondary, if a concern at all. Even when I needed money—before, during, after unemployment—I would write for free, telling myself that any work was good work, that at least I was getting my name out there, that maybe it might lead to something paid down the line. That was true, but more often what I was chasing was a *feeling*—the one where, after writing a piece and filing the piece and seeing the piece appear online, rainbow streams of dopamine seemed to be geysering out of nozzles lining the inside of my skull, flooding my brain, fizzing out all the junk like existential Alka-Seltzer (and then all the additional splurts that followed when the piece was tweeted and favorited and liked, even when the inevitable trolls rolled into the comments). With a day job, that feeling was more useful to me than whatever tiny amount of cash I would've received in a slightly more just world. You don't have to pay quarterly taxes on dopamine squirts.

That feeling, which I believe may technically be known as "happiness," was a bottomless, ever-widening pit. My rendering of the neurochemistry is cartoonish, but basically apt: You do whatever you do to make those good feelings flow, and you keep doing and they keep flowing, but to maintain them requires doing more and more, all the time. You're chasing something that gets further away the longer and harder you run. You can never catch up; you're always left wanting. In this way, hunger of the mind—or maybe what we're talking about here is "the soul"—mirrors hunger of the stomach. We consume, we digest, we begin again, as if everything that came before had never happened.

For a time I thought of myself as Mr. Creosote. I had eaten too much, too fast, for too long. My work felt rushed and cheap, my words a jumble, my ideas wafer-thin. I was sick of it all, and sick of myself. Then I began to feel more like Sisyphus, pushing the boulder up the hill and watching it roll back down and retreating to push it up again for the rest of time. The glutton and the damned. It took me so long to realize I was not stuck doing this for eternity, I was not pinned under my own weight—I had invited myself to the table and could excuse myself at any time.

§

I have never successfully subjected my actual hunger to the pains of a diet. Anytime I've come close, my body has won out—the griping gut, the fuzzy brain. The stomach wants what it wants. Even a simple fast for a blood drive or a doctor's appointment has the potential to turn ugly. But on those shaky occasions I've been reminded of the power of denial, the way an errant pang will drift away if ignored—a false flag revealing itself. What if I could begin to ignore the nagging need-to-work feelings the same way I can (only very occasionally) ignore the need-to-eat ones?

And so, after nearly a decade of gluttony, I found myself taking the advice I had scoffed at all along: I was hungry, and I was allowing myself to stay that way. It was an ambition fast, you could say, followed by ambition mindful eating. I stopped pitching, stopped trying to commit to the screen every half-formed impulse I had to write, stopped chasing those rainbow dopamine squirts that had already become elusive. I began saying no—to e-mails in my inbox, to editors, to myself.

I felt shaky. I still do. Often I feel I'm welcoming the symptoms of starvation, which seem as applicable to a human body as to a writing career: anxiety, depression, muscle atrophy, stunted growth, compromised immune response, death. (When I first stopped freelancing, I certainly ate more actual food to keep the uncertainty at bay.) For the first time, I began to ask myself what I was writing toward. It's a question I'm still trying to answer. Before, I may have said I wrote because it was all I could do, or because it was all I wanted to do—or, in more insufferable moments, because it was what I was *born* to do. Maybe that's so. But we are born hungry, too. The trick is learning how to feed yourself and not choke.

PORTRAIT OF THE ARTIST AS A DEBUT NOVELIST

Porochista Khakpour

1. JUVENILIA

When I was about eleven, I wrote my first novel, an epic about "a Victorian girl." Translation: a girl from a faraway time and place where human women wore big fancy dresses and sat around sulking. That lifestyle was so appealing to me. I was a sad kid, and the only excuse I could come up with was that I had been born in the wrong place at the wrong time.

My heroine happened to be eleven, with hair "the color of stallions" (translation: black) and skin of "pale wheat" (white or brown, depending on which Iranian you asked), and her name was knotty and yet "magnificent": Contessa Van Prgkhjiollzshdiyyiani.

Contessa VP was indoorsy and prone to fainting, her pockets weighed down with smelling salts. She was always perched gingerly on her windowsill, gazing at the outside world with mixed feelings. She eschewed friends—bores who mocked her "grand name" and her "odd secret beauty." But she had two distinguishing characteristics: melancholy and genius.

2. GIRL AWTHOR

I can be fansy.
I can be tall.
I can ware hi heel shoos when I grow up.
Who am I?
Answer: A GIRL AWTHOR!
   —My first documented riddle, 1983.

On Thursday, May 2, 2006, it's official. I am a girl author. I get a book deal.

It doesn't feel real—not for the obvious reasons, but because I am sleep-deprived, destroyed by crying and crying and crying about a nonliterary tragedy. The night before, I had seen a college friend at an East Village café that neither of us could really afford. We bonded over the sheer awkwardness of being nannies with master's degrees, liberal arts graduates with some of the most expensive educations in the world. At some point during dinner, a text came in from an old friend in Chicago. Just three words: a good friend's name—misspelled—"died" and "sorry." I called to clarify, but our chaotic voices canceled each other out. We had no vocabulary for this.

He had been a buddy of the most unlikely kind: the charming young ex-con, with tattoos from the edges of his face to his knuckles, who had a passion for bespoke menswear, obscure wines, and even more obscure books. He and his wife had adopted me because I was an Iranian to his Iraqi—*old enemies*, he'd laugh. He was also an unrehabilitated junkie on a downward path.

The night I learn of his death is the first night of pure, dead-black insomnia I have ever experienced. I spend the next day in a defeated fetal-squat. I hover over my laptop for hours, bawling and trying to write a eulogy, when my agent calls and leaves a message. "I have good news," she says.

By now, I have learned never to answer when my agent calls. I let her leave messages and then I throw my depressed fits in private. Before I call her back, versions of myself in jobs I've held since beginning work on my novel catwalk through my head with forced smiles and exhausted stomps: now, hostess; now, adjunct; now, tutor; now, hair model; now, bar reviewer; now, babysitter; now, nanny; now, shopgirl!

Yet here it is: good news, a book deal. There it is: everything, ever, answered.

Unicorns exist! Santa is not my parents! The world *is* just, Contessa! I have never broken $25,000 a year, and now some validation, hell, salvation has come. On the worst day, here it is, the happiest story of all time, a story so joyous I would have never written it.

3. THE VERY BAD SUMMER

There is a season where it seems like maybe I won't make it.

I spend much of the summer finishing the novel, in the midst of serious anxiety, panic, depression, chronic fatigue, gastritis, carpal tunnel, God knows what else, all the shattered states in the nightmare nation of chronic insomnia. Any normal person would assume I am on drugs, and I am. At any given time, it's a combination of two to five types of pills, prescribed by people who don't know about each other, given to me by my second general practitioner, all three of my psychiatrists, the ER internist from my third summer visit to the ER, and a gastroenterologist. I am sedated at all times yet so introspective I am paralyzed.

I turn the novel in. I go out to a celebration dinner with a very normal guy I have somehow fallen into dating. I pick at a whole fish and order dessert. I make bathroom visits devoted solely to dropping benzodiazepine crumbs under my tongue, licking any residue off my finger.

The novel made it, but I didn't.

Back at home, my parents' home, which was to be my summer editing and writing retreat, I look at the box of pills. *This isn't me*— Ambien, Ativan, Klonopin, Celexa, Trazodone. They are like names for weapons, an army of futuristic knives, jagged and unforgiving. They will get me a few hours of sleep that will keep me alive. I am terrified. My whole life is doctors and ERs and shrinks, and they all shake their heads when they hear the answer to their question, "Has anything traumatic happened in the last few months?"

Yes, I tell them.

"*Traumatic* means *bad*," one doctor informs me.

They seem skeptical when I say I have a novel on the way, like a washboard-stomached woman complaining about third trimester pains—just another part of the crazy talk, they must think. All they can recommend is shrinks, and I have four. I pay for the visits without insurance, in cash or with plastic gold. I collect cards, any card.

I have gone to post–book deal hell and all I got was this serious debt. But it's an okay place to be. There are no surprises in debt.

The novel is out of my hands and in purgatory before entering the world. I love that phase: the middle of the road trip, someone else driving, seeing a world outside pass by, deftly escaping resignation to thoughts, assignment to words.

4. AN ACTUAL PORTRAIT OF THE YOUNG ARTIST

Spring 2007: I am in New York, taking my author photo. I have known the photographer for more than half my life. He asks to see what I've got. I open my bag and out comes dress after dress, silk organza, crêpe de chine, satin, Italian wool, all impeccably tailored black dresses, fit for a modern Contessa VP.

Dollar signs flap their wings through the photographer's studio.

I wave them away. *Not what it looks like,* I tell him. *Just dating a fashion designer.*

Just! He groans, rolling his eyes.

I go to the bathroom to put on makeup, a lot. The second I meet my eyes in the mirror, the world starts to go black, and my vision is full of those psychedelic pulses that the world calls "stars."

5. WAITING

August 2007: My publisher tells me the *New York Times* is going to review my book, and it's tentatively slated for a date in September. I will lazily say that it is impossible to describe just how exciting that is, but it is also stressful, when there is a whole month to kill until the judgment.

Suddenly, there is time. Time has a way of injecting herself into the picture when there is waiting to be done. I remember this from childhood Christmases, a holiday we should have never celebrated in the first place. But there we were, my brother and I, with lists in hand and our eyes glued to the small department-store plastic tree and its ribboned droppings. Time kept on and on, like the cheapest toilet paper.

This time, though, because I am in it alone, the waiting is unbearable. It must be filled. I try yoga, massage, acupuncture, more therapy, but there is only one thing that does the trick.

Crank calls. This is a truth, sadly.

Even worse is this truth: I have a long history with this sort of thing. In elementary school with friends, calling an old man and telling him we were leggy blond Playboy models and being certain the joke was on him. International calls to Kenya, the globe seeming so surreal to me, a kid who was lonely in school and at home, never quite an American, never quite an Iranian. In college, I went through a phase of calling my parents at odd hours and saying I was with the IRS or the FBI or CIA or the local police, whatever could get struggling immigrants on political asylum really going.

But this time, I began crank-calling my friends. I created characters. I called famous people, professional contacts. Some never found out who it was. Some did. To this day, I have not patched up things with about half a dozen victims of the Great *NYTBR* Waiting Period. The review was good in the end, but I lost friends I'd had for more than twenty years. What do you say? How do you explain it?

There are very few people going through what I'm going through, you imagine telling them. *Very few people ever have, you know?*

CLICK.

6. STARS, PART II

Still August 2007: Panicking a bit about my finances—the final trickle of my advance doomed to coincide with my impending book tour—I apply for a job at a university in Long Island and am called back for an interview.

Just weeks before the launch of my book, on the day of the interview, I am what they call "all nerves." But in a good way, unlike the summer before. This time, I have hope. I assume all the gods are on my team, since I haven't been notified otherwise.

So far, a few blogs have said some nice things. I joined a gym I can't afford, but I have joined a gym.

Iran is in the news daily. I am eating and sleeping. I have an uncanny knack for looking at clocks at exactly 9:11.

I take everything as an omen, omens that could go either way.

I am at a Starbucks in Park Slope, reviewing my teaching philosophy, which sounds miserably fake even though I love to teach.

When I stand up, there they are again, the stars—not Park Slope literary luminaries, but again the hypoglycemia-diabetes-cancer-AIDS-godknowswhatIhave kind. I panic. I don't have much time before I miss the train to the interview. I am worrying about this as my vision wipes out in the aggressive sunshine beaming over the brownstone rooftops.

Fade in, and I'm slumped on the street quite indelicately, with some young hippie chick asking me *you okay you okay you okay.* Her eyes go back and forth from my squinting eyes to my hair that is partially bleached white.

You passed out, she says, and points to the left. *Let's go to the hospital.*

Evidence that nonfiction settings are sometimes less believable than fiction, the hospital happens to be across the street.

Not a chance, I tell her.

She protests, this girl I don't even know. Eventually, I tell her the truth.

She nods sympathetically. *I don't have health insurance either. But still.*

I fall four more times that day, but I get the job, the only job that will put up with my book-tour schedule.

Back at home, I watch my unsteady hands at the keyboard hit and miss over and over. During the spring before that very bad summer, a psychic told me too much anxiety surrounding the novel would breed disaster.

7. PORTRAIT OF THE STARVING ARTIST

October 2007: It is a fact that even a *NYTBR*-approved novelist can still find herself in highly undignified positions at certain times. Two months later, I am sitting Indian-style on the dirty linoleum floor at the JFK Delta baggage claim, hugging my carry-on like it's a pillow and trying to sob subtly into my cell phone.

I'm crying about money, something I have a negative amount of, according to a robot at my bank. I have some change in my jacket, but it is not even enough to get a cookie from the concession stand in front of me and I am starving.

I haven't had money for weeks. My paperwork from the new university job has not gone through. My publisher has paid for some flights and hotels, but I have not had more than what a struggling boyfriend could spare. I have a million fancy dresses to wear and a lot of good face to put on, but all I've been doing is eyeing the prices on every menu and pretending cookies and chips are my food of choice, that Subway is my adorably ironic passion, that the McDonald's breakfast menu is my kitschy little crush.

But the most disturbing part of being overdrawn is that it results from a certain check, made out in the summer, that I have no memory of. It is a three-figure check, written out to . . . *my psychic.*

I call people, but I don't want to ask for help. I want them to think of it as a humorous anecdote but not that it's real, that my life is that difficult. After all, certain friends who are not involved in publishing think I am rich and famous. Why burst that bubble?

In the end, I borrow money from a friend of my boyfriend and take that walk of shame to a yellow cab, when I know there are buses and shuttles and subways and all sorts of only semi-impossible ways to get back to Brooklyn.

Later, when my publicist finds out, she is shocked. *Why didn't you call us?!*

I give her some gloss-over answer, but I want to say, I don't know whom to call, when to call, why to call. I am learning everything over again. I have become what the publishing world and media suspect of a debut novelist—suddenly, I am new to the universe, not just to being a novelist. I suddenly don't know what the hell I'm doing.

Weeks later, I discover during another bad moment—as the value of the dollar plummets and oil is sky-high—that gold is at its peak. I sell what is left of family heirlooms to an old Iranian man in the Diamond District, who listens to a fraction of my story, gives me a decent deal, and tells me, "My boy in medical university; my girl, married and with baby. Your fault for being a starver of an artist, daughter."

8. PORTRAIT OF AN ARTIST WITH A CRAZY NAME AND ALSO CRAZY HAIR

There is the issue of my name, of course. To everyone who is not Dr. or Mrs. Khakpour, it is insurmountable—the ultimate hyper-ethnic polysyllabic foreign name, even foreign to "my people," who rarely recognize its Zoroastrian origin, the name of Zarathustra's daughter: *Pourucista.* My last name is the same as a famous Iranian soccer player—Mohammad, no relation—so people can handle it. It means *of the earth*, literally *dirt-full.*

No one can say it, and I even say it differently, depending on the person. In Farsi, it is best uttered in a low purr: *Poe-roh-chis-TAWH KHAK-pur.* (Americans—unless they speak Hebrew—are often disappointed to find out this is indeed the guttural *kh*, requiring more gut than a German *ich*.)

My name is such a mess of issues that it has been swept under the Iranian-American carpet, over and over and over, until I have forgotten it's there.

Until publication season, that is. Then I start really hearing and seeing my name again. It bends into its old bizarre forms: *Porchista, Prochista, Parochista, Kahkpour, Kkakpour, Khapour*, plus some I have never heard. People make fun of it like they did in elementary school; my book party gets linked on Gawker, and one of the first comments is the easiest on me: "Khakpour. I made that sound this morning before my first cigarette and coughed up last night's tequila binge."

Before my NPR interview, Kurt Andersen asks me how to pronounce my name, and I tell him. When we're on the air, he does the opposite of those who fumble it, who say it quietly and quickly, almost under their breath, like a bad thought they want to go away soon. He belts it! My first name is on target—go, Kurt, go!—but my last name is *KHHHHAWK-por*, which exactly rhymes with, say, "rock whore." Reading series hosts all fumble, and one even christens me *Chalkpore*. And, of course, many opt for what is still the general consensus among my closest hometown friends: *Hawkpurr*.

I do not change my name and never will. But one way I have battled the drama of a bad name is with other distractions. I've had piercings, tattoos, hair of every shade, cuts from nearly shaved to ass-length braided extensions. Just before my literary shit hits the fan, I go to my salon in SoHo and tell my skinny, scowling stylist to "ugly me up" and show him a sketch.

"Tough," he responds, racing both tattooed hands through my thick, black, disgustingly pretty hair.

"Totally fucked up," I elaborate. "A little badass, kinda burly. Y'know?"

"Sick," he shoots back. His face never changes, but he makes an approving squirm in his skin-tight black jeans. We have communicated.

Five hours later I walk out with randomly arranged chunks of white in my hair—paper-white—like some Persian-Californian Cruella de Vil in training in flip-flops and a sundress, instead of the razor-sharp stilettos and excessive furs of the Disney villainess.

People notice. Style.com applauds my "skunk-style highlights" and my "deliberately down-market look." A writer for *Pars Arts*, a young Iranian arts site, declares "my fascination with her as an author is slowly being overcome by a fascination with her hair." The name disappears a bit.

9. SUPERPOWERS

After my readings I generally get some people who just want to talk. This is fine with me. I like most comp lit students, and I can stomach the occasional misled housewife who wonders if I've ever read this book called *The Kite Runner*, by a guy whose name she "forgets" (i.e., can't say), which she read to know more about "us."

The other group is not as easy—they appear to be average middle-aged white males, but that's just their Clark Kent cover. They are really conspiracy-theory superheroes! They have seen the shadow of the World Trade Center in front of my novel and know I am Middle Eastern, and they have their own ideas about my religion, and so they want to share with me "the truth about 9/11." I politely decline going down that road every time, and still they carry on. Eventually, I excuse myself to visit the bathroom and put on my own superhero getup, my Invisible Snakegirl tube suit, which allows me to slither away undetected.

10. FOR A LIMITED TIME ONLY: MAHMOUD AHMADINEJAD INCLUDED IN THE PORTRAIT

On the afternoon of September 24, 2007, Iranian president Mahmoud Ahmadinejad, en route to addressing the UN General Assembly, gave a speech at Columbia University. It was a big deal.

Less of a big deal to the world, but a kinda big deal to me, was the next day: my technical publication date. One day later, my first book club appearance; three days later, the first day of my book tour. In all my interactions, the theme is Ahmadinejad.

One woman at a reading whispers in my ear, "Iran is hot—lucky you!"

Other people just want to hear something from some vaguely related horse's mouth. At almost every reading, someone inevitably raises her hand and utters, *So, Ahmadinejad . . . ?*

For a few weeks, I smile and nod. Yes, *Mah-moooood Ahmadeeeee-nezhaad*—deep Farsi phonetics—*my homeland's president. Well . . .* Every reading provides a challenge to say something comforting yet not bland, aware yet not activist, polished but not sharp. It gets old quick. I start wanting to ask people: *Can't we talk about anything else? 9/11, anyone?!*

At readings later that autumn I become what Iranians call a *bacheyeh powrooh*, which translates as "kid full of spirit," or a rather rude child. So I quip, "What about him?"

"Well," says the nervously smiling American, looking down at her sneakers. "What do you think of all this?"

In my imagination, I am Picasso declaring "I don't" when asked what he thought of the man on the moon. But in real life, humor—this time with a flushed face—is the only route I can take.

"I never dated Mahmoud Ahmadinejad and therefore have no insight into what he's like, what he's thinking."

11. PORTRAIT, AFTERMATH, 2008

After all I've been through, I give up and dye my hair black, my natural color.

After a few months of this old black, as fake now as it was real then, they come in bunches not unlike streaks. Not one, not two, but many and counting, the early and yet expected outcome, perfectly white hairs.

THE MERCENARY MUSE

Colin Dickey

*C*harles Dickens was paid by the word. This was junior high, we were reading *A Tale of Two Cities*, and this fact, when it was first uttered, raced like a rumor through the classroom, overtaking everything. Suddenly, every other word in Dickens's novel seemed like unnecessary padding, every sentence overstuffed, wasteful, filled with excessive detail. It didn't matter that *A Tale of Two Cities* is among Dickens's shorter novels; once we'd been introduced to the economy of writing, everything was tainted.[1]

How to trust each word from that point on? "It was the best of times, it was the worst of times, it was the age of wisdom, it was the age of foolishness, it was the epoch of belief, it was the epoch of incredulity, it was the season of Light, it was the season of Darkness . . ." How to tell what of this was necessary, and what was extraneous? At the same time that we young students were being taught to cut padding from our own writing, here we were forced to read the work of someone rewarded for piling it on. Once I'd formed this picture of Dickens in my mind, it became an easy way to discount his novels as superfluous.

Money obscures one's relationship to work; it distances us from ourselves and the things we make. Karl Marx, using the example of a weaver who sells a bolt of linen for £2 and then buys a family Bible with that £2, describes such transactions in terms of alienation:

"The linen, which in his eyes is a mere commodity, a depository of value, he alienates in exchange for gold, which is the linen's value-form, and this form he again parts with for another commodity, the Bible, which is destined to enter his house as an object of utility and of edification to its inmates."[2] Because the value of goods is dominated by the market, one's labor becomes subordinate to the ascribed market value, and once we begin to mistake this market value as true value, we lose any genuine connection we might have had to the work.

Money taints everything, why not writing too? Once its value is determined by the marketplace rather than the writer or the reader, our relationship to literature becomes estranged. From bloated celebrity advances to rejected masterpieces, the market is more than just a poor arbiter of lasting quality: it tends to obscure that quality behind purely economic motivations. Good writing, we're told time and time again, is born from love, not avarice. But this romantic picture of the writer, toiling without regard to money, is itself a fiction—one whose roots stretch back several millennia, and whose effects we're still dealing with today.

§

The first writer to charge by the word is thought to be the Greek poet Simonides, who became legendary for his stinginess. Prior to Simonides, poets relied on a patronage system. In exchange for food, lodging, and prestige, poets would provide wealthy bene-factors with writing that extolled their virtues, as well as act as general companions and creative writing coaches for the patron's own work. Amorphous and difficult to pin down, it was a system that allowed at least some poets to make a living without overly quantifying their art.

Simonides changed this. He wrote for money, and he kept precise books. Despite his undisputed literary excellence, this quality came to define him above all else: Simonides was thought to be parsimonious, a miser, putting money above all else. Ailian, his biographer, commented simply that "No one would deny that Simonides loved money." In Aristophanes's *Peace*, Simonides is described as one who would "put to sea upon a sieve for money."[3] It is to Simonides, agree most classical commentators, that we owe our current estrangement from our words. As Anne Carson puts it in the *Economy of the Unlost*, her study of Simonides and Paul Celan: "I like to think Simonides represents an early, severe form of economic alienation and the 'doubleness' that attends it."[4]

As Carson herself notes, the tension between a patronage economy and a money economy had been building for some time, and during Simonides's lifetime these two systems overlapped, despite being often described as diametric opposites. The distrust and distaste that Simonides garnered may have been due, in part, to his refusal to live in an ambiguous status afforded by these two contradictory structures, to play the game. Whereas previous writers and artists had negotiated the contradictions of a system that was intentionally not fully articulated, Simonides cut through the Gordian knot of such confusion, demanding a simple and straightforward equation of words and money. As a result, he appeared to all as avaricious—his love of money more central than his love of poetry.

The system Simonides spurned was one of patronage and gift. Goods and services were exchanged based not on their value but on the value of the relationship between giver and receiver. For Carson, the essence of Simonides's perceived greed "was the commodification of a previously reciprocal and ritual activity, the exchange of gifts between friends."[5] In such an economy, one's obligation to one's community and to one's writing trumps any obligation to cash.

Little is known about the actual Simonides. There are few contemporaneous accounts of his life, and he quickly became a stock figure for greed. As classical scholar Norman Austin notes, no other writer was so unequivocally associated with avarice, even though others (including Simonides's contemporary, Pindar) wrote about money with equal frankness.[6] All of this, Carson suggests, may be an indication that when it comes to Simonides we are not talking about a poet so much as we are talking about an idea. "Everything gets more interesting," she writes, "if we understand his greed as a biographical trope for the whole burgeoning fifth-century money economy."[7]

But regardless whether Simonides himself was responsible for this shift, or whether he simply became the straw man associated with a larger trend sweeping the classical world, the shift toward monetizing poetry had long-lasting effects. In short order, money became widely recognized as a corrupting influence; Pindar, in his second Isthmian Ode, nostalgically laments earlier times when "The Muses were not mercenary in those days, nor worked for hire, nor were the songs of Terpsichore for sale." And Horace, in his discussion of the poet Choerilus, whose pockets Alexander the Great filled "with lots of royal cash, as a reward for his misbegotten badly written verses," adds that writers who work under such economic motives mar both their subject matter and their writing.[8] There is a moral in the tale of pay-for-play poets like Choerilus, who was given a gold coin for each good verse he produced, and a beating for each bad verse: in the end, he was flogged to death for his writing.

No matter. We have continued to blur and smudge both good deeds and good writing with money more or less constantly ever since then. Pindar's lament against the Simonideses of the world has continued unabated to the present day. Writing for *The Telegraph* in 2014, Sameer Rahim complained: "You can't go on a writer's Facebook page or meet them for a drink without the discussion turning to what their publisher is doing—or not—to boost their sales, who the most ruthless agents are, or where to get the best-paid creative writing gigs." Simonides's original sin, for Rahim, continues to taint the work of writing, even to this day. Bothered by this endless avarice, Rahim wondered, "I know they have to eat, but when did it all become about the money? . . . Call me a romantic but it might actually benefit a writer not to rely on books as their main source of income."[9]

Perhaps this age of capitalist greed is coming to an end; with the rise of online publishing, the material costs of publishing have all but vanished, allowing for a world once again untrammeled by commerce. "Luckily, the freedom offered by the Internet offers a chance to resurrect the idea of writing for love, not money," waxes Rahim. "So far online self-publishing has been the preserve of fan fiction and erotica but it can't be long before high-quality fiction starts to emerge." In two thousand years, we have not strayed far from Pindar's long-ago complaint: "Men used to write for love alone; now they write for money."

§

It would seem, perhaps, easy enough to go back, to separate writing from commerce. Rahim's vision of writers holding other jobs and writing in their free time, their words no longer bound to feed them, is an easy enough solution. But the story of Simonides also suggests the way in which these two things—words and money—are closer in value than they appear. "Simonides appears to have been the first to introduce meticulous calculation into songmaking and to write songs for a wage," writes one commentator of his legacy. Carson notes that in the Greek, the word *smikrologia*, "meticulous calculation," can suggest not just "minute care about financial expense, miserliness," but also "minute care about details of language, exact expression." Dionysius of Halicarnassus, writing of Simonides, notes that one should "Watch very carefully Simonides's choice of words and the exactitude with which he puts things together"; the word *exactitude* here is *akribeia*, which likewise has a dual meaning: it can mean "precision, accuracy, exactness of language" or "parsimony, frugality, stinginess with money." Simonides, then, not only became the first to charge money for his words, but also, these sources suggest, awakened in Greek culture the fact that money and words bear an analogous relationship to each other.[10]

"Money had a radical impact on ancient culture," Carson concludes; "Simonides reacted to it by inventing a poetry of radical economy."[11] Rather than simply stating that Simonides interrupted a literary economy of gift and patron, of charity and reciprocity, one might perhaps suggest instead that he revealed, or at least cemented, a latent relationship between language and currency that was always there.

§

I have a small stack of gifts I've received from publishers I've written for: a few mugs, a tote bag, a T-shirt, some stickers, even a few 7" records. Primarily these are from small journals: places that weren't even paying editors, let alone writers. I'll write for free to help a new publication that I admire get off the ground, or because I admire their mission, or because the editor is a friend of mine. In a few cases I've been offered a small amount—barely more than an honorarium— that I've turned down to help defray the publisher's costs.

This is part of the gift economy of writing: Occasionally I'm asked to contribute a piece for no pay, and to do so as, more or less, a gift. And the implication here is always that one does such things out of love: love for new publications, love for new voices, and a love of seeing one's own words in print. In such cases, asking for cash, or turning down an offer for lack thereof, is always gauche.

Asked to write for love, not money, the writer is asked to exit the money economy and return to the gift economy. In 2007, poet Robert Hass suggested that this boomerang trajectory was the natural way of art. While institutions such as copyright exist "to put works of art on the market for a while," Hass sees the situation as temporary: "then they come out of the market and back into the commons, because the commons is where they came from. And the way they came there is just as anybody here who ever wanted to write, wanted to write because they got gifted."[12]

There's something beautiful and utopian here, but it's worth recognizing that this is not a true gift economy in the sense first defined by Marcel Mauss and other anthropologists. Gift economies, above all, are a means of keeping goods in circulation, as well as cementing bonds. Receiving a gift, be it a banquet or a poem, is only the first part of the equation. The receiver is then expected—more than expected, obligated—to return the favor. And not just return it, but to exceed it; the gift given in return must be more valuable than the original gift.

This obligation is a means of ensuring that goods and services stay in circulation in a given community, and it is also the means by which social status is determined. In Potlatch—a festival of elaborate giving practiced by various cultures of the Pacific Northwest—the goal is to give so much, and so lavishly, that your benefactors are perpetually in your debt. As Mauss notes, the gift economy may be "apparently free and disinterested but nevertheless constrained and self-interested." The gift, Mauss writes, appears generously given, but this is at best a "polite fiction, formalism and social deceit," behind which lies "obligation and economic self-interest." In gift economies, the obligation "to reciprocate worthily is imperative. One loses face for ever if one does not reciprocate," writes Mauss. "The individual unable to repay the loan or reciprocate the potlatch loses his rank and even his status as a free man."[13]

It may be that the term "gift economy" is a misnomer; it is a circulation economy, and it doesn't work if it consists only of gifts given in one direction. Georges Bataille describes potlatch as "the solemn giving of considerable riches, offered by a chief to his rival for the purpose of humiliating, challenging, and obligating him. The recipient has to erase the humiliation and take up the challenge; he must satisfy the *obligation* that was contracted by accepting. He can only reply, a short time later, by means of a new potlatch, more generous than the first: He must pay back with interest."[14]

Potlatch, like any gift economy, can never be a one-way process; those who receive gifts are indebted, and they are obligated to return the favor in order to save face. If editors and publishers—appealing to love, not money—ask for the gift of free words, then by the logic of the gift those writers can expect a return, with interest.

Largesse only makes sense when it is constantly returned, when it is part of a great wheel of motion. The accusation of a writer's stinginess can only be valid when it disrupts an already moving series of gifts and reciprocities. When this reciprocity is lacking, the humiliation lies entirely with those asking writers to give their words for free.

NOTES

1 The popular notion that Dickens was paid by the word is not, as it happens, strictly true: Dickens was paid by the installment, not the word; serializing his novels in periodicals allowed for a more sustained, steady income than waiting for book royalties.

2 Karl Marx, *Capital*, trans. Samuel Moore and Edward Aveling (New York, 1867), 1:105.

3 Anne Carson, "Writing on the World: Simonides, Exactitude, and Paul Celan," *Arion: A Journal of Humanities and the Classics* 4, no. 2.

4 Aristophanes, *Peace*, trans. Benjamin Bickley Rogers, in *The Complete Plays of Aristophanes*, ed. Moses Hadas (New York: Bantam Books, 1962), 238.

5 Anne Carson, *Economy of the Unlost* (Princeton University Press, 2002), 19.

6 Norman Austin, "Idyll 16: Theocritus and Simonides," in *Transactions and Proceedings of the American Philological Association* 98 (Cleveland, OH: Case Western University Press, 1969), 10.

7 Carson, "Writing on the World," 3.

8 Horace, *The Epistles of Horace*, trans. David Ferry (New York: Farrar, Straus and Giroux, 2001), 128.

9 Sameer Rahim, "Whatever Happened to Writing for Love, Not Money?" *The Telegraph*, August 14, 2014, Accessed November 3, 2015.

10 Carson, *Economy of the Unlost*, 19.

11 Carson, "Writing on the World," 3.

12 Robert Hass, "The Gift Economy of Poetry," Poets.org, Academy of American Poets, November 5, 2007, Accessed November 3, 2015.

13 Marcel Mauss, *The Gift: The Form and Reason of Exchange in Archaic Societies*, trans. W. D. Halls (London: Routledge, 2002), 4, 54.

14 Georges Bataille, *The Accursed Share, Vol. 1*, trans. Robert Hurley (Cambridge: Zone Books, 1991), 68–69.

RUNNING THE WIDGET FACTORY

Susan Orlean

in conversation with Manjula Martin

Manjula Martin: Do you remember the first story you were paid for, and how much you were paid for it?

Susan Orlean: Right after college I moved to Portland, Oregon, and I got a job at a little magazine, *Paper Rose*. It was a project funded through the Comprehensive Employment and Training Act. This federal act provided money for projects that presumably would help train people for jobs. And while it was mainly meant for people learning hard-core trades and skills, somebody came up with the idea of a proposal for a magazine, which would train writers and people on the business side as well, and they got the grant. I was on salary. This would have been 1978, and I have some memory of getting maybe $400 a month, or something like that. That could be wrong. . . .

Did you live off it?
I did. To be fair, my parents were helping me with a lot of expenses, like my car and that kind of thing, but I was paying my rent, and Portland was really cheap then.

And were you indeed trained to be a writer?
Yes. I got hired as a staff writer. I was not filing or making coffee;

I was writing. The first day on the job I came up with story ideas and was sent out to do them, and I really had no idea how to do either of those things, but that was my job.

What were your main influences when it came to your career?
I grew up with a dad who was an entrepreneur and his own boss. He was a real estate developer. So I grew up imagining not that you had some paternalistic corporation that took care of you and you'd retire and they'd give you this ongoing pension . . . none of that. My dad did very well, but he grew up during the Depression and definitely from humble beginnings. So I had that not-so-uncommon combination of upper-middle-class comfort coming from a parent who was very aware of what it felt like not to have that, and also imagining that I would make my own way in an entrepreneurial way, which I feel has been really helpful for me.

How?
The reality is, more and more and more, being a writer is running your own business. While I've had salaries, and I've been an employee, overall and ultimately and certainly increasingly so, being a writer is running a small business.

Do you enjoy running your own business?
I remember when I first started freelancing I hated the idea that I was both the manager and the product. I ran the widget factory and I was the widget. And if I ran out of paper clips, I was the one who had to go buy the paper clips.

So how did you learn to run the widget factory?
Pure experience. The longer you are a freelancer, the more you set up a system to make it more comfortable. One of the difficult things with freelancing initially was that I was nervous—where

was my next paycheck going to come from? So if any assignment was offered to me, my first reaction was, *I have to say yes, because I don't know what might come.* So I learned by managing that: Do you just take whatever comes? Do you hold out? How do you do that and how do you begin marketing your wares? It was an entirely new world that had nothing to do with making a beautiful sentence. And I don't necessarily think being a good writer suggests that you would be a good businessperson.

I do think that I found in myself a pretty good knack for business. The funny thing is that I felt like I had more in common with my dad in terms of being a businessperson than it would have seemed, given that I was doing something so different.

That makes sense. And obviously, you're very successful now. You're still officially on staff at the *New Yorker*?
Yes, but the definition of that is very different. For each person it can be a different financial arrangement. For a long time [at the *New Yorker*] I did what many of the writers do, which is agree in the beginning of the year to a certain number of pieces, and then that amount was paid out to me over the year—the aggregate of all of that. So I would say, okay, I'm going to do five five-thousand-word pieces, and we'd agree to this chunk of money, and then it would be paid in twelve monthly installments over a year. Then at the end of the year there would be a reckoning of, "Did you do all the writing or not?" And if you didn't, it would sort of roll over—you'd still have to finish before you started a new contract.

So there's some security there, although not in the traditional sense of a salary?
It's a predictability.

Like the magazine version of what a book advance would be.
Yeah, if you don't finish the work, you still have to finish the work.
So it's forfeitable in the sense that you pay it back in writing.

After I took a leave to finish *The Orchid Thief,* when I came
back I opted to switch to a different system where I didn't want to
get paid in advance, because I didn't like pushing to fulfill a quota.
I found the pressure very stressful. And I decided to instead say,
Look, don't pay me in advance; just pay me when I write a piece. It
meant giving up the predictability of the monthly check, but I was
more comfortable. I could say no more easily if I wasn't already "in
debt" to the magazine. I also had a kid, and I wanted the leeway to
make decisions with a little less pressure.

Also, I don't live alone. I've been with somebody for a very long
time—I was married before, and now I'm married to somebody
else, but it's been pretty continuous that I've been with another
person—which just changes the mathematics. I've always made my
own way, but there is a comfort there.

**After that first job, you landed at the *Boston Phoenix,* an alter-
native weekly newspaper. Like you, a lot of journalists get their
start at alt weeklies. And alt weeklies are not doing so well these
days; the *Phoenix* was shuttered in 2013. Do you think other
venues or training grounds are emerging?**
I talk about this a lot, because my advice to students and young
writers used to always be: look to the alt weekly world. It's a great
way to learn to write if your goal is to do longer narrative journalism. And while they never paid a lot, they would pay enough that
you could make that your profession. Alternately, I would say to
people: find a small- or medium-sized city and get a job at a paper
there and practice. Get jobs.

And you know, I haven't found a piece of advice to fit that

same place anymore, because I realize you can write a blog and eventually turn it into a business, but I don't see that as a good alternative to a job with the rigor of an editor and the ability to understand the audience as a readership that will respond and have expectations.

Finally, what I've been suggesting to people is that almost every publication now has a big online presence. I think there's a lot more openness to new writers on websites. I mean, I can see this with the *New Yorker*—the chance of getting something on the website is infinitely greater than getting in the print magazine.

You're very engaged online in general. That takes energy, and it takes time, and if time is money . . . how do you budget that?
First of all, I mainly do what I enjoy. To me it's an extension of a book tour. And even though it's a lot of work, I always found being on a book tour very exciting—to actually see people, hear from them, feel that connection.

And you know, the word here, which I cringe at, but it's reality, is *branding*. And the word follows the reality.

I think because I started doing books pretty early and started creating this other professional life for myself outside of the magazine, I began earlier than some of my colleagues there to imagine that maybe it was prudent and perhaps enjoyable to have a few irons in different fires. These are truly perilous times for magazines. And I suppose in a way I've been lucky that I've got other things going.

Sometimes I've been annoyed at myself because I thought, you know, oh, I'm so scattered, I could have just done the magazine work and had a very satisfying career instead of doing books and being on Twitter and doing some radio stuff and doing a lot of speaking engagements, but I don't know whether it's a certain amount of not putting all my eggs in one basket or whether it's just been that I'm curious about other platforms.

One quality that strikes me about your work itself is it seems like you're always saying yes. The stories you go after, the way you interact with people while reporting—yes is the go-to answer. So I guess it makes sense that, in terms of your career, you would say yes to more than one thing.
It is very much my personality to say, *Oh, I wonder, that'd be interesting, I'll try that.* I enjoy seeing where things go, not necessarily knowing if they will be remunerative. Lots of times they aren't, but it all adds up to some body of work that you're creating. And in this world, part of your body of work is you as a persona.

I think early on I had a knack for being strategic about choices I made. Either something was going to be really fun—the reporting or the experience—or it paid really well, or it would be useful in some other incarnation down the road. Like, this assignment maybe isn't so valuable in and of itself, but this is a good editor to know.

I recently pulled out my old copy of *The Orchid Thief,* which is an edition from after the movie came out. In it you did a prologue that was a very tongue-in-cheek self-interview. And you asked yourself, "Did you make a lot of money on the movie deal?" And you replied, "I don't think it's polite to talk about money."
I was joking, but I actually think, in the writing world, it's a very loaded subject. We're not talking about a profession that has any sort of systemized pay scale. In almost every other profession, people have a pretty good idea of what others are making, and I think, in writing, among the people I know, people have no idea. And the difference between people who do very well and people who are just getting along is a big range.

Would you put yourself in the former category?
Well, knock on wood, but yeah. My guess is, based on what I know, I get paid well. And I gather this from my agent, who probably knows a lot more than any individual writer about what people get. But I think it's, you know . . . if you're a union worker in a truck factory, you know exactly what everybody makes. With writers, we don't know, and we associate a lot of commentary about the value of the work, and it's very complicated. So it's a very personal thing. And I don't talk about it even with close friends.

I'm unsure whether you're suggesting that journalists should strive to be more like union factory workers.
I think unionization and standardized income works in professions where the work itself can be standardized. I think writing is by definition so individual, and each piece is so specific, the amount of work and the value of the work is so different. I do a certain kind of work. I'm not sure it really equates to what the guy at the next desk gets. As opposed to, if I'm literally doing the exact same job, I should get exactly the same pay they're getting.

One of the things union workers do have that freelance journalists don't is some level of protection against exploitation— standardized contract terms, job security, etc. And because workers know what everyone makes, they know how they're being treated categorically. They're a unit. What is your experience of these less-quantifiable types of job standards for journalists?
I don't think there's a solution right now that exists, that I know of. I've been places where there's talk about unions, and I've thought, it's not really a union type of employment. So I don't know what the solution is. I think it's difficult for people to negotiate for themselves, but not everyone can afford to have an agent negotiating, and that is one way to make sure you have a fair deal.

Do you identify as part of a particular class?
I would say that, more and more, class is defined not so much by income as by expectations and worldview and choices. I think that we need to reexamine the idea of class in that way.

In the creative class, the range of what people might earn is huge, but other similarities are pretty constant. You might have an actor who makes a lot of money or an artist who makes a little, but they probably have more in common class-wise than the financial advisor, who makes the same amount as the actor, or the factory worker, who makes the same as the artist.

It also used to be that class was somewhat divided along lines of religion, and those markers are so irrelevant now. I think it's so much more about profession and aspiration: Do you aspire to have a big house in the suburbs? It's not a question of whether you have one or can afford one. I think you can sort people out according to their goals, not whether they have the means to achieve them. That, to me, is a more interesting way of looking at class—rather than income.

What do you aspire to?
That's a good question. My aspirations are things like travel, time to try things that I haven't had the chance to try, stuff like that. I don't think, wow, I really want a bigger house or a fancier car or jewelry. I'm lucky. I'm comfortable. I'm not suggesting I haven't had those desires in the past, but I don't look at the Piaget ads in a magazine and think, wow, I want that. I love clothes, I love mid-century furniture—believe me, I sure could spend some money. I think my aspirations and interests—enjoying material comfort but caring more about great experiences and having the time to do interesting things—are aligned with those of my friends, whether they make more or less money than me. We all appreciate nice stuff, but probably dream more about having wonderful experiences.

What have you learned about class from your journalistic subjects, and has that changed over time as your economic situation has changed?
It's a huge subject that I'm very interested in both as a person and as a writer. And one that people tend to be a little reluctant to talk about or identify because we're hoping to be this classless society, which is certainly not true. I guess what I've done just continually reminds me of that fact. There is such a thing as class, and it defines who we are in every single aspect of our lives.

THE WIZARD

Alexander Chee

H ow do you know who you are as a writer? I think it is by how you make your living.

At some point in my education I remember being told that the correspondence between George Sand and Gustave Flaubert was one of the best correspondences between writers. I'd already enjoyed the letters of Mary McCarthy and Hannah Arendt, and the diaries of Anaïs Nin, so I figured this correspondence would be at least as interesting. And what I found *was* interesting—the two of them addressing each other as fictional personae, the use of all caps on Flaubert's part, as if he sensed the Internet was just 125 years away, or the way they fell into calling each other "Dear Master" (Flaubert's nickname for Sand) and "Dear Friend" (hers for him). But in particular I was interested in the way these two legends talked so frankly about money.

After reading the money parts, however, I remember I found them surprisingly dull. I didn't know enough about either writer at the time to understand the context. I reread them recently, and to the writer I am now, they are not dull.

I was moved by one letter in which Sand said she had not a sou with which to go to Cannes, to which Flaubert replied that he would lend her the money. But he led in with a little patter about how he would never have to worry about money. "I shall have enough to feed me and warm me until the end of my days. My heirs are or will be rich (for it is I who am the poor one of the family)." He then tells her he makes almost nothing off his writing and never expects to, and would lend her one thousand francs so she could also go to Cannes.

She rejects his offer in her next letter. "You offer me a thousand francs with which to go to Cannes, you who are as hard up as I am, and, when you wrote to me that you WERE BOTHERED about money matters, I opened my letter again, to offer you half of what I have, which still amounts to about two thousand francs; it is my reserve."

She goes on with various rejections of his offer and thank-yous to her friend before cutting to this point: "Only I tell you that if anyone ought to lend to me, it is Buloz [her editor] who has bought chateaux and lands with my novels. He would not refuse me, I know. He even offers it to me. I shall take from him then, if I have to."

Flaubert liked to act as if their relationship was entirely normal; a friendship between artistic peers of approximately the same social class, but the truth was there were differences that mattered. François Buloz was editor of *Revue des deux Mondes*, the magazine that ran some of the many serial novels Sand published, from which she made her income. Translated as "the review of two planets," the publication's title might also describe the different worlds the two friends inhabited. Sand was on a planet where she was the first woman in France to sue for and obtain a divorce, done so she could leave her husband and be a writer. When she says Buloz bought "chateaux" with her novels, she is just as much referring to how she has but one chateau.

Flaubert lived on a planet where he did not believe he had to worry as much as Sand did, thanks to family money, and while he made many financial mistakes, this was mostly true. In any case, she was likely refusing him out of pride as someone who made her living writing. He was probably offering what he did not have, as someone who was unsure of his income.

Today these letters are most of what is read of Sand's work; her reputation is much in decline by comparison with Flaubert's. Flaubert's novels are treated as classics, whereas Sand is treated as a historical oddity, a woman in pants with a cigar (and if you don't know her, she was famous for wearing men's clothes in order to go into places that forbade women). She wrote prolifically, sometimes publishing three novels a year in serial, for most of her life, and lived well enough, raising her children and keeping her lovers and her home in Nohant, never dependent on a man who wasn't paying her for writing. And her point, about what publishers take versus what writers make, or at least, their interdependence, is not lost on me today. Not much has changed. I don't have a single writer friend I write to about money the way Flaubert and Sand did. Instead, it seems to be a conversation we are all having all the time.

§

For those who are not writers (and many of those who are), there is an illusory "made it" point, the point at which the writer no longer has to worry about money. It doesn't exist unless you were born someone who didn't ever have to worry about it.

If you Google "one million dollar advance novel" you can see stories going back to the 1980s about writers who have "made it." See how many of the names you recognize. Some have definitely gone on to fame, perhaps as many have not. This is why I greeted a recent article in the *Wall Street Journal* about how publishing is making authors millionaires—a new trend!—with something akin to laughter. It's not a trend; it's just how the industry works. No one told the young reporter.

If I were going to write a cautionary tale about a writer earning a big payday, it would involve a story like this—told like a fable.

Back in the late '90s a friend of mine sold his first two novels for two million dollars. He talked about the deal so much that he became known in our common circles as The Man Who Talked About His Book Deal For Two Years. I never saw the novels in any store, was never invited to their release parties, never saw their reviews. After a few years, I stopped seeing him and then saw him one day downtown at a jewelry store, behind the counter. He seemed startled to see me.

"I'm just helping a friend out," he said. "She had to step away."

"That's very kind," I said. He seemed embarrassed, wanting to make sure I didn't think he worked there.

I had been near the jewelry store that day because I was buying myself shirts at Seize sur Vingt, a bespoke shirtmaker I didn't usually go to, but I was treating myself for having won an award. The shirts were to remind me of the victory.

The shirts no longer fit but I keep them. They now remind me of him and me both. They remind me that I don't know whether my old friend was working in that shop or not. That I don't know if he failed to write the novels or if he wrote them and they succeeded, just somewhere out of my sight. They remind me there is no "made it" point. There is only ever the making of work.

§

No education in being a writer should be complete without someone teaching you how to make a living as a writer, but this is less common than one might think. I was lucky to have undergraduate professors who were all very frank with me. I have tried to do the same with my own students.

My three first teachers of writing were all very successful and all lived well, within the life of the university, but each offered a very different model of how to live and work as a writer. Phyllis Rose was a biographer who typically spent a long time between heavily researched projects; Kit Reed is a novelist, short story writer, and screenwriter who has produced a book every other year, if not every year, for decades; Annie Dillard is an essayist, poet, and novelist who has frequently appeared on bestseller lists throughout her career. All had faculty housing at Wesleyan, where I was an undergraduate—lovely homes that I envied and I hoped someday to have one myself. Annie was rumored to own three other homes in Cape Cod, purchased with her book money and rented out for income, which struck me as incredibly wise, if true. All of them seemed comfortably middle class, or possibly better off than that.

When I decided to be a writer, I decided I too would pursue a life writing and teaching. I wanted a deal like I'd heard Annie had: teaching one class a year, a house on campus, a writing cabin in the backyard. I would write like Kit did, keeping my mornings to myself, opening up to teaching class or to visitors and friends in the afternoons and evenings. And I would be as strict as Phyllis was, keeping careful boundaries around my own writing time versus my teaching time. But it didn't quite happen that way.

Instead, over the course of my career, I have had to watch as both teaching and writing have suffered from twin crises of income destruction. I am now, as a result, in a future where my teachers' advice and example do not serve me.

At present, I am a visiting writer, which is a sort of high-class adjunct—the pay is roughly three to ten times more than adjuncts make but there is still no job security. Some years I am in New York, where I live, sometimes not—a semester away in Germany, or Texas, or Iowa, or Hawaii. Mark Doty lived this way for a while, as did Edmund White, and I watched them carefully as I set up my life: I have a home base I return to that costs very little when I'm not away—I don't move from place to place to place, as I did for a while. I sometimes have access to benefits and funding. I have no faculty housing as I'm not on tenure track—faculty housing, once standard, largely does not exist anymore, or if it does, it exists in a few premium locations where the real estate market is high—the Stanford faculty, for example, typically receive financial aid from the university when buying homes or they could not afford to live in Palo Alto. The Columbia and NYU faculty receive apartments or they likewise could not afford to live nearby. They become professors living in multimillion-dollar homes, which I imagine is its own kind of irony museum—if also very pleasant.

Annie was the frankest of my three professors about money. She made it clear in her nonfiction class that we could make more money with nonfiction than fiction; that when we were starting out, even if we didn't have clips, we could write an essay and send it to an editor, and it would be our introduction. The editor might not take the essay but like it enough to assign something; if the essay was good, it could create a new relationship. Nonfiction paid about three to five times as much as fiction, in her estimation, and this is still, to my mind, true. She taught us to use the *Best American Essays* collections as a guide to submitting work—to note the places that placed the most essays in the collection and focus there. And to always check the editors' names.

My first major publication was an essay in the anthology *Boys Like Us*, which is still in print. The fee was not high—I don't recall it at this point—but I remember the contracts were scrupulously drawn up. Edmund White was in the anthology also, and I met him at the release party. He told me he'd admired my essay and later invited me to be a part of his anthology *Loss Within Loss*, for which I was paid $1,000, the most I'd ever been paid for a piece of writing at that time (this was 1998). That essay, a memoir, ran to about three thousand words. At thirty-three cents a word, it was low for the '90s, but I was too young to know better, and I felt rich. It wasn't the kind of nonfiction that usually paid well: an essay about an artist who'd died of AIDS in the last days before the advent of the drug cocktail which saved so many lives. White asked us to take stock of the epidemic's human cost.

I mention this because in the years since, nonfiction has become my other day job apart from teaching. With these very literary beginnings, I made a steady source of income that could get me through, regardless of what else was happening with my fiction.

I've since written for outlets ranging from *Martha Stewart Living* to *Garden Design* to *Departures* to *Tin House* to the *New York Times Book Review* to the *Wall Street Journal*. I have made as much as three dollars a word and as little as nothing. Most of what I have to endure as a writer is the asymmetry between effort and reward: the travel piece that flies me to have dinner in Shanghai at an avant-garde French restaurant with ten seats, paying three dollars a word for three thousand words alongside the memoir of teaching myself to use the tarot, written at the same length, for which I was paid $250, a flat fee.

The most mysterious arrangement: the op-ed I wrote for free in an hour, for which I later received a $1,400 check because it had been republished. This will never happen again, though, the reprint fee no longer possible, as the media company I wrote it for had me sign a contract recently giving away, retroactively, any reprint rights to anything I wrote prior to the new contract as well as anything I'll write afterward. The contract is probably indefensible, but for now it stands. But when I say things haven't changed much since the days of George Sand's complaint, this is what I mean. Much as in gambling, the house, if not always, usually wins when it comes to money. And I believe this is because they know no one will remember them. And it may be no one will remember us. But we don't have Sand's editor's letters in translation. We have Sand's.

§

I was at a panel recently on the topic of how writers make a living and it quickly became clear to me that everyone was younger than me by at least ten years and did not know any writers who made a living at writing. Everyone was speaking of side jobs and having them for their whole lives, invoking famous writers who had worked at other jobs their whole lives as if this was virtuous and not the result of an at least decades-long scam on fees for writers.

Back in Maine, where I grew up, before I moved to New York, I knew just one writer who made his living at writing. His name was Bill Caldwell and he was a popular syndicated newspaper columnist who lived in a beautiful house in Portland with a view of the ocean, and he was well off enough that he even lent money to my mother when we went through a difficult time as a family. I remember when I would visit him I would think, *Everything here is made out of writing.* It was like visiting the home of a wizard who had cast a spell to make everything he owned come into existence.

Only when I moved to New York after college did I meet many other writers who made their living at writing—it was arriving in a city of wizards. It was the early 1990s and I was working at *Out* magazine as an assistant editor during the start-up. I was paid $800 a week, which felt like a lot of money then. I was learning how to listen to the people around me for the clues I needed. The writers I dealt with in my job made their living writing the sort of things I was learning to edit, and I could see it was possible then to be a writer for magazines and write books, and to make a good living at it, even while writing adventurous things—risky fiction or journalism, film criticism, and, of course, columns. I met writers who were putting their kids through New York City schools and colleges while writing and living mostly on the income from their books and speaking gigs.

These writers were very different from my undergraduate professors. To them teaching was something you did to get you through. My dreams of teaching and writing, if described to them, would have seemed quaint, even alien. If they were ever interested in teaching, it was in the short term, something they did to get through. Teaching requires accommodating yourself to a set of values that has nothing to do with writing, like pedagogy and earning an MFA or a PhD, which takes time away from writing. Teaching jobs have to either be worth missing the writing time or allow for more time than most teaching allows. To writers like this, adjuncting for low pay was out of the question.

Despite admiring and studying these writers, I did not, I remember, feel cut out for what they were doing. I wanted something more contemplative. I wanted to be around serious conversations, I told myself. I wanted to be around people who wrote no matter what they were paid and yet I also wanted to make a living at writing. I was young enough to think this was a serious approach. I was young enough then to think there were only one or two ways of doing these things.

I needed to go to another city of writers to learn how to do what I wanted.

§

The Iowa Writers' Workshop was my first lesson in making my own house out of my own magic. I had been paid for other writing work before graduate school—freelance journalism, even poetry—but the stipend I had at Iowa was pure sorcery to me. I rented a modest basement apartment by the graveyard at the edge of town, a former ROTC unit tiled in linoleum, furnished with rented furniture. It was a cave, but to me it was my cave—my magic cave—I had made it out of my writing, after all. And it was there I wrote a story that became my first published short story in a magazine that paid money, a magazine called *Big*, which somehow made it even a little hilarious—a "big" deal.

When the check came, I bragged to the man I was dating about it—all fiction writers, I think, love to imagine we can make money at fiction, and the people around us love this also. He is one of my favorite ex-boyfriends. He was a terrible fit but we were very fond of each other—we still are. He looked and dressed a bit like a hero in a movie about a World War I air force pilot—a big square jaw, wavy blond hair that sat high on his head. I looked like the guy the hero would chase through the tunnels—shorter, darker, dressing in the post-punk way I was sure was the only way to dress for the rest of my life. The first day he came over to my magical ROTC apartment cave, he took one look at the T-shirts I was using as pillowcases and said, "Alex, my brothers live like this. But they're hockey players."

Which is why he said, "I know where that money's going." And he drove me all the way to the Ralph Lauren Factory outlet where he made me spend it all on bedding: sheets, pillows, pillowcases, a duvet, a duvet cover, and a big black wool blanket I still have to this day.

There was a feeling of unleashing something when I cashed that check, a force unlike any other. When I sell a piece of fiction, it feels different from selling an essay and I think of it as the clearest way for me to know who I am. However I'll be remembered by others, this is how I remember myself. Selling fiction feels like I've cast a spell on the world and made it give me something that didn't exist before. It's the closest thing to actual magic I can think of. And that blanket still keeps me warm in the cabin I bought in the Catskills with my partner Dustin. Each night I go to bed there, I feel as rich as I did on that day Shawn made me spruce up my bed. The magic of that day, that achievement, is in that blanket—born from the story, a blanket I made up. And then went to sleep in, for years, every night.

Maybe I'll be buried in it.

YOU ARE THE SECOND PERSON

Kiese Laymon

You know that any resemblance to real places, spaces, people, time, or things is purely coincidental.

Alone, you sit on the floor of your apartment thinking about evil, honesty, that malignant growth in your hip, your dead uncle, letters you should have written, the second person, and stretch marks. You're wearing a XXL T-shirt you plan on wearing the day your novel comes out. The front of the T-shirt says, WHAT'S A REAL BLACK WRITER? The back reads, FUCK YOU. PAY ME. You open your computer. With a scary pain in your hip, you inhale and force a crooked smile before reading an e-mail from Brandon Farley, your fifty-four-year-old black editor.

The success of your book will be partially dependent on readers who have a different sensibility than your intended audience, he writes. As I've already said to you, too many sections of the book feel forced for the purpose of discussing racial politics. Think social media. Think comment sections. Those white people buy books, too, bro. Readers, especially white readers, are tired of black writers playing the wrong race card. If you're gonna play it (and I think you should) play it right. Look at Tarrantino [sic]. He is about to fool all these people into believing they were watching a black movie with

Django. *I guarantee you that whiteness will anchor almost every scene. That's one model you should think about.*

Also, black men don't read. And if they did, they wouldn't read this kind of fiction. So you might think of targeting bougie black women readers. Bougie black women love plot. They love romance with predictable Boris Kodjoe–type characters. Or they love strong sisters caught up in professional hijinks who have no relationships with other sisters. Think about what holds a narrative like Scandal *together.*

In 2012, real black writers make the racial, class, gender, and sexual politics of their work implicit. Very implicit. The age of the "race narrative" is over, bro. As is, the only way your book would move units is if Oprah picked it for her Book Club. That's not happening. Oprah only deals with real black writers.

You begin typing, "Hey Brandon, this is my fourteenth thorough revision for you in four years. I know I'm not changing your mind and that's fine. Thanks for telling me what real black writers do and what Oprah likes. You never told me you met her. Anyway, the black teenagers in my book are actually purposely discussing 'racial politics' in awkwardly American ways. Their race and racial politics, like their sexuality and sexual politics, is somehow tied to every part of their character. My book is unapologetically an American race novel, among other things. I'm still not sure why you bought the book if you didn't dig the vision."

You push send on the e-mail before opening up the Word doc you just defended. You jump to Chapter Nine. Thirty minutes later, a section of the book where an older queer coach tries to impart a strange "them versus us" racial understanding on your narrator is cut because it "explicitly discusses racial politics."

You call your editor names that hurt, muddied misogynist names you pride yourself on never calling any human being while looking out the tall window of your second-floor apartment in Poughkeepsie, New York.

A barefoot white boy with a red and black lumberjack shirt is outside sitting under an oak tree. He's doing that walkie-talkie thing on his phone that you fucking hate. You can tell he's telling the truth and lying at the same time.

"*You* fucking hurt me more than anyone in my whole life," he says. "I couldn't hate *you* . . . I just don't trust *you* . . . You're the second person who has done this to me. *You're* the one who said *you* tell the truth . . . *You* started this." The white boy is scratching his sack with his left thumb and using his big toe to make designs in the dirt in front of him. "*You* ruined my life and hurt me way more than I hurt *you*. It's always all about *you*."

You wonder about the second person on the other end of the phone. Is the second person a woman or a man? Is s/he listening to the lumberjack on speakerphone? Is s/he wishing the lumberjack would hurry up and finish so s/he can run and get a two for one special on Peanut Buster Parfaits from Dairy Queen? You know far too well why a first or third person could self-righteously claim innocence in matters of love and loss but you can't figure out why the lumberjack is scratching his sack with his thumb and making dirt rainbows with his big toe.

Looking down at the browning S key on your keyboard, you think more hateful thoughts about your editor, your ex-girlfriend, skinny people, and fat young black men. These thoughts distract you from the pain in your hip, the dirt on your hands.

For five years, Brandon Farley, your editor, has had you waiting.

You remember the acidic sweetness in Grandma's voice when you told her you'd just signed a two-book deal with "KenteKloth Books," the most popular African American imprint in the country. New York fall felt like Mississippi winter as Grandma came out of her second diabetic coma.

"We are so proud of you, baby," Grandma whispered over the phone from Forest, Mississippi. "Just remember that God gave you five senses and whatever health you got for a reason. When they gone, they gone, but if you don't use them best you can while you got them, ain't a bigger fool in the world than that fool in the mirror."

Six months before your first novel's initial publication date of June 2009, you stopped hearing from Brandon Farley. He didn't answer your calls or respond to e-mails. You gave up and called the publisher of KenteKloth in February.

"Oh, Brandon didn't tell you?" his boss, Ms. Jacoby, asked. "He's no longer with us, but your book has been picked up by Nathalie Bailey. She'll call you in a few days."

Your lungs whistled, crashed, and slipped into the heels of your feet. You told yourself it would be okay. Then trudged your sexy ass to the International House of Pancakes.

Three hours later, you were full, fatter than you wanted to be, less sexy than you were, and you found a way to reach Brandon Farley at home. Brandon apologized for not telling you he wasn't seeing eye-to-eye with his boss. He promised you that Nathalie Bailey was a friend of his who would do right by both your novels.

§

A week later you got a call from Nathalie. "It's a hard sell for black literary fiction these days," she told you. "But I like what you're doing. You're on your way to becoming a real black writer. It's a gorgeous book with big messy ideas and we've got to work hard and fast. But I'd love for you to let me take this book to publication. It's a winner."

You felt a comfort with Nathalie but you didn't want to be impulsive like you were with Brandon. "Can I have a few days to think about it?" you asked her. "Just to make sure."

A few days passed and you planned on calling Nathalie at

4:00 P.M. on a Thursday. At 3:00 P.M. you got a call from a 212 number. Before you had a book deal, 917 and 212 numbers were like slimming mirrors; they made you think, *Damn nigga, you ain't that disgusting at all.*

On the other end of 917 and 212 numbers were agents, editors, or an ex telling you she was sorry and she missed sharing a heartbeat.

"Hello," you answered, trying to sound busy and country at the same time.

"Hi."

It was Brandon Farley.

After a few minutes of spin where Brandon Farley showed you how much he remembered about your book and how happy he was to be the new senior editor of young adult fiction at the widely acclaimed "Duck Duck Goose" Publishing Company, he said, ". . . all that to say, we really want your book."

"Word?"

"Word up, bro!" Brandon laughed. It was the first time any black man on earth had ever called you "bro" with a long *o*.

"Bro," he said it again, "I will pay you more for one book than you got for two over at KenteKloth. I'll want an option of first refusal on the second. But that'll still give you the kind of flexibility you want."

"Are you serious?" you asked. "Only thing is I'm a little worried about changing the subtext and the darkness and the metafictive stuff if it's gonna be marketed as a young adult book. The ending ain't really pretty."

"You'd be surprised at the possibilities in young adult fiction," he told you. "Listen, bro, young adults will read it. This is adult literary fiction with mass appeal. You won't have to make many changes at all and we can get you a pub date of June 2009."

"But what about Nathalie?" you asked.

"Bro, you're the second person to ask me about her," he scoffed, sounding like a hungry hip-hop mogul. You hated even imagining using the word *scoffed.*

"It's business, bro. Never personal. You'll have to get out of that contract over there. And I've got the perfect agent for you. She's this wonderful fine sister over at Chatham Ward & Associates named Bobbie Winslow. Look her up. Bobbie'll take care of everything if you decide to go with us."

You smiled and forgave him for four or five "bros" too many.

§

Later that day, Bobbie, the perfect agent/fine sister, called from a 212 number and asked you to send her the other pieces you were working on. By 8:00 P.M., you sent her the book Brandon wanted, another novel, and a rough draft of some essays you'd been working on. By 3:00 A.M., she e-mailed you and said, "We want you. You're the second person I've said this to in five years but I think you could change the trajectory of African American contemporary literature. You've got the makings of what Brandon calls 'a real black writer.' I'm so excited about the new projects you're working on. If you sign with Chatham Ward, we'll have our lawyers get you out of the deal with Nathalie in the next week or so and Brandon says he can get us half the advance in three weeks. I'll be in touch."

You never contacted Nathalie, but a few days later, Bobbie, the perfect agent/fine sister did. "Nathalie is so fucking pissed," she said a few days later, "but all's fair in love, war, and business." As you wondered whether this was love, war, or business, you and your perfect agent/fine sister waited and waited and waited for Brandon to deliver.

Six months later, three months after your initial publication date of June 2009, Brandon offered you substantially less money than he promised and a publication date two years later than the one he verbally agreed to.

"Pardon me for saying this," your perfect agent said over the phone from a different 212 number, "but Brandon Farley is a bona fide bitch-ass nigga for fucking us out of thousands of dollars and pushing the pub date back to June 2011. He's just not professional. I'm wondering if this was just some ploy to get you away from KenteKloth. He's been trying to take all his authors away from there as a way of fucking the company."

"I don't get it," you said, shamefully excited that your agent used *fucking, bitch-ass,* and *nigga* in one conversation.

"So Brandon acquired this wonderful list of new literary black authors at KenteKloth, and they were all going to work with Nathalie after he was basically fired from the company. Nathalie and the house were going to get credit for a lot of his work. Do you get it now? We got caught up in something really nasty."

You got your first edit letter from Brandon Farley in July 2011. In addition to telling you that the tone of the piece was far too dark and that you needed an obvious redemptive ending, Brandon wrote, "There's way too much racial politics in this piece, bro. You're writing to a multicultural society, but you're not writing multiculturally."

You wondered out loud what writing "multiculturally" actually meant and what kind of black man would write the word *bro* in an e-mail.

"Bro, we need this book to come down from 284 pages to 150," he said. "We're going to have to push the pub date back again, too. I'm thinking June 2012. Remember," he wrote, "it's business. I think you should start from scratch but keep the spirit. Does the narrator really need to be a black boy? Does the story really need to take place in Mississippi? The Percy Jackson demographic," he wrote. "That's a big part of the audience for your novel. Read it over the weekend. Real black writers adjust to the market, bro, at least for their first novels."

By the time you found out Percy Jackson wasn't the name of

a conflicted black boy from Birmingham, but a fake-ass Harry Potter who saved the gods of Mount Olympus, you were already broken. Someone you claimed to love told you that you were letting your publishing failure turn you into a monster. She said you were becoming the kind of human being you always despised. You defended yourself against the truth and really against responsibility, as American monsters and American murderers tend to do, and you tried to make this person feel as absolutely worthless, confused, and malignant as you were. Later that night, you couldn't sleep, and instead of diving back into the fiction, for the first time in your life, you wrote the sentence, "I've been slowly killing myself and others close to me just like my uncle."

Something else was wrong, too. Your body no longer felt like your body and you doubted whether your grandma would ever see your work before one of you died.

Two years after the first pub date for your first book, there was no book. Questions fell like dominoes.

Why would Brandon buy the book? you kept asking yourself. "Why would that bitch-ass nigga get you out of a contract for a book he didn't want?" your perfect agent kept asking you. "Why'd you promise stuff you couldn't deliver?" you asked Brandon on the phone.

"The book doesn't just have Duck Duck Goose's name on it," you told him, slightly aware of what happens when keeping it real goes wrong. "My name is on that shit, too. That means, on some level, it ain't business. I feel like you want me to lie. I read and write for a living, Brandon. I see the shit that's out there. I've read your other books. I see your goofy book covers looking like greasy children's menus at Applebee's. I ain't putting my name on a fucking greasy Applebee's menu. I'm not. Don't front like it's about quality. You, and maybe your editorial board, don't think you can sell this book because you don't believe black southern audiences read literary shit. And that's fine. Maybe you're right. If you didn't believe in it, why buy it in the first place? Look, I can create an audience for this novel with these essays I've been writing," you tell him. "It sounds stupid, but I can. I just need to know that you're committed to really publishing this book. Do you believe in the vision or not?"

After a long pause where you could hear Brandon telling his assistant, Jacques, to leave the room and get him a warm bear claw with extra glaze, he said, "Bro, you're the second person to complain to me this morning about how I do my job. The first person had a bit more tact. Honestly," he said, "reading your work has been painful. It's business. Take that folksy shit back to Mississippi. I did you a favor. Don't forget that. You're just not a good writer, bro. Good-bye."

The next morning you got an e-mail from Brandon with the following message:

Hey Wanda,

I finished the revision this afternoon. It totally kicks ass. Congrats. I've sent back a few line edits, but it's brilliant. Move over Teju and Chimamanda. There's a new African writer on the scene showing these black American writers how it's done. I'm so proud of you. Always darkest before the dawn, Wanda. It feels so empowering to work with the future of contemporary diasporic literature.

Tell David hi for me.

   Best,

   Brandon

Your name was not, and never will be, "Wanda."

You logged into your Facebook feed and found that Brandon, your Facebook friend, had posted the covers of recently published and forthcoming books he'd edited. Wanda's book and all the other covers really looked like greasy children's menus at Applebee's. Your eyes watered as you googled the published authors Brandon had signed two years after you. You wanted your name on an Applebee's menu, too.

Even though you were fatter than you'd ever been and the joints in your hip got rustier and more decayed every day, parts of you were a rider. Yeah, Brandon bombed first, you thought, but right there, you felt determined to get your novel out by any means necessary so you could thank him in the acknowledgments:

> . . . And a special thanks to that shape-shifting cowardly ol' lying ass, Brandon Farley, the untrustworthy editing-cause-he-can't-write-a-lick ass Tom who'd sell out his mama for a gotdamn glazed bear claw as long as the bear claw had been half eaten by a white librarian named Jacques or Percy Jackson. I know where you live. And I got goons. Can you see me now? Gooooood. Congrats, BRO.

Instead you wrote:

> *Not sure why you sent that e-mail intended for Wanda Onga-Nana, Brandon. I hope we both appreciate the distinction between what's marketable and what's possible. Glad you're having success with some of your authors. I think you should give my books a chance to breathe, too. Thanks for the inspiration. Tell Wanda congratulations.*

Brandon never responded to your e-mail.

You stayed in your bedroom for weeks writing essays to your dead uncle, your grandma, the son and daughter you didn't have. Outside that bedroom, and outside of your writing life, you'd fully become a liar, unafraid to say I love you, too willing to say I'm sorry, unwilling to change the ingredients of your life, which meant you'd gobbled up your heart and you were halfway done gobbling up the heart of a woman who loved you.

You'd become typical.

One Tuesday near the end of spring, you couldn't move your left leg or feel your toes and you'd been sweating through your mattress for a month. You knew there was something terribly wrong years before your furry-fingered doctor, with tiny hands and eyebrows to die for, used the words "malignant growth."

"It won't be easy," the doctor told you the Friday before your spring break. "You're the second person I've diagnosed with this today, but there's still a chance we can get it without surgery. You said you've been living with the pain for three years? Frankly, I'm worried about you," the doctor said. "You seem like you're holding something in. Fear is okay, you know? Do you have any questions?"

You watched the doctor's eyebrows sway like black wheat. They looked like a hyper four-year-old had gone buck wild with a fistful of black crayons. "I like your eyebrows," you told the doctor. "I don't know what's wrong with me. I just want my grandma to think I'm a real writer."

"I'd actually like to recommend therapy in addition to the treatment," the doctor told you before he walked you out the door.

§

For the next few months you took the treatment he gave you and prided yourself on skipping the therapy. You told no one about the malignant growth in your hip, not even the person whose heart you were eating. Though you could no longer run or trust, you could eat and you could hate. So you ate, and you ate, and you hated, until sixty-eight pounds and five months later, you were finally unrecognizable to yourself.

You accepted, on a ride through Georgia that ended with you

falling asleep and crashing your car, that you had sprinted away from the hard work of being the human being and writer you wanted to be. Like every hater you've ever known, you shielded yourself from critique and obsessed with wading in the funk of how people had done you wrong.

One Sunday near the end of spring, after talking to your two family members who were both killing themselves slowly, too, you made the decision to finally show the world the blues you'd been creating. You also decided to finish revising the novel without Brandon.

"The whole time I'd been in those woods," you wrote in one of the last scenes in the book, "I'd never stopped and looked up."

You spent the next four months of your life skipping treatments for your hip and getting a new draft of the novel done. You didn't dumb down the story for Brandon, for multiculturalism, or for school boards you'd never see. You wrote an honest book to Paul Beatty, Margaret Walker Alexander, Cassandra Wilson, Big K.R.I.T., Octavia Butler, Gangsta Boo, your little cousins, and all your teachers.

You prayed on it and sent the book to Brandon. You told him that you had created a post-Katrina, Afrofuturist, time-travelish, black southern love story filled with adventure, metafiction, and mystery. You wanted to call the book *Long Division*, after two of the characters' insistence on showing their work in the past, present, and future.

"It's a book I'm proud of," you wrote in the letter attached to the manuscript. "It's something I needed to read when I was a teenager in Mississippi. Shit, it's something I need to read now. I'm willing to work on it. Just let me know if you get the vision."

Brandon responded the same day that he would check it out over the weekend and get back to you with his thoughts.

Four months later, he finally sent an e-mail: "Ultimately, the same problems exist in this draft that were in the other drafts." Brandon ended the e-mail, "We need more traditional adventure. We need to know less about the relationships between the characters, less racial politics, and more about the adventure. You need to explain how the science fiction works, bro. No one is going to believe black kids from Mississippi traveling through time talking about institutional racism. It's way too meandering. Kill the metafictive angle. You haven't earned the right to pull that off. This is still painful. I'm convinced you really do not want to be a real black writer, bro. The success of your book will be partially dependent on readers who have a different sensibility than your intended audience . . ."

Still too ashamed to really reckon with your disease or your failures, and too cowardly to own your decisions, you stretched your legs out on the floor of your living room and cried your eyes out. After crying, laughing, and wondering if love really could save all the people public policy forgot, you grabbed a pad and scribbled, "Alone, you sit on the floor . . ."

After writing for about two hours, you wonder why you start the piece with "Alone, you . . ." You are the "I" to no one in the world, not even yourself.

You've eviscerated people who loved you when they made you the second person in their lives, when they put the relationship's needs ahead of your wants. And you've been eviscerated for the same thing.

You're not a monster. You're not innocent.

You look down at the browning S key on your keyboard. You don't know how long you'll live. No one does. You don't know how long you'll have two legs. You know that it's time to stop letting your anger and hate toward Brandon Farley and your publishing failure be more important than the art of being human and healthy. You know it's time to admit to yourself, your writing, and folks who love you that you're at least the second person to feel like you're really good at slowly killing yourself and others in America.

"Sorry your reads have been so painful, Brandon," you start typing. "I want to get healthy. That means not only that I need to be honest; it also means I've got to take my life back and move to a place where I no longer blame you for failure. I've thought and said some terrible things about you. I've blamed you for the breaking of my body and the breaking of my heart. I hate the word *bitch* but I've used it so many times in my head when I'm thinking about you. Women deserve better. You deserve better. I really believed that you and your approval would determine whether or not I was a real black writer, worthy of real self-respect and real dignity.

"There was something in my work, something in me that reso-nated with your work and something in you. We are connected. I'm not sure what happens next. No young writer, real or not, leaves an iconic press before their first book comes, right? Whatever. I can't put my name on the book that you want written and it's apparent that you won't put your company's name on the book I want read. We tried, Brandon, but life is long and short. I've written my way out of death and destruction before. I'm trying to do it again. I think I'm done with the New York publishing thing for a while. I'm through with the editors, the agents, and all that stress. No hate at all. It's just not for me. I can't be healthy dealing with all that stuff. I'll get my work out to my folks and if they want more, I'll show them. If not, that's fine. I'm a writer. I write.

"I'm sorry and sorrier that sorry is rarely enough. God gave me senses and a little bit of health. It's time for me to use them the best that I can. Thanks for the shot. Good luck. I hope you like the work I'm doing.

"Not sure if it's good, but I know it's black, blue, Mississippi, and honest. I'm a not a bro, Brandon. You ain't either. Thanks again for everything."

You look up.

You close your eyes.

You breathe.

You look down and you keep on writing, revising, reading, reckoning, working . . . because that's what real black writers do.

FIVE YEARS IN
THE WILDERNESS

Cari Luna

In 2010 my first literary agent fired me after five years together. The end of our relationship felt as big as any breakup, nearly as devastating as the end of my first marriage, even though we parted on the most amicable of terms. Comparing a business relationship to a romantic one sounds like ridiculous hyperbole until you take into account that I had put all my professional and artistic hopes and dreams into my agent's hands. Or, rather, I had projected that power on to her. I wanted to publish books, and to publish them well. I wanted to be read and respected as a novelist. I wanted to put books out into the world and have people read them and care about them. I believed that having a literary agent was the only way to make that happen. And then I didn't have her anymore.

My agent had taken me on right out of grad school in 2005, agreeing to represent my first novel, *Drowning Practice*. Though it came close a couple of times in the two years that she shopped it around, the book was never published. When I graduated from the MFA program at Brooklyn College, armed with my big MFA ego, and immediately signed with a *big New York* agent, it hadn't occurred to me that the first novel I wrote might not be the first one I published. Yes, I knew it happened to other people all the time, but that wasn't going to be my story. I had the first line of

Drowning Practice tattooed on my lower leg in my own hand-writing, to mark my commitment to the book "no matter what happened with it," but in my mind, there was only one way things could go, because I had a Real New York Agent in my corner. If she believed in my book, it would sell, and sell well. I thought, having cleared the agent obstacle on the road to publishing suc-cess, I was all set. I granted my agent the power to create a career for me. And if that was true, then it followed that there was no way to navigate without her.

While *Drowning Practice* was failing to find a publisher, I was writing *The Revolution of Every Day*, a novel that follows the lives of five squatters living on New York's Lower East Side in the mid-1990s as the city is attempting to evict them. I was pretty proud of it. I remain really fucking proud of it. It's a good book, and a much more ambitious one than *Drowning Practice*. But my agent (who is a wonderful person and an excellent, smart agent) couldn't get comfortable with the squatters. We went through a couple rounds of revision and she just couldn't click with the book the way she would need to in order to sell it. I was adamant about not setting *The Revolution of Every Day* aside in favor of a more marketable project. Ultimately, she sent me a long breakup e-mail saying she couldn't represent the book, and it would be doing me a disservice to take *Revolution* on when she wouldn't be able to pitch it to editors with honest enthusiasm. She wrote, "This is heartbreaking, difficult for us both. . . . I'm not your guy." And with that one e-mail, our five-year partnership was over. No matter that we genuinely liked each other, no matter that she'd loved my first book. She wasn't my guy.

The summer of 2010, when she and I split, was a low, low period for me. My first book had failed to sell, but I'd comforted myself with the knowledge that at least I still had an agent in my corner who believed in my work. And then my agent fired me and I didn't even have that. I was back to the beginning. I felt humiliated, as if I'd been demoted. It seemed essential that I find a new agent as quickly as possible, as much to cover the shame of rejection as to try to get my novel out into the world. My savior had cut me loose, but I would find another. I spent over a year trying to find a new agent for *The Revolution of Every Day*, but no one wanted to represent it. No one, it seemed, cared about a bunch of squatters.

In the spring of 2012, I said *Fuck it*, and I started submitting the book to small independent presses on my own. That July, I accepted an offer from Tin House Books and negotiated the contract myself. I had spent most of my adult life working in book publishing, at Penguin and HarperCollins, and though I worked in production editorial and didn't have direct experience with contracts, my general background in publishing proved useful. The language and terms of the contract were familiar to me, and I did some Internet research to figure out what rights to retain and what to sign away. (My general rule is: Sign away foreign rights if you don't have an agent to handle them for you. Keep film and theatrical rights. Always.) In hindsight, I wish I'd asked for a slightly larger advance, if only because it never hurts to ask, but I'm pleased with the contract I signed, and I'm proud to have negotiated it by myself.

Tin House proved to be the perfect publisher for *Revolution*, and my experience with them was wonderful. I published a novel I believed in, and readers found it and embraced it. It received excellent reviews and won the 2015 Oregon Book Award for Fiction. It's been a huge privilege, a fantastic experience all around. And I did it without an agent.

I reread *Drowning Practice* a couple of years ago, at age thirty-nine, and could do nothing but cringe. My editor at Tin House wanted to see it, and I refused. I loved it when I wrote it and in the period when my first agent was trying to sell it, but looking back now I have no idea what either of us saw in it. I mean, the sentences were pretty, because I do that well. But who cares about pretty sentences when the substance of the book is a hot mess? *Drowning Practice* boils down to this: a thirty-year-old woman (guess how old I was when I wrote it?) walks around Park Slope and feels sad about her dead father. Which . . . you know . . . fine. Perhaps every novelist has to write that thinly veiled auto-biographical first novel, if only to get it out of her system, but I'm glad that mine never sold. I was crushed when *Drowning Practice* failed to find a publisher, but in truth *The Revolution of Every Day* is a much stronger debut.

I see now that it was a very kind thing for my first agent to do, to recognize we weren't a good editorial fit and to set me free. Because I never would have walked away on my own. What unpublished writer just walks away from a top agent because the editorial fit isn't quite right? I'm so grateful to her for passing on the book, because that led to my finding the exact right home for it. And by being forced to go it alone, I learned that I am indeed capable of building and managing my own career. If an agent didn't believe in my novel, well, that was okay. I believed in it. Turns out I didn't need a savior. My career wasn't sunk when I couldn't get an agent. My career is doing just fine.

And yet there were times in the process of representing myself when I wished I had a little more help, when I wanted an advocate in my corner looking out for the big picture.

And so when I finished my new novel, I decided I wanted to find an agent again. It's a lot easier to find an agent once you've published a novel. Rather than throwing myself onto the slush piles of Manhattan again, I was able to send the new one to two agents who'd contacted me after *The Revolution of Every Day* was published to good reviews, as well as to two agents who represented friends of mine. A short time later, I accepted an offer of representation from my first-choice agent, one of those who'd approached me after *Revolution* came out.

And so now, after five years on my own, I have an agent again. She gets my new book. She's enthusiastic about it. We're a good fit. I look forward to working with her on many books, for years to come. But having had much more success on my own than I did with my first agent, I'm now more aware of what an agent can and can't do for me. I'm not putting all my hopes and dreams on my agent's shoulders. That's more of a burden than I should expect anyone to bear. I haven't found a savior. What I've actually done is outsourced the business-negotiation aspects of my writing career to an expert and acquired an advocate and ally. That feels a hell of a lot better than clinging to the idea that someone else has the power to make or break my career.

FREEDOM

Richard Rodriguez

in conversation with Caille Millner

Caille Millner: You grew up in an isolated place. Your parents were immigrants. There wasn't a lot of money. When did you realize you wanted to write?

Richard Rodriguez: In high school. I was ugly, overweight, lonely—and yet as a columnist on the student newspaper at a boys' Catholic high school I was able to achieve some visibility and notoriety as a public voice. Words gave me the first sense of what it was like to have glamour.

How did your friends and family react?
My family didn't know what to make of what I was doing. My father was almost completely silent, in both languages. But my friends in high school were all talkative. They may not have had the athletic glamour that some boys have. But they had conversation. And their parents had conversation.

I decided quite early that one of the ways to get into their houses to see how rich people lived—that was my notion, rich people—was to chat. Especially to the mother. And the mothers of my friends were really interested in this boy who asked them questions about the movies they were going to and the books they were reading, because their own children had no interest in these things.

So I kept getting invited to come over to these houses because I'd romanced the mother. Even in cases where the kid was no longer my friend, the mother would ask me to come over. And then I started getting invited on summer vacations with various families. It was language that took me there.

And language is what took you through your struggling early years, isn't it?
Yes. After I got out of school, I was floating around Los Angeles. Talking my way into dinner parties. One of the things I learned with very wealthy people was, first of all, how bored they were. And second, that what was most important was whether or not you could entertain them with words. And if you could, it gave you enormous social power. I learned that quite early.

Were you interested in rising above your class?
Oh yes. Words were my passageway out. And you must realize that it was my taste, too. The books that interested me were in some sense way out of my class—eighteenth-century British fiction, for example.

But I don't want to give the impression that those were my only concerns. At the same time, I had a keen sense of language as the only way out of the things that were happening in America. I was reading my eighteenth-century British fiction, but I was also very interested in the rhetorical tradition that was coming through the television sets at the time because of the civil rights movement—this amazing rhetorical tradition that came out of the black Protestant church. This capability of language to literally move people, to lead them in a procession through danger, past danger. I'd never seen anything like that.

But where did you—a child of immigrants, a native Spanish speaker, a boy trying to rise above his station—where did you get the authority?

This is where it was helpful that I was so lonely. The world opens itself up to those who are willing to be lonely. No one was paying any attention to me when I was a teenager. I didn't go to the junior prom. I didn't have peers who shared my interests. Neglect gave me the sense that the world was mine, because no one knew who I was or what I was doing. I felt the freedom to take risks.

What did you think the financial realities of being a writer would be?

I didn't think. I was supported by various people early in my writing life. I spent a lot of time lying by swimming pools at other people's houses, housesitting, looking at Italian fashion magazines.

And then I realized I couldn't write the book I wanted to write if I continued to live in that world. That I had to give it up. And I wrote *Hunger of Memory*, my first book, with no expectation. I wrote it because I was haunted by the story of my parents, and because of my own anxiety about being a scholarship boy. I didn't expect money for it.

Was it difficult, to give up this charmed existence for years of poverty while you were writing your first book?

It would have been harder if I'd stayed in Los Angeles, that's for sure. All the temptations that were there. And I do like to do things well. I like a nice dinner party. I still like to travel well. When I was younger, I liked to dress well.

But I needed to write something I could be proud of. That's not to say that it was easy. We're very jealous, human beings. I remember one night when I was doing very badly with my work on *Hunger*

Richard Rodriguez

of Memory. I was crossing Fillmore Street [in San Francisco] with my bicycle. While I was waiting for the light to change I watched a very comfortable-looking man about my age pull up to the corner in a nice car to pick somebody up. I thought, *That's my generation in that car. And I'm on this bicycle.*

Ah, those moments of envy.

It didn't last long, fortunately. In one important respect I was helped by something that was devastating in many other ways.

In Los Angeles I'd gotten into a world that was both gay in the descriptive sense and gay in the physical sense, in terms of aesthetics. In time this became the world of AIDS. I've been in some extraordinary bedrooms—helping people die.

I'd notice the beautiful objects in the room, I'd write about them, I'd think about them. And I'd notice the irony of beautiful bodies being corrupted by illness. So a lot of that materialism that I might have been attracted to once, I was less attracted to after the AIDS epidemic.

How old were you when *Hunger of Memory* came out, in 1982?

In my midthirties. It wasn't a career choice. I wrote it to explain myself to myself, to save myself.

It was rejected by nine publishers. I thought that was it, that it was over. But fortunately it got picked up by a small publisher where the editor loved it so much that he walked it over to the editor of the *New York Times Book Review.* That's the luck I'm talking about. It could have been handed to an editor at a big house who didn't love it.

There was quite the firestorm when that book came out. It must have made you a lot of money.

I don't know about that. I know that it gave me a lot of notoriety.

Suddenly I was invited to give speeches and go on television. On a number of occasions, when I'd give a speech, there would be a policeman escorting me because there were demonstrations or protests where I was speaking. And I remember what the policeman would always say—he'd say, *Just walk right behind me. Don't walk to the side of me; don't walk in front of me.* That was happening in my life for a season.

Something I've always wondered about your career is why you didn't make more of that period. You could have been a darling of the Right, getting paid big money to go on the speaking circuit. That season in my life, when the policeman was always following me? That wasn't what I wanted.

Look, I really think that the writer really should pry and investigate the limits of what's acceptable speech, acceptable opinion. But I don't find it interesting to go to a school and be shouted down. That's what you have to do in order to take on that pundit role. And on the other side of it, sometimes when I go to very conservative places there's a whole negotiation about what I can speak about there, because I'm gay.

So I never wanted to be pinned down. I always want to surprise people. Our lives are too complicated to be frozen on this kind of political chessboard.

But did you ever take on other types of work for strictly financial considerations?
I did a lot of TV. I was very fortunate to have my gig on the *MacNeil/ Lehrer NewsHour* for eighteen years. That job gave me money, it gave me travel, and it gave me visibility. I also had an opinion column at the *Los Angeles Times* for many years. That was a stable source of income for a long time.

Now that I think about it, it is and was the journalism work I did, in print and television, in the United States and Britain, that supported my literary essays. Journalism often required compromises: there were deadlines, and there were severe restrictions about what was allowable on air, but I loved working as a journalist.

Were there other things that helped you sustain yourself over long periods between books?
Royalties. I've been lucky; some of those essays have been serialized a lot.

I find it interesting that you speak about luck so often in terms of your career.
Only because no one ever talks about how crucial it is.

Here are a few other things younger writers don't hear about this career: If you're going to become a writer, you have to start introducing yourself to people. You have to know how to talk. People need to like you in this business, to remember you well.

Here was some more of my luck: I was Latino at a moment when nobody knew what that meant, and I spoke English in a way that didn't frighten white people.

But speaking as another writer of color, writing about race and ethnicity can be very fraught. There's always someone who will pay for you to do that, but maybe not in the way you want to do it. Or if you don't feel like writing about it at all, good luck.
I notice that, when I have an elderly upper-middle-class white audience, when I get introduced, there will be this caution in the audience until I establish that I'm someone not to be frightened of.

And I do that with my voice. It's a theatrical effect. I do it consciously and deliberately and theatrically: I want you not to be afraid of me so I can tell you about yourself.

So if I talk to that audience about being white, they're not afraid to hear it. You have to get that point of trust for that. Because if they see a brown man with a big nose, they're going to be shaking with fear. So it's a rhetorical trick.

But doesn't that make you feel a bit . . . weird? Like, you're expected to do all this anthropological work for other people?
I believe that race is an erotic category; it's the record of our parents' lovemaking. So there's all this potent possibility in it that's not reflected in the political discourse.

Look, I'm not saying it's not frustrating. I go on and on about where my books are shelved in bookstores. Why are all the essayists white and the writers of color are in their ghettoized sections?

You live in the most expensive city in the country, San Francisco. You've started to write some essays recently about technology and the new tech billionaires.
I don't know why more writers don't. This is the most interesting shift happening in the country right now. All these newly minted billionaires in hoodies, emerging into the limelight from our erotic relationship with the computer.

Is it a reasonable city for a writer, though?
Not if you don't have rent control already. But as far as subject matter goes, I find it really interesting to be in a city where no one is interested in me. It's really interesting to be in a city where no one reads.

It's like what I learned from being a teenager—if nobody's paying attention to you, the world is yours. You can go anywhere you want, observe anything you want. You're free.

WORK HARD, READ DEAD

Yiyun Li

in conversation with Manjula Martin

Manjula Martin: What kind of an economic environment did you grow up in?

Yiyun Li: I grew up in China, so the attitude was that you work hard. And that's it. So I would say I'm a hardworking person!

Did that mostly come from your parents or was it more from the general culture?
I think it was from the culture. My parents, yes, but also the culture. I was very self-disciplined when I was a child. I really succeeded in school so that I could have less supervision from grown-ups. If you do well, then you don't have to be supervised!

Money-wise, we didn't grow up rich or well provided for. Coming to this country, my husband and I lived in Iowa City on a University of Iowa student stipend for nine years, and I didn't feel that I was poor.

How much was the student stipend at that time?
It might be more now, but when we were there [in the late 1990s] it was like $14,000 or $15,000 a year.

I really don't have a good sense of money, and I don't think about money so much, as long as I can buy food.

When you first came to Iowa from China in 1996, you were studying to be a scientist, but gave it up to study at the Iowa Writers' Workshop. What did it feel like to switch careers as an immigrant in a new country?

When you were in a science program, you knew you would have a future, right? After your training you would get a stable job, either teaching or doing research. So that's a sense of stability. I think I did give up that stability for writing.

Why would you give up that stability?

I think I had an early midlife crisis!

A quarter-life crisis?

Yes, I was in my late twenties and I thought, *God, I cannot have a PhD! I cannot become a doctor!* I wanted to be literary.

Giving up that sense of stability—knowing as a scientist that there are jobs, concrete jobs, that you can go get with this degree—was it scary?

I thought I must be really stupid! Sometimes I thought, *You know, you were really stupid to do that—to never really plan your future.*

Well, you must have really liked writing.

I did. I love writing. I remember telling my PhD advisor I was leaving to be a writer. He said, *Stay with me another year. You're gonna get your degree; you'll get a good job*, and I said, *I would probably regret it my whole life if I stayed.* And he said, *Okay, but in science, you can never come back. It's not that you can wait for three years and then come back to do the same thesis.* And I said, *I understand that.* And I just went away.

At that time, did you have any idea what kind of literary job you might have or how you might make a living?

No. I mean, again, I come from a hardworking background, where you want to have a job. So I told my husband I would try it for three years and if at the end of three years I did not get published, I would go to law school or get an MBA, or one of those very useful degrees. That was not completely serious, but it was sort of the plan: We'd try it for three years.

By the end of the third year, I got published. I gave up science in 2000, and in 2003 I was published in the *Paris Review* and the *New Yorker*.

How did that happen?
The *Paris Review* one was just in the slush pile. And they picked it up, and I thought, oh, that's very good! [Laughs.]

I thought it happened all the time. I'm probably the only one.

How did being published in prestigious magazines right out of the gate change your outlook?
When you go into something so blindly, you don't know what will happen; you just work at it. Now I always think that my students know too much about the business. I feel they're too savvy, always thinking about money, and . . . I don't know. I just went in so blindly. And the story was picked up by [the] *Paris Review* and I got an agent, and he sold my next story to the *New Yorker*, and I got a two-book deal all within six months. I had just started at Iowa and I wrote my first collection while I was there, and then the second book I finished a year after school.

So I didn't know it would happen and I didn't expect it to happen so fast. In a way I think I was just oblivious. Very oblivious.

Why do you think that young writers now have more of an awareness about the business part of being a writer?
Well, the Internet, I'm sure. People exchange information. But the more you know about these things . . . I think there's some massive

panic about things or problems that don't exist. I just always think, well, you know, maybe look at Graham Greene. His first two books didn't really get published, right?

It happens all the time.
Not everybody started at such a high or successful place. People used to have this expectation: you'd graduate from college, you'd write your poetry collection nobody read, and then you just went on with your life until you made it, right? Now, I think . . . I don't know why, but it seems there's so much pressure.

I'm often tempted to associate it with the larger economic situation, where there's just a lot less certainty in general about being able to have a job and a career after college. And I think that's changed within this generation.
I think that's true. Then, on the other hand . . . there's the hardworking part. Work hard! And there are two aspects to that. First, one has to get solid work done rather than looking around to see what others are doing, what others are getting as rewards; in a sense, one has to avoid comparing oneself to others. Second, hard work does not always pay off, which seems inevitable in life, so one has to avoid measuring outcome against effort.

My mentor, James Alan McPherson, when he was writing, he was doing custodial work. He was throwing everybody's shit out and cleaning up everybody's apartments. And he was happy, because he could feed himself.

Some young writers have an expectation that they can just do nothing but write. And you don't seem to be a fan of that expectation. Why not?
I think any kind of experience is good for a writer, except sitting at home all the time. If my students have a character who does

nothing, I always ask them, "Well, where does the money come from? How does he live?" And they cannot answer. They would have someone sitting in the house for five weeks, having all sorts of crises, and I said, "Does he go out to buy food? If he goes out to buy food he has to interact with people. And things will happen."

Young writers seem to forget that there's a big world out there. And you have to be in the world.

With regards to the panic you say your students have—the desire to know all about the publishing business—do you think there's also a lack of confidence behind that?

That's a very good question. Lack of confidence, yes. Also, again, perspective. There's this really beautiful essay by Lawrence Weschler, and he said that in the '60s and '70s when he was at Harvard it was the antiwar time, right? And all the students were having this gathering, and everyone went up and said, *This is the moment. This is the moment for humankind.* And finally, he said, a visiting professor from Europe came up and said, *I think we need to put this into perspective. People in history, they died from, you know, black fever!* [laughs] I always liked that. You have to put everything into perspective.

When E. B. White first saw television, he said, *This machine will destroy writers,* and I just love that. Because I mean, yes, so many things will destroy writers, but real writers are not destroyed in any case.

You mean we're not delicate flowers?

I mean writing is strong enough. The reason I was thinking about perspective is that in Chinese history—in many countries' histories—there would be a period where writing would not be allowed. Every book would be burned. And every single writer would be buried alive. But I think writing survives. Writers survive.

You have said before that you primarily read dead writers, yes?
I do. I read dead people. And for a reason. They're tested by time. And there's that perspective again.

So if you were oblivious, how did you learn about how the publishing business works?
I still don't know! No, I mean, I've published four books and I still say, what's the difference between marketing and publicity? I don't really know how publishing works and I prefer not to know. And I think the more you know, the more panicky you become, and you're thinking about all these things that have nothing to do with writing. And really all I can control is the quality of the writing. That's all I'm responsible for.

I'm curious about how much of your life is about teaching and how much is about writing. How are you feeding yourself and your kids?
Writing doesn't feed anybody.

I always assume that to be the case! But I have to admit I don't really know how well your books sell.
Oh, I have no idea! I will probably always have to work, to teach.

Brigid Hughes [former *Paris Review* editor and current editor of *A Public Space*] once told the *New York Times* that you're a very stubborn person. I'm curious if you think that stubbornness has served you well, or not served you well, in your career.
I think it has served me well. I mean, this is always a fight between me and Brigid; she always says I'm too stubborn! [laughs] But you know, I think there are different kinds of stubbornness. Stubbornness is like a double-edged sword. In my career, I just want to be a writer, and I don't want to think about stability and money. So all

these really unrealistic, impractical things come from my stubbornness. And that's probably not very good for life, so . . .

So how's that working out for you?
So-so. But wouldn't it be nice if I were not as stubborn and would be *a very good girl*? Do all the things a writer should be doing to promote herself?

Somebody has to do it, right?
Well, it's not me! I mean, I know some people are really good at it, and some people are dedicated to it, even if they don't enjoy it. And that's my stubbornness: If I don't enjoy it, I'm not going to do it.

There's this great scene in "Eat, Memory: Orange Crush," a personal essay of yours published in the *New York Times*, where all the families in your childhood apartment building [in Beijing] cook dinner in the hallway. Everyone can tell how everyone is doing economically because everyone can see how many times a week their neighbors eat meat. I think that's true everywhere—there are these markers of money that are visible to everyone, and I'm curious about how you think of the American ways of "marking" wealth.
I find Americans very cagey about this topic, which is interesting to me, you know? I think people are very open about other stuff—race, immigration, gender, all these other things you can put on the table and debate. Except for class. Americans want to think you can be a self-made man no matter what your background is. But the truth is, actually, whatever class you were born into is more important.

When you were growing up in China, what were your perceptions about money and class?
Well, of course, it's different in China. When we grew up, there

were privileged people and there were common people. That was all. Which means everybody who was not an official—a Communist Party official—everybody else was underprivileged.

What was going on for you culturally at that time, with art and literature?
I would say we had limited knowledge of the world. As it opened up, we got more, but still, we were underprivileged in that sense.

As a person who makes culture, how do you see your place in the cultural economy of America now?
I think I was well served because I wasn't really interested in money or fame. But I have this student—he's in his twenties and he's a strong writer for his age—and I was talking to him one time and he said, *You just don't understand me. At my age, I just really want to get published.* And I said, *Why? Writing is not a race. What's the hurry?* And he said, *You don't understand. Young people have ambition.*

And I thought, *That's the wrong ambition.* If you get there first, it doesn't mean you're the best.

What do you have ambition about?
Because I read mostly dead people, I try to match what I write with dead people's work. There are certain sentences where I think, well, maybe I can compare this to Chekhov and see the distance between me and Chekhov, or the distance between me and Graham Greene or anyone else, and most of the time I'm still way behind. But there are moments where I think, *Hmm, this sentence is really good!* So my ambition is to always measure myself against these dead people. And that solves all my problems about money and fame, because they're all dead!

WRITE TO SUFFER, PUBLISH TO STARVE

J. Robert Lennon

I write for my pleasure," Vladimir Nabokov wrote to his publisher, Maurice Girodias, in 1955, in an effort to extract from him the delayed second half of the advance for *Lolita*, "but publish for money." This beloved quotation serves as a succinct abstract for an aspirational philosophy most writers at least sort of embrace: We create our art without regard for its extrinsic value, deep inside our Batcave of rectitude; and only once the work has met our approval as a fully realized expression of our aesthetic ideals do we issue it into the world in the hope—shruggingly expressed through professional intermediaries—that someone might be willing to pay us for it.

On the face of it, this philosophy seems unambiguously useful: fiscally pragmatic and mojo-positive. The work's worth, in dollars, to publishers and readers is immaterial, in this conception of the writer's purpose. Whether we are given a "six-figure advance" (industry parlance for "ninety-five thousand dollars") for our blue-crystal-meth art object, or a virtual stack of mildly insulting rejection e-mails, matters not at all. There is writing, and there is commerce, and between them stands an impenetrable wall of inestimably thick bulletproof glass. The writer can make out the agents and editors and publicists over there, on the other side, if she presses her nose to the wall's scratchless, ungouged, greasy, and slightly bloodstained surface; the wall—its integrity-preserving inviolability bending and scattering light—diffuses and warps their horrifying corporeal forms as they intermingle like eels in a tank, their mouths opening and closing, their chests convulsing with silent laughter, their meaty pink hands coming into direct contact with actual money.

But don't peek. It's not healthy. Indeed, the writer should stand as far from the wall as he can, facing away into the black void of creation, where all that can be made out in the cigarettey gloom are the slightly crooked contours of a battered desk; the squat, platypusian outline of a manual typewriter; a minor Alp of scribbled-upon and balled-up paper; and a secondhand pine bookshelf, sagging from the weight of every word every other writer has managed to publish since 1439, when Johannes Gutenberg brought to Europe, from the Holy Roman Empire, the device that would eventually be employed to transform our profoundest thoughts, emotions, and desires into a form that insects can comfortably nest in and that doubles in size if you drop it in the bathtub.

Here's the problem, though, with the Nabokovian dictum: for most of us, writing is not particularly pleasurable, and publishing does not make us much money. Most writers I know work in a state of perpetual anxiety and self-disgust, and regard the products of their labor as profoundly disappointing. I don't wish to embrace the cliché, as pernicious as the one I've so far spent this essay mocking, of the tortured artist (in the self-mythologizing and eye-rollingly hackneyed words of Paul Auster) "bleeding words onto a page." Writing is not coal mining. It is merely a pain in the ass, albeit one that tends to invite psychic distress, especially given the bewilderment with which it is greeted by a writer's loved ones, once they realize what one actually does all day while writing: i.e., not much. Maybe a more appropriate rallying cry would be, "Write to suffer, publish to starve."

In all honesty, I've quoted that Nabokov line to graduate students hundreds of times. In the hothouse environment of the writing workshop, it's a handy reminder that, despite our career ambitions, we should focus on the work when we're at work, and worry about publishing later. But I'm wary of discouraging students, or any writer, really, from developing a relationship with the idea of commerce. The separation of art and commerce, while a noble aim, is in reality an endeavor akin, in the rarefied and impoverished professional universe where writers actually reside, to the separation of smoking and drinking. A nice thought, but yeah, good luck with that.

Besides, commerce is more than money. It was fine for Nabokov to tell his publisher that he published for money, for it was money Nabokov was trying to secure. But money isn't the only reason he published, or that anyone publishes. We publish because we are exhibitionists. We publish to be admired. We publish to be part of something that excites us. We publish to feel special, to feel real, to feel brave, to feel afraid. We publish to evoke emotion in others, to prove Mom wrong. We publish because other people publish, and that's what is done. We publish so that we can talk about publishing to other people who publish. We publish so that we can get contributors' copies, so that we can get a job, so that we can get laid. We publish for an excuse to go to New York, to have something to flog at conferences, to have something to brag about on airplanes. This is all commerce. Our cocktail party banter with other writers is commerce. Our blog posts about books we like, or loathe, are commerce. Our barroom readings and subtweets are commerce. We parlay our genetic predisposition to language, and our hard work developing it, into companionship, attention, admiration, criticism. This is normal, and we all do it.

It is the rare serious writer who does not wish to publish. There is only one in recent memory: J. D. Salinger. Certainly it is possible to regard Salinger as a paragon of literary integrity. He wrote precisely what he wanted, for decades, and showed it to no one. But the posthumous masterworks we have hoped for have so far failed to materialize. Perhaps they're forthcoming. Or perhaps they fall further along the axis of disconnection from reality established by Salinger's last published story, "Hapworth 16, 1924," an epistolary novella that appeared in *The New Yorker* in June 1965, and which, aside from its inalienable lastness, is noteworthy mostly for its tiresome digressions, obscure stylistic flourishes, and twee self-absorption. It's pretty bad. It reads like the work of a man who hates to be read.

Our commerce with the world is not corollary to our art. It is, rather, a vital component of our art, perhaps our art's reason for being. If we regard writing as an act of empathy that presupposes and celebrates the existence of other people, then its commerce with humanity must represent its consummation. The money is just so that we can eat, or to keep a roof over our heads, or (in the pitiful amounts that are typically involved in an exchange between writer and publisher of literary product) a mildly apologetic acknowledgment of labor. But money isn't the real currency here. The real currency of literary commerce is love.

Now, I'm not singing Kumbaya to litbiz, saying that we all have to be besties, plump for each other on Facebook, and get drunk together at AWP. I'm not advocating short stories with happy endings (although, seriously, try one sometime) or schlock poems about adorable animals. I'm saying that every writer needs to conceive, develop, and maintain a literary relationship to her family, her country, her community, her peers. A writer ought to be thinking about this, yes, when he sends his work out to be published, but *also when he's writing it*, and when he's contemplating writing it. A literary work unconcerned with the desires of its audience is like a thoughtless gift, a crass experiment in social engineering, like the statue of Jesus your pious aunt bought for your atheist front garden and expects a thank-you note for.

What the theoretical separation of art and commerce is meant to prevent is, of course, pandering. Good art is not supposed to service the lazy reader; it's supposed to challenge, surprise. It is supposed to change the world. But you aren't going to change the world without loving it first, even if you love it in the most resentful, confused, exasperated imaginable way. Respect the world, even as it pisses you off. Otherwise you'll produce nothing but hermity manifestos, bursts of static from your own private Yaddo.

Art and commerce are not separate. They are not even different. Write to suffer, publish to starve. And have the courage to give your work a purpose, to want a future for it, however painful it may be to hope.

THE DAILY GRIND

THE BEST WORK IN LITERATURE

Manjula Martin

I. IN THE BASEMENT

I began as a "stock girl" at eleven years old. My job was to run up and down the stairs to the basement of my grandmother's upscale housewares store and fetch customer purchases—sets of wineglasses and unassembled wire drawer units, mostly. Every summer weekend of 1987 I carried outgoing boxes up the stairs and newly arrived UPS boxes down. Between laps I flattened and bundled cardboard, tallied inventory on a clipboard, and filed purchase orders. I worked hard, but nepotism had its privileges: I was paid $5 an hour in cash under the table, a fortune for a kid and on par with what the grown-up clerks made. (California minimum wage at the time was $3.35.)

Even then, I viewed my summer gig as work I would one day leave behind: when I grew up, I was certain, I would become a full-time artist of some sort. (I cycled through the dream jobs of ballerina, actor, rock star, and, finally, writer.) While I was working in the basement I visualized my future Artist's Life: I would have a postindustrial living space with high ceilings in a large city; I'd share it with a cat and a partner, both of whom would adore me but value my independent spirit and leave me alone to work. My work would be popular yet retain its authenticity. There would be cocktail parties and ceiling-to-floor bookshelves. Above all, I would never "have to" flatten cardboard boxes again.

My family's store was housed in a grand 1910 sandstone build-ing, formerly a bank. The basement was cool and dark. It smelled like damp cement and Styrofoam, but to me it was the shadowy secret headquarters of capital. My grandparents had repurposed the old bank vault as their office, its original meter-thick door permanently propped open like a steel monument to the place's past as a retailer of money. When I delivered my packing slips to the manager's filing cabinet, I could see an intricate interior system of old locks and gears in the door's cross section. Prior to working at the store, I had been enchanted by the mechanics of the cash register, by its percussive flashes of bells, sliding parts, and coins. But in the basement I realized the sales floor operations were a façade: the real work of business was happening downstairs. The basement was both the physical and fiscal seat of power in the store. This was where the money lived, in the heavy lifting that made those wineglasses shine for the yuppie newlyweds shopping upstairs, and even deeper, behind a steel door as thick as I was tall. I wondered then if everything I knew and experienced might have a similar duplicity—another thing, a working and sweating mechanism beneath the surface.

In the business of literature, the people who mind the store—from writers to editors to Tumblrs—often have other jobs, too. For writers and other creators of culture, the "day job"—a means of in-come for an artist that is not the production of her art (leaving the definition of art aside for the moment)—is viewed as a temporary step on the ladder to artistic success. Many young writers hold the conviction that a day will come when they don't have to do anything but write. When we speak about our "Work," we mean our writing. We treat this work with reverence and hold it up as the work that makes us who we are: artists. But beneath the surface of our art is a life largely spent doing other work: basement shifts, rent gigs, and adjunct positions whose earnings shore up our literary work. Day jobs are a mechanism beneath the business of literature. As such, they don't just pay our bills; they're what we do with most of our lives. Is there value to be found in a day job beyond its paycheck? Why are writers so eager to leave work behind?

II. MOVING ON UP

In high school, I scored a legit job at the local used book and record store. There, I still had to flatten cardboard, but I also shelved pocket books—sci-fi, fiction, mysteries, and Westerns—in their delineated sections on the basement level of the store. I got my hands on the work of Flannery O'Connor, Emily Dickinson, Joan Didion, and Anaïs Nin, and the fantasy of leaving behind my day job grew. I could see so many potential iterations of myself as a successful writer: I might be the sensitive introvert composing my work in a window seat while watching the light fall all day long; the cultural critic, always traveling and observing, a notebook and chic sunglasses my most constant companions; or the continental sensation breaking literary hearts with every breathless epistolary I penned. Regardless of the details, I was certain I would soon be illuminating the human condition with impeccable prose while living a life far removed from the drudgery of "regular" work.

I was sixteen and about to graduate from high school by the time a coworker said to me, "So, what are you gonna do now?" I'd soon be leaving to attend college back East, but I already had larger ambitions. (And had recently added Kerouac to my roster of role models.)

"I dunno," I said, "maybe drop out of college and move to New York and become a famous writer by the age of twenty-one?"

My coworker, a bookseller with two kids, a man who has read and understood all of Proust, *Finnegans Wake*, and John Fahey's liner notes—and an agreeable clerk who was kind and sincere with even the most hostile of customers—rolled his eyes. He handed me a stack of paperbacks and said, "Yeah. Right. Don't quit your day job, kid."

Did I really believe I would be a best-selling author with a sweet SoHo loft by age twenty-one? No, but I didn't believe I wouldn't be. Any artist who produces work for public consumption must navigate a tenuous balance of ambition and pragmatism. Ambition requires dreaming; sometimes dreams veer into fantasy. Fantasies, once they take root, are difficult to remove. Weedlike, they devour the productive environment around them. They are fertile and robust. Sometimes, they even flower.

The Writing Life is one such fantasy; another is quitting your day job. Both scenarios imply there is something else—something more—for artists around the bend. Freedom, unfettered expression, fame. Legend, even. Take my high school–era hero: Emily Dickinson, hard at work at her little table, free from the bothers of having to earn a living (and an unseen maid hard at work cleaning up after her, no doubt). I know it's not real for me, but also, even now, I believe in it a little.

Recently I was living the Writing Life by clicking on a link to "10 Writing Rules from Some Canonical Author Dude" on one of the literary websites I frequent when I came across an item about a newly discovered letter by Oscar Wilde. Among a reported thirteen pages of advice to a younger writer was Wilde's admonition to secure a steady income: "The best work in literature is always done by those who do not depend on it for their daily bread."

In other words, don't quit your day job, kid.

III. THE BEST WORK

I did drop out of college, and I did move to New York. I wrote. I published a zine. I typed poems on my old typewriter and taped them to the walls of bedrooms and bars. I scribbled letters to friends back home and kept carefully Xeroxed copies in my journal just in case I needed to plunder them later for my memoir. I wrote a few okay, earnest short stories that weren't published and some snarky cultural criticism that was. I sold some articles for money, to the magazine where I was a receptionist. I moved cities a few more times. And I worked.

During my illustrious one year of college, I'd had a job as a seam-stress for a theater company while many of my mostly wealthy peers were occupied with burning their parents' money in bongs. My coworkers at the shop, two middle-aged women, preferred listening to public radio to talking. They were kind to me: although I was only a stitcher—my job was to iron and baste pattern muslin—the shop manager walked me through the process of crafting a 1940s noir bombshell's dress from raw white silk. On opening night of the play in which the dress was featured, I had to pick up the costume from the dry cleaners and deliver it to the theater; when I slipped and dropped my pristine creation into the dirt-filled snowpack of the city street, I cried. I had made that dress, the first physical thing I ever entirely made, and I had done so in the tradition and company of other working women. Then I had ruined it. And I had to tell my boss. She came in to help me spot-clean the garment while the analog sounds of the radio warmed the quiet cold of the empty shop. After I left, that warmth became part of the fabric of my experience as a creator of things.

As an official college dropout, however, I was soon a server of things: At a busy NYC restaurant I learned when you don't show up, your boss might dock you, but it's your coworkers who suffer. That's called solidarity. At a downtown nightclub, I learned to carry a full tray of cocktails on one hand above my head, and I learned what it smells like when the tray drops down the back of a well-perfumed nightclub patron. That's called going home with no tips.

At multiple retail gigs I developed the ability to read a person's mood in one glance, to ask them what they wanted and then perform customer service triage. I learned to fake friendliness, to flirt strategically, and to be smart about what I stole. I met kind and talented friends. I asked stupid questions: while I couldn't possibly pretend I'd heard that rare 7" record my coworker was raving about, if I swallowed my ego and asked about it, I'd be gifted with a mind-blowing music history footnote. The next time someone asked, I was the expert who passed it forward.

As a personal assistant, I performed other people's intimate tasks: I bought socks for a successful visual artist, walked her dog, and separated out her paintbrushes from those of her soon-to-be ex-girlfriend. As a receptionist at a magazine, I did similar tasks for the founding editor, and I learned about reporting and editing along the way. My Queens-born coreceptionist and I became friends, and she taught me how to make sandwiches from nothing but a deli roll, a spoonful of mayonnaise, and salt.

I was in the passenger seat of a white van in far-flung Brooklyn in 1999 when I realized a place can contain a multitude of realities. A temp job installing corporate signage in bank branches had me driving around the outer boroughs for six weeks starting at six in the morning every day. While I compared my site list to the map I'd found in the door of the van, my signage partner, a thirty-year-old painter with permanent hangdog eyes, sped through other worlds: Hasidic enclaves, beach neighborhoods, middle-class Caribbean suburbias, and streets that looked more like Dickens's London than the downtown Manhattan I thought of as New York. While we stood on ladders in ATM vestibules, the people who lived in those neighborhoods talked to us. I listened.

The whole time I wanted to quit. Work was keeping me from my true Work, I thought. I was really a writer. Not a reporter or a copywriter—a creative writer. An artist. Yet despite my intolerance for it, all this un-writerly work was what allowed me to understand that people and experiences other than mine exist. Empathy is perhaps the most valuable skill a writer can possess, and I found it at work. There, I was becoming myself, figuring out my values, where I stood in relation to the world, and what I wanted to say about it. My art wasn't doing that for me; art was what boomeranged off me while I processed real life.

Would I quit working if I could? Of course I would. But I'd do so with the knowledge it might make me a person who is less engaged with life, and possibly a lesser writer.

While I was at work, the '90s passed. I moved back to the West Coast, and I kept working. The aughts were fully underway. I was in my thirties, and I was still largely unpublished. I had a bundle of life experience to write from, a bifurcated class identity, and a résumé full of holes bigger than the ones in my unfinished manuscripts. As in memoir, there was no big epiphany, but somewhere along the way, in small doses and messy life changes, I started to realize work wasn't what was holding me back; the ideal of the Writer's Life was. Once I let myself understand that statistically I would probably never—yes, never—be able to quit working, the hours I had spent agonizing over having a day job became hours in which I could write. I began to transfer the energy behind my fantasy into real ambition.

The work I performed at my day jobs also became more valuable to me. I started asking for more—saying no when I should, demanding pay for the minutes I spent counting out my register off-shift, seeking transparency in personnel policies, asking to be paid as much as men. And I began asking these questions at all my jobs, writing included. Work is work, even when we call it art, or love, or culture, and even when it's not. I want my work to be valued, as much and as often as possible, regardless of which clock I'm punching.

Manjula Martin

IV. COSTS AND COMPLICATIONS

A conversation about work is also a conversation about class. There's an implied choice behind "day job" narratives like the one Wilde suggests—whether to have a day job or be a "starving" artist hustling and living off connections. Such options don't exist for a lot of artists. I'm a straight white woman with friends; I was raised in a safe, supportive middle-class environment by people who valued literature and the arts. It's presumed my story is authentic when I speak about work and art and say I was once a seamstress. It's also presumed Emily Dickinson's maid didn't go home and write poems after work. I bet she did.

Remember the girl in the basement? The one who made as much as her adult coworkers? I could choose a different way to narrate my "history of day jobs" that doesn't sound as scrappy and working-class. This other story is the unvoiced half of a sort of writerly code-switching, a privilege I enjoy as a person who lives on the poverty line but hangs out with intellectuals. In this narrative I still work as a receptionist at that New York magazine, but I get promoted to an editorial position by the founding editor, who happens to be a distant cousin of mine. I start attending editorial lunch gatherings at the iconic Meatpacking District restaurant Florent and leave my coreceptionist behind at her desk. After a couple of years, company reorganization and cubicle-inspired restlessness send me back to waitressing (at Florent, because I know the owner now) and other poorly paid service jobs, but I retain a connection with literary New York that still serves me today.

I eventually move back to the West Coast. I work in bookstores and record stores making minimum wage alongside other artists. Through a personal connection I become the in-house copywriter at a large nonprofit arts organization. Salary ($38K), benefits, the whole works. After a few years, I decide to finally go straight and finish my college degree, and I take out student loans I will likely never be able to pay back in order to intern at a prestigious literary magazine where I'm the same age as the editor. I work nights at home editing a porn star's memoir, but I still feel far away from Anaïs. When I graduate into the Great Recession in my early thirties, I'm "forced" into the freelance economy, which welcomes me due to my now-extensive professional network. This story is not the Writing Life story either, and its lessons are perhaps less romantic than the ones I learned in the van in Brooklyn. Today I make a living from a mix of freelance writing, copywriting and copyediting, and consulting work. I live paycheck to irregular paycheck, but I never go hungry. Do I have a day job? Honestly, I'm not sure. I do know I work all the time. Sometimes with a capital *W*, sometimes without.

Oscar Wilde's advice is still making the rounds, one more cliché among listicles. It may be cribbed from a different economic era, but he does have a point. A writer needs financial stability—a paycheck, preferably steady—to enable her "best work." This is fairly self-evident: people need money to live, and writing rarely pays well or at all, so it follows that a day job will "free" a writer to concentrate on writing instead of earning, and hopefully she'll write something amazing. At the same time, our sped-up culture and sluggish economy are overflowing with cautionary examples of people who spend so much of their selves and time earning a living that they have nothing left to give to the very thing they work to sustain, be it family or poetry. Going for the Writing Life might put you in a position of economic uncertainty (or, likely Wilde's true concern, selling out), but the realities of the working life aren't exactly a deus ex machina either.

Since my stock girl days, I've poked around in the machinery churning beneath the surface of many realities. The only clear truth each of my jobs has taught me is that the working life—real life—is just as important as the Writing Life. Here's why: they're the same thing.

THE INSIDER

Kate McKean

I have always been a writer, and I have always been practical. My career plan was to have a job and write and keep doing both until I reached my goal: publishing novels and living off those earnings.

While I was still an undergraduate earning my English degree, my sister, who is always right but never gloats about it, suggested I get a job at the university press. I did—adding a check to the *work* column—and I worked there full-time for a year before going to grad school. After, I earned a master's in fiction writing. I was still sticking to my path, but I hadn't written a novel yet. I couldn't live off something that didn't exist, so I leaned into the *work* part of my plan, feeling very adult because I recognized that sometimes you have to do what you have to do, instead of what you want to do. I was reading a lot of Raymond Carver at the time.

So I moved to New York to work in book publishing. My experience at the university press and my master's degree helped me get a job as an assistant at a literary agency. My hope was that eventually, sometime in the future, I would be a literary agent with a flexible schedule and I would be able to write and work, and earn a living by either or both. In the meantime, I would write in the morning and on weekends. I also thought that experiencing publishing, and especially agenting, from the inside would give me an advantage as a writer and get me published faster.

I was wrong.

Building my career as an agent ate every spare moment I had. There would be no writing on mornings and weekends. I was making barely $30,000 a year as an assistant and I was struggling to pay my $675 monthly Brooklyn rent. A few years later when I became a full-time agent, I went from a small salary to commission only, so I didn't get a paycheck unless I sold books. I made less than $5,000 my first year and I hustled freelance like I had never hustled before. I wrote manuscript reviews for a self-publisher that no longer exists. I wrote blurbs about Norwegian death metal albums I'd never even heard of for a big subscription-based music company that no longer exists. I worked at a wine store. I blogged for a tea company under the pseudonym Betty Bergamot or something like that. I was writing and even earning a little money from it, but it wasn't the kind of writing I thought I'd be doing. There was still no novel. Being on the inside was doing nothing but exhausting me.

Eventually, when I started selling more books and the checks started to come in, I had more time to write. I still had to do it in fits and starts, like most writers with full-time jobs. But I did what I could do. I went on a weeklong writer's retreat with my aunt, also a writer, and banged out over twenty thousand words in a week sitting on the floor of a condo in Florida. Sometimes, I wrote in the morning or on the weekend. That year, about seven years after I left grad school, I finished my first novel, a YA novel about teen coders and Internet entrepreneurs in hoity-toity Long Island that inexplicably had a robot in it. (I modeled it after Conky from *Pee-Wee's Playhouse*, even though no reader in the book's target demographic would get the reference.) But, finally, there was a novel. I was back on track.

I let the book sit for a month or two, and then edited it the best I could. This was where my experience as an agent finally kicked in. Thanks to the dozens and dozens of manuscripts I'd edited for my clients, I felt very prepared to edit my own work. I am fond of all my clients, but I have to be objective about their work when I edit. I used the same tactic on myself.

I shared the edited draft with some close friends and a few industry acquaintances, and they had nice things to say about it. They did not whisk it off to an editor who then offered me a six-figure deal. (Even I am not immune to this fantasy.) I agreed with the suggestions made to me, and could even see the point of the ones I didn't agree with (or didn't like hearing). I've written dozens of dozens of extensive (but kind!) editorial letters to my clients, and even with that experience, it wasn't easy to hear the critiques of my own work. I was just better prepared for it. I knew I needed to do a heavy rewrite if the novel was going to be in any shape to share with editors.

This did not surprise me. As an agent, I also know how rare it is to sell a novel with no edits, even after a round of revisions on my own. By the time I felt ready to tackle a big revision, I knew in my heart—as an agent, and as a writer—that the market for a book about teens and the Internet and apps had passed me by. What had been exciting to me in the moment of writing (teens know more than adults about the Internet!) was going to age badly on the shelf. By the time the book came out, people could be using totally different phones, or be online in a completely new way. After the excitement of finishing a whole novel had worn off, my agenting experience had kicked in: I could see the hook and topic and theme of my novel wasn't going to work. And even if it worked, it probably wouldn't *sell*. You'd think I would have caught this sooner, but I fell prey to what all writers easily fall prey to, the conviction that *my novel would be different*—that the rules didn't necessarily apply to me, because I was that good or smart or clever. Nope. I was not immune to any of that, regardless of the insider knowledge I had about the publishing market.

So I scrapped the book. All seventy thousand words of it. I printed it out and put it in a nice binder and it's still sitting on my shelf. I will not try to get my first novel published, even though my contacts list is full of publishers and editors. And I'm okay with that. I've read a lot of authors' first novels, and I have seen up close how many first novels just do not work. I have to tell people every day that I don't think their first novel will get published. Because I am an agent I knew it was a distinct possibility that my first novel would not get published from the day I started writing it (of course, I believed I would be the exception). And once it happened to me, I was able to deal with it. Because I've sold dozens and dozens of writers' *second* novels. I already knew I could do the writing part, so all I had to do was write another one. I felt exhilarated, not discouraged.

So I did. I wrote a nonfiction "how to get published" kind of book that's also sitting on a shelf in limbo and I've also started writing three or four other novels. I have a good start on another YA novel that I feel is promising and also on a novel for younger readers that I feel *really* good about. But along the way I've nixed many more ideas, because as an agent I know too much about the industry to fool myself into thinking every good idea will make a successful book.

At work I am watching the development of books that won't make it to bookshelves for a year or more. And so when I see a market trend, I'm seeing it a good two years before the general public sees it. This bird's-eye view of the business saves me from following trends before it's too late, as an agent and a writer.

From time to time, I make the mistake of thinking I can capitalize on the trends I see emerging. (There's that writerly exceptionalism again.) When I have lunch with editors, we talk about what books they're looking to publish. It's hard not to go home every day and plot out something that will fit the bill. I know so many writers who say, *"Just tell me what to write and I'll write it!"* I do have that information, but it's not that easy. I can follow a sure-to-be-marketable idea and realize I have zero passion for it. If I have no passion for it, the writing will suck. That is a truth for me as a writer, and for many of the writers I know and work with. It's not just about the idea. So my advantage as an agent doesn't help me as a writer unless I feel as strongly about an idea as a writer as I do as an agent.

While passion is important, so is money. In trying to find my next novel to write I couldn't not think about money. That was and always has been my goal—to write a novel that earns money. As an agent I have a general idea what a book will sell for, give or take. Whenever I had a new idea for a novel I thought about how I would pitch it to editors, what kind of publisher would publish it, and what they generally paid for a novel (even though I would never represent my own work). My quiet literary novel ideas, for adults or kids, were not going to pay off, and I still had to consider what kind of time publishing a book was going to take away from my day job as an agent. The big, commercial, heavy-on-the-hook ideas sounded fun for a while and made dollar signs dance in my head, but when I tried to plot them further, I realized I had the same problem—I just didn't care about the story enough to warrant spending years working in that world and with those characters.

What I know about the financial side of publishing has definitely affected my work as a writer, even as some people say that writers shouldn't think about money. That's bullshit. Not thinking about money wastes my time, and I only have so much time to write. Thinking about money has saved me from writing another novel that probably won't sell. Of course, none of us, even those with insider knowledge, can guarantee that books we think will be successful will actually be successful. But that's a risk I'm willing to take in order to do a thing I love. And I'm going to mitigate that risk by using the expertise I've gained as a literary agent to help myself in any way I can.

There's another aspect of working in publishing that people tend to talk less about: being a writer has helped me be a better agent. All those years of workshops and literary magazine rejections and tough criticism of my writing have made me a kinder editor of my clients' work. I spend more time on building them up when I send an editorial letter, instead of just sending a list of everything wrong with their novel. As a writer, I've also gotten inexplicable editorial advice like "fix the middle section," and I'm left with no clue how to do that. As an agent I try to be as specific as possible with editorial advice, so my authors know what issues I'm addressing and so that we can find ways to fix it together. When I do have good ideas for books I know I can't write, I dole them out to clients or friends more judiciously. I know how long it takes to write a whole novel or even a book proposal, and I don't want to send people on a wild goose chase. I've submitted books to editors written by clients who I adore, but which don't earn a publishing contract in the end. I've watched my clients lick their wounds and bounce right back. They've shown me that I can do that, too.

Most people assume being a literary agent gives me an advantage in getting my own work published. That's both true and not true. I know a lot about the industry. I know a lot about how a book is conceived, created, produced, and sold. But I am still, as yet, an unpublished novelist. My experience has shown me what to spend more time on (craft, editing) and less time on (chasing trends, daydreaming about advances). But I don't think I'm significantly more likely to be published than anyone who does a great deal of research about publishing and reads a lot of recently published books. I may be a literary agent, but when it comes to getting published, I'm still just a writer.

AGAINST "VS."

Leslie Jamison

I moved to Iowa City when I was twenty-one and New York when I was twenty-three, then back to Iowa City when I was twenty-six, and back to New York when I was thirty. If you were someone versed in the binary of "MFA vs. NYC"—the publishing/ academia polarity that's become a hot topic over the past few years (at least in the tiny worlds it purports to describe)—you might say I've gotten MFA vs. NYC whiplash, or seen the distinction from both sides. Or perhaps I've simply seen enough to understand that, insofar as that binary maps a set of tangled distinctions between two highly privileged communities, its rigorous pursuit can start to feel like a narcissism of small differences.

To me, the most interesting part of the MFA vs. NYC model— first proposed in an essay written by Chad Harbach in 2010, then explored more fully in an entire anthology edited by him in 2014— was never the question of literary culture (Brooklyn brownstones vs. midwestern dive bars; obscure short stories vs. high-profile debut novels) so much as the question of money. The binary points to the two major means by which American writing is funded: the publishing industry and the university system.

Like most binaries, Harbach's is ultimately more useful in its dismantling than its original formulation. To my mind, the MFA vs. NYC distinction is both more *and* less than a binary. It's less than a binary because its cultures are heavily crossbred, and it's more than a binary because each of these distinct "cultures" is in fact composed of multiple forms of attachment to a single economic engine. Each culture on either side of the "vs." is actually an intricate blend of attachments, and the "vs."—at this point—is something of a toppled wall.

There are several distinct ways of being attached to "MFA" culture—as a student and as a teacher, as starving-grad larva, caterpillar adjunct, or tenure-track butterfly—and at least two distinct ways of being attached to "NYC" culture: by living there, or by being supported by its publishing industry—represented by a New York agent, published by New York magazines or houses, edited by New York editors.

But these two literary cultures are intertwined in economically structural ways; and what it means to succeed in either world is often quite contingent on the other. Success in NYC publishing is an important part of getting a good academic job (the cred of getting published by a big house, getting good reviews in major media, getting major awards from literary institutions based in NYC), while many of the writers granted success and credibility by NYC publishing venues are still dependent on the MFA world for monetary support. Few writers can live entirely off the one-two punch of advances and, maybe, royalties (if you're impossibly lucky, or get a fairly low advance and earn it out quickly). Which is to say: Neither literary culture is an island. Both are inescapably subject to the influence of the capital (monetary and cultural) the other offers. If MFA or NYC are the workplaces that fund literature, then most writers have two jobs.

My own tax returns from the last ten years show an even split between these two worlds: a first-book advance in three installments from a Big Five publishing house; paychecks from four separate academic institutions, including my MFA stipend, my doctoral stipend, my paychecks from teaching undergrad creative writing and low-res MFA creative writing; paychecks and expense reimbursements from glossy New York magazines; much tinier paychecks from *un*-glossy literary magazines; and an advance from a large indie press based in Minneapolis that either counts as *neither* MFA nor NYC, or else somehow counts as both. I've also accrued a slew of tax stubs from so-called actual jobs, most of them part-time, none of which I kept for more than two years: innkeeper, tutor, baker, medical actor, personal assistant, Citigroup temp—all of which testify to the alternate income streams of writers in both cultures; the other work performed outside publishing *and* the academy to support the heart's labor of writing. I've lived in both team dugouts twice (IC and NYC), and having some success with my second book only entrenched me more deeply in both worlds: I have another two-book deal from a big NYC house and will tour the country talking to university students. At this point I work at the nexus where the binary collapses most literally: I have a tenure-track job at an MFA program in NYC.

What just happened in that last paragraph, when I stopped making an argument and started telling the story of my tax returns? Argument turned to anecdote—or rather, turned to anecdote to do its dirty work. It seems less responsible to talk about how it works for *everyone*—how the money flows for everyone—and more possible, more responsible, to talk about how it has worked for me; how I've worked, how I've tried to make it work. The question of money and anecdote is tricky like this: If we want to talk about the economics of writing, we can only speak with authority about the muck of our own financial lives, but our financial lives often feel tactless to talk about in public. I feel especially tactless talking about my financial life now that it's become less difficult than it used to be.

Why is this worth talking about at all? For starters, looking at where the money comes from points to how much privilege is still deeply embedded in the American literary scene—how many incredible voices aren't funded by either of these economic engines. Talking about money forces us to acknowledge aspects of the creative process that feel uncomfortable, that push back against our sense of what pure *making* might look like: the hustle, the shame of contingency and context.

Asking where the money comes from—and what kinds of literary culture and community its channels produce—also means asking: How does funding affect the work we make? I'm interested not only in the question but in the discomfort I feel—in myself, in others—at its asking, a discomfort about the relationship between creativity and collectivity and capital: the ways in which we are not simply producers but produced. We are anxious about our influences.

§

In a 1981 essay called "Fires," Raymond Carver replaces one notion of literary influence with another: "I can't talk about books or writers who might have influenced me . . . I don't know about literary influences," he writes. "But I do have some notions about other kinds of influences."

He says that the fact of having two children influenced his writing more than anything else, and speaks in quite frank—and often shockingly pained—ways about the pressure they put on his money and his time. He describes one clarifying moment in a Laundromat in Iowa City, while he was doing his family's laundry, desperately afraid he'd never become the writer he wanted to be:

> I remember thinking at that moment, amid the feelings of helpless frustration that had me close to tears, that nothing—and, brother, I mean nothing—that ever happened to me on this earth could come anywhere close, could possibly be as

important to me, could make as much difference, as the fact that I had two children. And that I would always have them and always find myself in this position of unrelieved responsibility and permanent distraction.

I'm talking about real *influence* now. I'm talking about the moon and the tide.

I'm moved by the bold truth of his piece—the tension it articulates—but also saddened by its tone, the ways in which his children come across as an unremitting strain, like tiny slave drivers: "Somehow, when we weren't looking, the children had got into the driver's seat. As crazy as it sounds now, they held the reins, and the whip."

But mainly I'm struck by Carver's willingness to speak against certain taboos—he openly resents his kids, and says so—and I love the way he upends the question of influence. *Fuck the canon*, he says. *I was influenced by having to pay the bills, for myself and for my family.*

Discussing "influence" in terms of literary models is beholden to a more romantic vision of writing—as an ongoing conversation with other authors, and with the tradition of literature itself—but tax returns and day jobs are "influences" that feel less constitutive of creativity and more in competition with it.

But what happens when we bring financial necessity and financial constriction into the conversation? We have to look at William Carlos Williams's relationship to his career as a doctor, Zora Neale Hurston's relationship to her patron, and James Agee's relationship to *Fortune* magazine. We have to look at Jean Rhys living in impoverished obscurity; Nellie Bly angling for a story that would get her on staff at the *New York World*; David Foster Wallace's entire career in the academy.

Looking at these financial contexts feels less like ripping away the curtain to show that the Wizard of Oz is actually an ordinary middle-aged guy and more like widening our vision of genius—not stripping it of its brilliance by suggesting that genius was prostrating itself before its gravy train(s), but offering that brilliance in a different kind of context: messier, dirtier, more ecstatic. I remember a friend telling me that the notebooks for Marilynne Robinson's *Housekeeping* held the jam-smeared fingerprints of her young son alongside the early traces of that book: a book that has always felt so entirely *of* its world, to me, so brilliantly apart from this one. But it lived in this world, once. That's what those smears of jam tell me. It was born here.

In his autobiography, Williams writes about the relationship between his different kinds of work: "[A]s a writer I have never felt that medicine interfered with me but rather that it was my very food and drink, the very thing which made it possible for me to write. Was I not interested in man? There the thing was, right in front of me. I could touch it, smell it. It was myself, naked, just as it was, without a lie telling itself to me on its own terms." He says the "poet's business" is "not to talk in vague categories but to write particularly, as a physician works, upon a patient, upon the thing before him, in the particular to discover the universal." It's not just that the poet has his own "business" too, but that he works like a physician upon a patient—that he finds, in this work, the residue of another profession. It's not a staining residue but rather an analogous form of attention.

Zora Neale Hurston's wealthy, white patron was interested in "primitivisms," and when she gave Hurston a stipend and a Ford to drive around the southern states collecting folktales from African American communities, her support came from that troubling interest; but that doesn't cheapen the fruits of Hurston's work. It only exposes how deeply Hurston was aware of the ways in which folktale culture could be sought and traded like a commodity; and gives us another way to see Hurston's intelligence at work in the field and on the page: how intricate and savvy her relationships to her subjects and her material were. James Agee started writing for *Fortune* but couldn't finish writing for them—they didn't want what he'd done—so he wrote against his assignment instead; he made the economics of the journalism industry, and how they troubled him, part of his subject instead of simply allowing their machinery to remain invisible.

If our mythology of romantic inspiration is disrupted by an attention to logistics and circumstance, I think that discomfort is not just a question of money but a question of collectivity: recognizing the shaping influence of money also means recognizing the shaping influence of institutions. It means acknowledging the ways in which larger collective bodies make art; that art doesn't get made simply by the isolated body of the individual artist. At the end of *The Program Era*, his book about MFA programs' effect on American literature, Mark McGurl urges us to "[lay] aside our anachronistic prejudices for the One over the Many Ones," which makes me think of that moment from the gospel of Mark, when Jesus asks a man possessed by demons for his name. "My name is Legion," the man says, "for we are many."

Our abiding discomfort with the idea of art produced by context is the inevitable flipside of two strands of privilege: the American privileging of individuality and agency and an aesthetic privileging of uniqueness and distinction. If you're a writer, being produced by an institution means you might be just like your fellow institutional products, and that you aren't even responsible for your own productions. This carries a certain shame, and makes coauthors of us all. It's the artistic equivalent of that old saw from sex ed: When you sleep with someone, you're sleeping with everyone s/he has ever slept with. We're forced to confess we're not just making art with everyone we've ever been to bed with—we already knew that—but with everyone we've ever been in *school* with; everyone we've been edited by, everyone we've gotten drunk alongside. Everyone we've gotten paid by. It's why the MFA crowd gets defensive when "MFA fiction" gets invoked as a homogenous entity—an endless parade of cookie-cutter fictions stretching from Charlottesville to Iowa City to Tuscon. It's why writers funded by the NYC publishing industry are made to feel self-conscious about writing for "the market"—as if wanting to be read was a crime, which it isn't, or writing for a readership is necessarily an aesthetic compromise.

When I say *We are anxious about our influences,* maybe I should just own it: I'm anxious about my influences—not simply the fact that money may have influenced my writing life but that I wouldn't necessarily know if it had, or how it did.

I'm going to close with a return to anecdote: the story of the last thing I wrote. It was a response to the work of the Colombian sculptor Doris Salcedo, an essay I delivered as a talk at a symposium at the Guggenheim devoted to her work. The project was very much "from the heart," as they say. Meaning what? Meaning that it was my attempt to express a genuinely powerful response I'd had to her work—an almost mystical connection I'd felt to a funeral shroud she'd made from thousands of rose petals, preserved between death and life, sutured together with thread. The talk was also my attempt to link her work to certain questions that had been troubling me for a while—namely, how can an artist's work respond to the suffering of others?

At the time I wrote the piece I was teaching a seminar in my MFA program about documentary writing, and this class started seeping into my talk: How was Salcedo's work responding to suffering in a different way from the documentary writers we'd read? There was a genuine connection between Salcedo and these writers, but the link was also efficient: I didn't have infinite time; these writers were on my mind. They were on my mind because they were on my syllabus, which was part of my job; I had my job

Leslie Jamison

because I was paying my rent. The presence of the sculptor and the documentarians in my essay was a function of their intellectual relevance, but it was also a function of money.

In fact, money lurked in every corner of this talk. Not only was I getting paid by the Guggenheim to give it, I was also getting paid by Columbia to teach the texts that had become central to it. My job was also helping to pay for my daughter's afterschool program, which allowed me the time to give the talk at all; but spending the afternoon with my daughter the day before I gave the talk was part of why I hadn't been able to edit it as much as I would have liked.

Here again, the shameful residue of *constraint, constraint, constraint.* The idea that work has been hobbled by constraints on time or of money depends on some faith in a kind of Platonic form—that the work has some hypothetically perfect shape it could reach, if only time and freedom were infinite—and that these questions of money and daily responsibility were simply chipping away at that form, rendering it more imperfect with every coveted dollar or lost hour. But art has no Platonic form; it has no perfect shape in another world—only its imperfect shape in this one.

What if we stopped thinking of money as the dirty secret of creative pursuit and instead recognized money as one of its constituent threads? Whether we like it or not, money's presence in art doesn't depend on whether we consider its presence. It's always already there anyway. My intention isn't to suggest that the demands of work and finance always make the work better, or easier, or to sugarcoat the often brutal terms of financial necessity: Zora Neale Hurston died in a welfare hospital, Jean Rhys lived out her alcoholism in deep poverty. I just want to admit money entrance into the room, to think about what it might reveal. What's exciting to me about allowing the question of money more fully into our vision of creative production is that it forces us to acknowledge how art rises from life, and how it rises from collective enterprise.

When she got on stage after I spoke, Doris Salcedo talked about the essentially collaborative nature of her work: not just because she has studio assistants who help her stitch together thousands of rose petals or weave burnt needles into shimmering metallic shirts, but because her art rises from every single voice she's ever heard.

And now, of course, this essay has become a kind of collaboration with her, and with Harbach and McGurl—whom I will quote here. Near the end of *The Program Era*, he takes us back to one of the core promises of creative writing as a discipline:

> To perform in the world is to say "I am," and to say "I am" is the most essential motive of every human performance, no matter how mundane. As an exercise of the human imagination, creative writing supplies a special effect of personal agency in that performance, a way of saying not only "I am" but "I am whoever I want to be," which unfortunately I am not.

McGurl's gloss on creative writing as an institutionalized articulation of individual potential—"I am whoever I want to be"—becomes, in actuality, some complicated version of: *I am whatever these worlds wanted me to be.* Part of the fear of looking at the relationship between art and its financial context, perhaps, is the fear that something else is true as well: *I am whatever these worlds paid me to be.*

When we stand up to say "I am," we declare how much more than *I* we actually are: we stand up to perform our influences, the shadow of our peer workshops and our marketing meetings, the aggregate of our friendships and our Facebook friendships, the residue of our Twitter feeds and our Park Slope cocktail party small talk and the long comet trails of our W-4s. Whether we publish or not, whether we *write* or not, we contain these multitudes. We are all legion.

LOVE FOR SALE

Harmony Holiday

LOVE FOR SALE

Griot/poet Amiri Baraka is seventy-five years old and out in the mid-November cold on Harlem's 125th Street. With him are two large boxes full of copies of his most recent book. The books come direct from the publisher, gift economy editions of what belongs to them now back in his possession, as if it belongs to him again, reproductions of the content he made, that they own/believe to have earned the "rights" to for having turned it into an object that can be sold, distributed, muted, and amplified at the discretion of their copyright. A publisher rendered his writing a sturdy rectangle by way of several factories and hired hands and now he's privy to the outcome, he gets the pretty/petty mercy mirror that is a bundle of copies of his own work to admire and distribute autonomously. Amiri Baraka is selling his own books on the street for money. We call him hood rich. We call him free. We call a job a slave. We call him a slave. A nigga with a job to do. A prophet. A savior.

LOVE CAN BE MANY THINGS

Prophets become profits, reveals religion, give way to Capitalism, obscene rich motherfuckers who fuck up the world for money, Amiri begins in his poem "Money." We call him valuable. We call him the will and owl of our value, poet, griot, gangster, bohemian if need be, master of this American/un-American slow drag to falling up, of the mask and the unmasking. Our fathers had some nerve to let the retribution match the contribution, to give us him, as mercenary and vessel. And Amiri has some nerve, out in the November empty after seventy-five journeys around the illusion/sun, selling his books for cash/money, for rational compensation, because there's a lien on his on-the-record earnings—any royalties coming from the publisher to him are intercepted and instead go direct to the US government because he allegedly owes the government money for back taxes. Is irony our safest ladder yet? And where do we get to on that clan/destined climb?

If you were always right would it be easier or more difficult to live in the world?

§

They have no god, no perceived good but, money.
No god, nothing they would live or die for but, money.

In explaining the impetus for his poem "Black Dada Nihilismus" Amiri recounts the story of his grandfather, a shop owner, lynched in the South for being too successful and black. This incident is why his parents fled to Newark, he explains. To shroud their excellence in a safe humility. His father a mailman, his mother a social worker. Theirs was resettlement to escape certain murder for the certain talent running like tender danger through the (then) Jones bloodline, making them double-conscious escape artists. This is why Amiri grows up working class with the name LeRoi, king, echoes of whitey on his bling, and then becomes middle class, blood prince, beyond hierarchy and addicted to transcendence. That tree. That treason. The mob of mentally ill white men who burned down Amiri's grandfather's shop and then hung him from a blues tree are why we have Amiri Baraka. The casual tragedy. The common story. Every nigga's grandfather was lynched or something, or light-skinned or both, they think. And we think: If they didn't have us to look at, maybe they would look at themselves. Hanging out under trees. Loving trees. Loving niggas. No mirror having but us. Is irony our climbingest ladder yet? White men looking for their reflections in the glare and glow of electric black flesh. Craving our blood enough to spill it. Inventing everything with their ignorance. Loving to unite niggas with trees and fall in love doubly, with our blood again, with the docile militancy of our corpses, the number one product of white labor here, broken black bodies.

So pathetic a pathology it's beyond greed, it's lack, Amiri Baraka's grandfather was a martyr to white American lack. White men walked toward their fear and murdered him. "Black Dada Nihilismus" echoes the tale eternally *for Jack Johnson, asbestos, tonto, buckwheat, billie holiday. For tom russ, l'overture, veset, beau jack / (may a lost god damballah, rest or save us against the murders we intend, against his lost white children, black dada nihilismus.* And critics unaware of its history would call the poem too violent, most of his poems, and affronted literati would call his imaginary revenge deranged, just out of range, too powerful, too warranted, too mythic, too possible, too obvious. But revenge is impossible. Amiri would hold his grandfather's limp body out as candor and nightmare for his life entire, he would secretly fear trees and breathe factory air more comfortably than the rural air of black death. He would seethe, tenderly. He would wonder at the difference between territory and landlessness as the difference between his grandfather's body and his grandfather's shop, both gutted, became clearer, became more important. His body would become his business, and none of yours. He would march his books onto the blackest, most hood-rich street in this heartsick nation and wave them like flags with a price tag and an urgent message, humming *The evening breeze / caressed the trees, tenderly,* medleyed with "Strange Fruit": *Blood on the leaves and blood at the root.*

What numb pain it had to be. To understand danger that acutely, to truly understand the phrase *love is a dangerous necessity.* Mafia at his feet, prophecy at his feet . . .

GHETTO LOVE KNIGHTS: A HISTORY

Black men and women newly "freed" from slavery were meant to become "productive" members of a society built on our blood, on our perceived excess, which thus perceived makes oppressors guiltless for turning our free labor into profit, jealous we are so capable of labor, so free. But once the traditional plantation has been disbanded, with what resources would we transform from slaves living on some white man's obscenely opulent land in the service of some white man's family and lifestyle to men and women, families, tribes, and dynasties again, laboring in the service of our natural black selves—how would we remember what true improvisation of feeling and action feels like, *against what light*, would our shadows dim and flicker triumphant? Free of contrived hubris. Free of kitsch Egypt. Where and how could we be that free in a United States that still refuses to apologize in the form of actual land and currency, for the crimes against our bodies, minds, and spirits, the crimes that turned us into worshipers of self-doubt, of white jesus, of white excellence, walking in such fear of our own capacities that that fear became amnesia and that amnesia became self-destruction, us turning our creative powers against ourselves or using them to assimilate rather than to reinstate value systems that serve us? Amiri thought about all these things when he decided to feed and clothe his children or do whatever else he needed to do with his money, before paying any of it back to this hideous government as taxes that would likely help fund the genocide of black, brown, and beige peoples abroad, and surely not education, or health care, or the rebuilding of black cultural centers like Harlem and Newark.

Until the United States gives every black "descendant of slaves" (a phrase we fetishize the weight out of) land to do with what we will, whether that be to build a school, build a factory, repair ourselves, or drum and dance in the splendid isolation of decolonized space, until then it is my belief that we do not owe this government taxes at all and certainly not any back taxes from years past. Each and every one of us should be tax exempt until the idea of reparations transforms from high concept to mandate. Until we have a payment plan from the government on what is owed us. No black-earned income should fund the United States' incessant attempt to do overseas, to populations rendered virtually invisible, what is done to black, brown, and beige people born and raised on US soil, under the tired tyranny of a bought and sold mainstream media and FCC; no fraction of any size of any black American citizen's paycheck should be given back to the government for the sad and meager handouts deemed services in this country. Let our collective sense of entitlement flail like one of those niggas we might glimpse at the bus stop in any run-down "urban center" in the United States, freely on PCP and beating the Vodun down in a monologue about the murders he intends against his lost white children. As entitled as we feel to be strung out on anger and the literal and metaphoric drugs we turn to for solace, let us apply that entitlement to our earnings, to what we are owed as citizens of a country that we built, that intends to break us. Let us cross-pollinate James Baldwin with Amiri with Malcolm X with Zora Neale Hurston and populate the land with writers immune to the seduction of prestige and reckless/beautiful enough to get a kiosk together on 125th Street.

LOVE IS ALSO A METHOD OF WORKING
AND WORKING THROUGH

As conscious as Amiri Baraka was of the horrors of contract and copyright law, even he was not above falling victim to it (though he was no victim but a savior). Even he, when faced with the choice between not publishing his work widely and getting a book deal with a "reputable" New York publisher, chose the deal. He wanted his message and his method accessed, at times at the expense of his fiscal autonomy. And there's a way in which whenever we go against what we know, whenever we compromise, we end up feeling like low-key prostitutes for it one way or another, down the line, especially if we are fortunate enough to possess as much integrity as Amiri did. And yet we must move through these transactions of spirit without the crutch or curse of pathos, as Amiri did. Out on 125th Street on any given day no matter the season, you will see griots with rented kiosks, selling incense and self-published books, moringa powder, sea moss smoothies, CDs, LPs, agitprop, salt peanuts, whatever needs distributing, whatever went underground. This is our factory. This is where we reclaim our practice of using public space or the commons to tell our stories and hand down our culture. All the allegories meet here and thrive. And in this way, every time the white world tries to steal our dignity from us we end up one-upping the attempt, uncovering the secret pleasures of being down and out in the form of being forced to face our charisma and interdependence. Amiri Baraka was master of this. His seventy-five-year-old self occupying Harlem's one-two-five with a stack of his books to sell is, as I see it, one of the great triumphs in the history of Black American publishing. When those with the power of nomination made Baraka famous after his 1964 play *Dutchman* it was in part in order to watch him, to keep an eye on him, to clip his wings with the weight of scrutiny, because his power was a threat but he was otherwise too charming and correct to demonize. Feigned alliance was easier. Fetishization was less effort than true understanding. And with the fame came separation from the very communities he was out to save. And when the visibility threatened to be his undoing, he was forced to go back into those communities as an elder, to deliver his urgent messages in person.

In West Africa creative genius enters the gift economy in a most automatic way, and showers are held for new writers, storytellers, and ministers in the same way that we now hold them for wives- and mothers-to-be. Here too we should (re)claim such rites of passages but we lack the language to even acknowledge them. Until the pang of one of our elders out in the cold under the threat of destitution reminds us. Until we see this and acknowledge that Amiri Baraka's economic suffering should be as impossible as all revenge is. Rather than death and taxes, death to black taxes. En masse. In the name of the legacy of Amiri. In the name of black radical writers who do not want to fund the systems their words seek to dismantle. Come after us if you got a problem. Meet us up in Harlem with our reparations. Take the A train.

UNLIKEABLE

Emily Gould

In 2005, when I was a young publishing assistant, I attended the PEN foundation's annual gala in New York City, held under the giant whale in the American Museum of Natural History. As I walked into the lobby and took a glass of wine from a passing tray, I tried to tell myself that this situation was normal and all in a day's work and that I was not awed by any of it, but of course I was mind-blown, starstruck. (It's funny to remember now that there was a time when being in a room full of famous authors and editors could still thrill and impress me.) I had borrowed a long strapless bridesmaid dress that showed the tattoos on my upper back, and during the cocktail hour before the seated dinner Margaret Atwood came up to me to compliment me on them. In my wildest dreams I had never imagined being in an environment of what seemed to me then like such glamour and elegance. I drank all my wine every time they refilled the glasses, and they refilled the glasses constantly.

Each publisher had been allowed to invite an author, from a list distributed by PEN, to sit at their table. My boss had selected a female author I'd never heard of before, but whose two published novels I'd bought and read in the weeks leading up to the event in order to prepare for the possibility that she might want to, I guess, discuss her work with me. As it turned out, neither I nor anyone else was required to discuss her work, or indeed anything else, with her, because she didn't talk to us. She wasn't rude, exactly. She simply participated in conversation at the absolute minimum and didn't encourage anyone to speak to her more than necessary. She didn't do any of the things women usually do, that I spend so much of my life doing: try to draw others out in conversation, smile receptively, laugh at jokes or even non-jokes just to show you are listening attentively. She didn't draw attention to her silence or deliberately snub anyone; she simply wasn't playing the game. She took a lot of cigarette breaks.

When this author rose to national prominence a couple of years later with a long, best-selling, hilarious, and true-seeming book that skewered the mores of several different types of Manhattanites, I thought of that evening. As I read and loved her popular book, I remembered what she'd been like—or, more accurately, how I had no idea what she was like, in spite of having met her. This made me admire her. In a man, of course, the aloof author's behavior would have been completely unremarkable. I doubt I would have remembered it. In fact, I know I wouldn't have.

I've worked in and around publishing for almost fifteen years now; I've met countless male writers who are socially careless or even blatantly offensive and who suffer zero professional censure for it. But women don't often get the luxury of acting that way, not if they want their careers to grow. To be like the female author I met in 2005 seems like it would require constant effort, a policing of the borders of self and persona and maybe also a constitutional immunity to caring what others think of you. In order to be successfully un-nice, an author would have to be so confident in her talent and skill that she was willing to risk alienating influential peers, editors, and agents—not to mention actual readers. To be un-nice might also require her to ignore the very real possibility that her likeability will be reflected by her bottom line.

For all authors, and especially for authors who live in the publishing industry's capital, New York, the continual awareness of a network of traded back pats and favors and blurbs and likes and faves is a background noise that's hard to ignore, and at times becomes deafening. Authors know we'll always have to sell another book, and with editors and publishers' hierarchies and jobs constantly in flux, we never know whether the assistant sending a halfway-decent galley for a blurb might one day be the editor who'll buy our book for six figures. Or whether the publicist we wish we could ignore might be our publicist someday, or whether we'll end up on a panel with or being judged for an award by an author whose latest book we think deserves a savage pan rather than the lukewarm review we end up writing. Et cetera. Most everyone, except conscientious objectors, the very un-astute, and people with unshakeable confidence or inherited wealth, plays the game. Women are less likely than men to fall into almost all these categories. For us, playing the game is less a choice than a default. It's a part of the job.

So we bake cookies for our readings. We express love on social media for books we find to be only okayish. And once in a while, in person, we vent to each other about how we really feel, but instead of feeling relieved by these sessions I end up feeling disturbed. Not only am I a phony, so is everyone I know! And of course, these back-channel chats end up on the public record sometimes, undermining years of assiduous anodyneness. After all, the business of publishing is not about being nice, it's about seeming nice, and no one is really *that* nice.

While my literary heroes have always been the kind of women who don't or can't pander, I've never been able to muster that kind of courage or tunnel vision. The way I see it, there are two ways to be a female novelist: play the game and ply everyone you encounter with sugar, or be a cool, distant ice queen, ideally ensconced for much of the year at some remote liberal arts college, disseminating your opinions only to your rapt students and never to, say, Facebook. It's much too late now for me to decide that I will be one of those ice queens, or like that PEN gala author, and it's also so emphatically not in my nature that it's kind of hilarious to think of myself approaching the world that way. I mostly like that I am naturally friendly and somewhat extroverted; I'm interested in people and I enjoy talking to them and engaging with them rather than observing them from a cool distance. I like (or am addicted to, however you want to say it) social media because I am a social, sociable person. I am somewhat less fond of my tendency to be constantly worried whether so-and-so secretly hates me, whether I'll be blackballed at some influential publication or other if I make my real opinions known. But I also realize how much of this behavior is gendered, conditioned, like my tendency to temper my statements of opinion with "I feel like" or "kind of," or to apologize to men who bump into me on the subway.

If likeability equals profitability, I'm probably headed in the wrong direction. Not only am I incapable of keeping my niceness veneer consistent, I'm also increasingly not in the mood to do the work it takes to seem perpetually likeable in person. It takes increasing effort for me to maintain a friendly, inviting persona at moments when I would much rather be alone, working, or with my family. Sometimes in situations where extroversion is professionally required of me—when I'm doing a reading or moderating a panel, or even just attending someone else's literary event—I am called upon to Be Emily Gould by someone I've just met who's read a lot of my writing and who has the not-entirely-inaccurate impression that she knows me already. But *I* don't know *her*, and the imbalance puts the onus on me to close that distance and put the person at ease. A lot of the time I don't mind doing this and over the years I've made friends this way. But sometimes after an evening full of these encounters I feel like the marrow is being sucked out of my bones. Still, I fear that avoiding such vampiristic feelings is not exactly an option if I want to sell books.

Being an extremely social, sociable, accessible person should not be the price of being a professional writer, but for women it almost inevitably is. No one ever explicitly *says* you have to send friendly notes to critics along with your galleys, maybe even on cute stationery, or bake cookies for your readings, but when you see your peers doing this and it seems to be working, it's hard not to feel like that's the standard we're all being held to, unless we want to do the mysterious and uncertain work of crafting the opposite kind of unapproachable/distant persona. It's galling how often we think of writers as people we either would or would not want to be friends with. Understandable, but still galling. I don't want to be friends with everyone; why should everyone have to want to be friends with me? I don't want to be friends with Philip Roth or Clancy Martin but I still want to spend time in the worlds their minds have created. Refusing to extend that kind of intellectual curiosity sans yearning for personal connection when it comes to work by women is wrong.

I wonder what would have happened if I had still been a smoker in 2005 and if I'd followed the antisocial female author out onto the steps of the museum and casually asked her for a light, then pretended to recognize her. "Oh, you're [her name]! I loved [name of her book]," I would have said, then segued naturally into a great icebreaking question about some kind of irresistible gossip. She would have seen me, recognized my true full self, the proto-novelist light flickering behind my eyes, and she would have given me the rare gift of one of her smiles. Ha ha, no she wouldn't have. She would have muttered something under her breath and then walked a few steps away to smoke the rest of her cigarette in peace, and she would have been right to do so. But claiming that right, for most of us, is harder than it looks.

SAD BIRTH LADY™

Meaghan O'Connell

A few weeks before I found out I was pregnant I was on a walk with my best friend, a TV writer who was also just starting out. Like many other afternoons, we were away from our laptops and walking in circles, berating ourselves for not writing. Tomorrow we would get up early. Tomorrow we'd go to the gym, not waste time, not read Twitter. It was difficult to take ourselves seriously, to take our work seriously, to believe we would do it, when we hadn't yet. We were so confident of our talent, of our future selves' inevitable success, but unsure of how we'd get there. We were tortured, hating this middle part.

Just promise me, I said to my friend as we stood on some New York sidewalk waiting for the light to change, *if I start talking about trying to have a baby as a way to distract myself from writing—just slap me*. She knew what I meant, and agreed. Most women, I think, would know what I meant. Writing and motherhood take up the same sort of space in a woman's life—that shrinking, typically non-remunerative space that we reserve for fulfillment, for reinvention, for growth. Both writing and motherhood are sentimentalized and undervalued in the market; both seen as a choice, a lifestyle, something you should feel lucky to do if you get to. I wanted them both, and I suspected this was too much to ask. I suspected the only way to have it both ways (a baby and a life) was to do everything else I ever wanted, then get pregnant—to build up my life and then, when I was good and ready, throw a bomb in it.

After all, writing was merely vital to my sanity, which wouldn't hold much water in the face of a child, who, as feminist author Tillie Olsen famously put it in *Silences*, "needs one *now*." I didn't know what "one" referred to yet but I figured it was not "to lie quietly in my crib while my mom finishes a personal essay she won't be paid to write."

§

When I got pregnant accidentally, I had just quit my full-time job at a tech company to finally pursue freelance writing. I was going to apply to get my MFA. I got engaged to my longtime boyfriend, and we were going to take an extended honeymoon and then move to some midwestern college town and live off my grad school stipend. Or so went my fantasy. When I found out I was pregnant I was elated, but full of dread. I felt emotionally ready to have the baby, which was perhaps naive, but I didn't feel practically ready. And by that I mean I had not achieved everything I wanted to with my career. I had not, in fact, achieved, or written, much at all.

Still, I kept the baby. I applied to MFA programs, naively holding on to the idea of going to grad school with a newborn, but I didn't get accepted anywhere. I was offered a part-time job editing a personal finance site I loved called The Billfold and took it without hesitation. It paid $1,000 a month for work I knew I'd spend most of every day doing. *But I could use their office space!* I justified to Dustin, my newly deemed fiancé. I never went into the office. We canceled our wedding plans. I got Obamacare. I swore I'd start some big work in progress that I'd be able to come back to after my (unpaid) maternity leave, but that never happened either. In reality I managed only to edit the website I worked for. Instead of starting a novel, I let myself be obsessively consumed by birth stories, baby forums, and the endless sea of pregnancy-related Internet content.

The birth story is a genre of writing that has flourished on the web, one that I was obsessed with long before I ever got pregnant. Once I did get pregnant, I was, despite my better efforts to be "empowered" (the classes, the books, the meditations!), terrified to give birth. I read birth stories obsessively and watched videos of births on YouTube as a sort of exposure therapy, as if the image of having your body split open as another human exits it would ever lose its power. I burrowed in deep, rubbernecking really, but it was no use. Pregnancy, childbirth, and all that came after have left me hugely affected, hugely unmoored.

My writing life, though, has never been better. This has been a great relief to me, and a great irony. After birth, something shifted. My relationship with my work became the urgent, focused love affair I've always imagined it could be.

§

My birth experience was nothing like the stories I'd read. There was no slow dancing with my husband by the light of a full moon. No baking cookies for the nurses during early labor. No triumph, no cake. I was greatly supported but felt very alone as my labor went on and on, lasting nearly forty hours until I finally threw in the towel and consented to a C-section. When visitors came to see the baby afterward, and would ask what it was like giving birth, I would just shrug. *It was insane*, I'd say. I couldn't quite manage to communicate much else, though I wanted more than anything to explain, to relate, to feel known.

A month postpartum, I walked out of our studio apartment alone and shuffled to a coffee shop to try to work for two hours, and I may as well have heard angels singing. I'd never felt freer. I would've liked to have spent hours sitting in a dark hole with my laptop until I had made sense of all the changes that were happening in my life. I wanted to write more than ever but logistically speaking, I had about ninety minutes, twice a day, between feedings. Logistically speaking, I had a newborn baby. He needed one now.

"One" was me.

When I wasn't in front of my laptop in a coffee shop, which was most of the time, I was thinking about writing, fantasizing about it. Stuck in the low-down dailiness of caring for a baby, I wrote essays in my head. I ran out the door as soon as the baby was fed and stayed at my computer until my breasts started leaking milk. I solicited essays and wrote a blog post a day for my editing job. My writing for this blog about money slowly became all about having a baby: the cost of my hospital stay, my phone calls with the health insurance company, our trip to see a pediatrician, the funny comments from neighbors about leaving my baby behind to do work. Reading these dashed-off blog posts now, I am a little bit in awe—there was a ferocity and a focus to them that was totally new for me. All the confidence I was missing in childrearing I found in writing.

How to get more time to write was all I thought about. Not where to publish, whom to pitch to, what rates I'd earn, or deadlines; there was no self-loathing work avoidance, no second-guessing, no envy (in short, all the things that tormented me before and continue to torment me now). *I feel like my beautiful son is distracting me from a deeply transformative journey of self-discovery*, I wrote to a writer friend. I was emboldened, full of righteousness and bad news and dark jokes. I also no longer had time to procrastinate or second-guess myself. I had to take my writing seriously if I was going to justify taking the time to do it. And I had to keep doing it for my sanity. I had to keep doing it so that I could keep doing it. Amid the chaos of new motherhood, I clung to what I knew, and I knew that I needed to write, to defend it against everything else in my life. It was a time of great confusion for me, but in this alone, really, I had total clarity.

Time, of course, was another story, but during this passionate extrafamilial affair with writing I did manage to finally write my birth story. As it grew close to twenty thousand words, I couldn't believe how much fun I was having. Writing it, I felt the kind of catharsis we are all supposed to pretend is not part of the writing process, even as we still seek it. I could have kept writing forever; I wanted to.

§

Despite feeling proud of myself for finishing my birth story, and despite my urge to share it with a safe audience (I sent it out as a newsletter with a few hundred subscribers), I was hesitant to publish the piece more widely. It felt so new and vulnerable, for one. And I had received the same cultural message I imagine most ambitious women with children contend with: that writing about motherhood wasn't serious, or literary, or something non-parents wanted to hear about. But when Longreads asked to publish the essay, and said it would only be lightly edited (by my friend and boss at The Billfold), I agreed. The day my birth story was published was one of the most rewarding days I've ever wasted on Twitter. It was also, in retrospect, the start of my writing career.

People were rapt, tweeting all-caps reactions, demanding that their friends read it, laughing, crying, sending me overly intimate e-mails, swearing they would sew up their vaginas. I was so taken aback by the response and how rewarding the whole process had been. I had been feeling so alienated and overwhelmed I had forgotten writing had always been my way to cope, and that hadn't changed.

When the piece blew up—it was the most popular original writing that Longreads published in 2014—I knew I was onto something. That my first "viral hit" was fifteen thousand words (a fifty-seven-minute read!) and called "A Birth Story" strikes me as both hilarious and perfect. Soon, editors from publications I'd dreamed of writing for my whole life began to solicit me for work. Book editors and literary agents asked if I was writing a book, and I told them that, well, I wasn't, but wanted to. Soon, *New York* magazine's women's website The Cut asked me to write a weekly column for them about parenthood.

The months after my son was born marked one of the hardest periods of my life. I suffered from what I think was postpartum depression and what I know was postpartum hypothyroidism, but career-wise, everything was happening. Before Dustin and I moved across the country in search of more space, milder weather, and affordable childcare, I met with six different agents at six different coffee shops in New York City. I was nervous, still wearing maternity leggings while Dustin sat at home with Henry, but my nerves gave way to a quiet, calm excitement when I met Sarah, the woman I decided to work with. She compared my writing to Cheryl Strayed's, and on the G train on the way home to my family I cried with happiness.

There wasn't much time to celebrate. I had a column and a book proposal to write, not to mention a baby to take care of. Writing a book proposal, ultimately an argument for why someone should pay you to write a book that doesn't exist yet, required a confidence I didn't always have. I could take my time and my need to write seriously. But could I take this book seriously?

I often had these second-guessing conversations with myself on midday walks to my son's day care. One afternoon I was listening to a writing podcast while I walked; the guest was a successful journalist, a woman who profiles A-list celebrities and wins every industry award. This is a woman I look up to; I'd love to write a little bit like her. She was talking about how she had written a few personal essays about her birth and postpartum experience, and opportunity after opportunity had fallen into her lap. I was laughing and relating to her so much, my heart was soaring. I felt like,

Wow, I am *really doing this, too.* The weather was beautiful that day and I was so full of hope. The journalist started talking about how editors approached her back then, wanting her to write a book. She laughed and explained that she had said no, "Thank God." I turned red. "I didn't want to become the sad birth lady," she said, laughing. "I didn't want to be pigeonholed." As I inched my way down a hill in my clogs, I began to feel ill. Here I was, walking to my son's day care to breastfeed him in the middle of the day because he refused to take a bottle, alternately full of hope and filled with dread. Was this me? Am I that woman, the rightful heir to "Sad Birth Lady"? I didn't want to be pigeonholed either. I didn't want to be dismissed. As soon as I got home I pitched a web editor a book review that I'd written in my head on the way home, one that I didn't have time to write. Take that, pigeonhole.

§

On a phone call with my agent that same week, we went over the part of my book proposal where I explain why I want to write the book—what is my message, and what do I want the book to be "about." We called this document "Why This Book?" and when I had trouble with *Why This Book?* the document, I also had trouble with *Why this book?* the larger question. This trouble happened often throughout the proposal process, moments when I wondered if I was making a huge career mistake. How to parse self-sabotage from self-preservation, fear from knowing better? When I was filled with insecurity, or self-loathing about my new maternal identity, I came back to this fact: the book was something I would have loved to read. Writing about motherhood, sad or no, has been creatively fulfilling and professionally rewarding.

And when that reasoning didn't work, there was always the money. I'd just signed a real contract with The Cut and they nearly doubled my rate. Since quitting my start-up job eighteen months earlier, I'd been in a race against my dwindling savings account. I was lucky to have enough savings from stock options to give it a real shot, but I knew that to keep writing long term, and to pay for my son's childcare so I could take time away from him to do it, I would have to make real money.

To make enough money to live by writing one essay a week, well, it felt like a faraway dream—something in my distant future, maybe, if not a bygone era. Add in my book advance, and it's now my reality. If all goes as planned, in 2016 I will make $5,000 more than my highest tech salary. I am now contractually obligated to get over myself, to forget my fears about being the Sad Birth Lady. Being paid enough to devote real time to it, for writing to be sustainable, helps keep it in the bucket of "work." Being paid enough to devote real time to my writing makes it sustainable and possible but also lends it proportion. The money grounds my writing in the realm of "work." Work I'll go to lengths to avoid, sure, but still it's a job, and I have to show up for it. I have to get over myself so I can get paid. *It's just work. You have a child to provide for, think of him if not your own ego.* This is what it took for me to take my writing seriously, to justify it to my smallest self.

I've gone from being a copywriter to a financial blogger to a parenting columnist to an author with a book contract within the course of eighteen months. I can reinvent myself later, if I'm so inclined. But for now this is what I am in the middle of. This is the subject matter and the readership—full of searching, funny women—that is closest to my heart. This is how I make my living. The essays I used to write in my head were always better and cooler and less easily dismissed, but they didn't exist. Instead I have vowed to get out of my own way, to be the most rigorous, most insightful, most empathetic mommy blogger I can be, even if the "M" word still sends a little chill up my spine, even if some days I would rather be something, anything, else.

GHOST STORIES

Sari Botton

A controversial homebirth midwife; a woman cop who took six bullets as she helped stop a terrorist attack; a young woman making the best of life despite a disfiguring disease; a sixties-pop-music buff who, after his fourth bout with cancer, decided to live out his dream of writing about his encounters with his idols. Those are the kinds of people I have ghostwritten books for—not people like V. C. Andrews or ex-presidents. You don't get rich ghostwriting for regular people. In many cases, you also don't get rich writing for the big names, either. You'd be surprised—sometimes it's the wealthiest and/or best-known clients who pay the least.

Exactly how much do I make writing other people's stories? For most books, I receive a flat rate—anywhere from $10,000 to $40,000 in my case, plus or minus a percentage of the author's royalties. Sometimes I get a percentage of the author's advance—twenty-five to forty percent in my experience, plus or minus a percentage of the author's royalties—but I am told the top ghostwriters get fifty. In the best cases I have gotten forty, with twenty-five percent of the author's royalties. Here and there, I charge by the hour, $50 to $90, for what I call "editorial hand-holding" for clients who can sort of write, but need a lot of guidance and editing work.

For me, ghostwriting is a job—one I wouldn't do if I didn't need the money. Like any job, it has its pros and cons, its ups and downs—lots of freedom, the satisfaction of helping someone tell their story; but also, frequently, having to handle intense personalities with kid gloves.

And yet, I still have not given up on ghostwriting entirely. For every bad client there's also an instance of grace—mostly people grateful for my ability to help them express themselves, even if their books haven't been blockbusters. There have been moments that made it all worthwhile, like helping an author's daughter, who had severe learning disabilities, write an afterword that made her feel proud. Not to mention it's a way for me to use the skills I have to make at least some money, while working at home, at my own pace.

Here are a few of my most memorable deals from almost two decades in the trenches.

THE FIRST TIME

It's 1996 and I'm looking for a way to leave my full-time job as a writer for fashion magazines *Women's Wear Daily* and *W* and go freelance. I meet a young agent at an Authors Guild event I'm covering. She's looking for someone to ghostwrite a book for a wedding planner. It sounds pretty easy. I've been interviewing people, writing profiles, and doing lifestyle journalism for a decade already. I know how to listen, how to construct a story arc, how to keep a story moving. I've also dabbled in nonfiction MFA programs I ultimately dropped out of—Sarah Lawrence and City College of New York—and have been working on a memoir. This seems like something I can easily do, and something that can supplement the money I'll make freelancing, so I quit my job.

If we land a book deal, the $3,000 I get up front to write the wedding planner's book proposal will be deducted from the $15,000 in total I'll receive for writing the book, in three increments: on signing, on delivery, and on acceptance. I'll also get fifteen percent of the author's royalties once she earns out her advance.

I get that job, and at the same time, another—$10,000 for a book about hair and beauty styles for weddings by a hairstylist. Again, I will be paid in three increments, and this time I secure twenty-five percent of the author's royalties. The hairstylist is my first client to muse aloud, from the beginning, about what he is going to say when he appears on *Oprah*. He is even paying for media training for this express purpose. He is far from the last client I will ever have who verbally anticipates an impending star turn on *Oprah*.

Doesn't sound too bad, right? But after I write four very different versions of her proposal, the wedding planner's book never secures a deal. And the hairstylist's book never earns back its advance. He never makes it to Oprah's couch.

THE GREAT MASCARA CAPER

In 1998 I get a gig writing a book for the multimillionaire founder of a major cosmetics company. He's paying $25,000, but no royalties. However, I am told it's going to be an easy job—probably taking no more than a couple of months—because the author has all his information and research ready to go. As a consolation for my missing out on royalties, he also promises me the employee discount—seventy-five percent—on the company's products, for life.

On three separate occasions I spend three weeks working with him in a tiny town in Wisconsin (population: 650). I do what I do with all my clients: a combination of recorded interviews—which are then transcribed by a professional transcriber (the client balks at paying the fees, but my agent insists)—and getting my client to do some freewriting (free-associating on paper) because sometimes people brainstorm better that way.

I keep waiting for him to give me some big folder full of all the research, but it turns out it's all conveniently stored in his brain. Some details come out a little different each time. So I interview the scientists at his company myself. I learn to translate into layman's terms why curly hair tends to be drier than straight, and other secrets of beauty science. The job seems like it will never end. It ends up taking nine months, monopolizing my life, and leaving me nearly broke. Within a year, the client has sold his cosmetics company, and I promptly lose my discount.

THE BEST (AND WORST) DEAL

This is the memoir of a mother whose son had become quadriplegic after an accident. I race through the proposal so my agent can have it in time for a big international book festival. She's hoping to get offers in the $200,000 range. That sounds good to me; I'll receive forty percent of the advance. My agent calls three times from the festival, first to say she's gotten an offer of $250,000, but will keep going. The second call, she says she's snagged a $750,000 offer, but she isn't stopping until she has $1 million. By the third call, she's made good on her word.

This is it. I am going to make $400,000 in six months for writing one book, plus twenty-five percent of the author's royalties. I am stunned. But I am also so scared. What makes a memoir a million-dollar book? How would this have to be different from a book I would have delivered for $200,000? How the fuck am I going to do this?

I receive my first of three scheduled payments: $113,000 after my agent's cut. I have never made that much money in a year, not even when I was an advertising copywriter.

But that's the only check I get. The editor gushes over early glimpses we give her of the manuscript. But then she changes her tune. She rejects two different drafts of it. This is now 2008. The economy is changing. The business is changing. The publishing house wants to kill the book. It seems they've realized they've been too loose with their money. The agent campaigns to not have the book killed. *How can you do this to a woman in her situation?* she argues, pulling out the author's backstory for sympathy. Instead of killing the book, they fire me.

I wonder if there's some kind of lesson I'm supposed to learn from this: I have made the most money I have ever made in ghost-writing on a book from which I was fired. The book eventually comes out, and it's a huge flop. (And no *Oprah* appearance.)

THE $20,000 BESTSELLER

At a time when I am fairly desperate for work, a celebrity's wife comes along. She wants to write a memoir about raising a kid with a disability. She's offering $20,000 with no royalties. Subtract my agent's fifteen percent and taxes. Know that this work is very taxing with even the best clients. Know that I need a job. My agent presses for royalties, but the woman and her people refuse. *Don't worry*, my agent says. *This book won't be big. There probably won't be any royalties.*

I go to meet the author and resentment rises up inside me as she proudly shows me around her ten-bedroom mansion. At the end of our first interview, I ask whether she's ever tried a gluten-free diet for her son. *No, I can't do that*, she says. *He'd freak out if I served him something different from his brothers and sister. Tonight, for instance, I'm making spaghetti. It's his favorite. I can't deprive him of that.*

A half hour later, we walk into her kitchen, and there, in front of the stove, is an older woman in an apron making spaghetti. *Oh, my god*, I think, *my client thinks she's making spaghetti. She's so used to having people do things for her, she doesn't even know she's not actually doing them!* I feel like another one of the many people she pays to live her life for her, and it doesn't feel great.

After the book comes out, my client reportedly tells interviewers she didn't have a ghostwriter—that the publisher had hired someone, but her work on the first chapter was unsatisfactory, so they fired her and the author wrote the whole thing herself. In five weeks.

That false claim amounts to a public retraction of the acknowledgment stipulated in my contract. I am advised to have my lawyer send her a cease and desist letter. To add insult to injury, not only are there royalties for the author, the book lands on the *New York Times* bestseller list for several weeks.

I get nothing for it beyond the $20,000. That sours me on ghostwriting for a while, at least for stingy quasi celebrities.

§

A couple of years later, I'll have a very gratifying experience working with an unknown author on his memoir about his struggle, in his twenties, to come out. I don't get rich on it by any means, but I am fairly paid and enjoy the work. There are aspects of this client's story that resonate with the memoir I've been struggling to write, and so I feel personally invested.

This job leaves me feeling hopeful about ghostwriting as a means of supporting myself. Helping people tell their stories, writing books in one of my favorite genres—memoir—feels like the most logical and best possible use of my skills, in cases where I am being remunerated decently and treated fairly. It keeps me from having to acquire new skills to stay afloat, like some colleagues who have become real estate agents and lab techs, or are studying nursing.

Since then, I've had a couple of easy, small gigs, and one nightmare job that would have put me off ghostwriting forever if I weren't lacking other skills that are as lucrative. As of this writing I'm considering another longer project. The woman who reached out to me has said two things that caught my attention: *Money is no object*, and, *The client is . . . well . . .* emotional. Here's hoping that, at the very least, the former makes up for the latter.

ECONOMIES 101

Susie Cagle

part one:
The Grift Economy

There's no way I can ever know just how much I stole.

It started early, on the desktop PC in the living room of our house in the late '90s. After I'd filled the hard drive, I stored my stolen treasures on an infinite series of burned CDs that teetered in a precarious stack against the dusty monitor, a physical manifestation of my thousands upon thousands of tiny teenage crimes.

I stole until I knew who I was. I was not on the web; I was of it.

This was in no way a gift economy, but a confused economy: one where communication and property had accelerated into a future era far faster than payment had, and where new territories were not governed by old ethics. I didn't take any distinct pleasure in my crimes—they were an investment in my cultural development, a means to an end at a price I could afford.

I spent little if any time thinking about the economics of MP3 theft or the long tail of its repercussions. While I downloaded hundreds of copyright-protected pieces of art, I was working hard to create my own, in long blog posts that I wrote and shared almost daily. I sat cross-legged and hunched a few inches in front of that computer until 1 A.M., 2 A.M., 3 A.M., reading and writing as much and as fast as I could, until my eyes burned and I could feel the heat and the static from the monitor on my oily skin.

The Internet was more than I could have ever hoped for, administered by a romantic kind of anarchy and expectations of reciprocity, equity, and community. Or at least it seemed that way in 1999.

There's no way I can ever know just how much I stole. There's no way I could know how much would be stolen from me. I assumed that everyone was surviving. I assumed I would too.

part two:
The Gift Economy

Eight years later I started to give as much as I got.

I only made comics because I wanted free comics. This is a well-known strategy in the comics community: If you expend even a middling effort at making your own comic book, you can pawn it off on others who will feel obligated to trade you theirs in kind. It's an excellent scam for a new artist, and one I took full advantage of. Comics are often a closed economy regardless, but barter made this reality even starker, if no less useful to me.

I made my first three comics in three months. I squatted at empty tables at conventions, ones for which other, less thieving artists had paid hundreds of dollars. I traded with abandon, and sold my tiny, hand-stapled books for a dollar each to men who looked at my breasts or looked like they had the money.

Giving away those physical objects, even at thirty cents each, felt like subterfuge. But it was also a pain. I made enough to cover my costs, but those costs seemed unnecessary—a twee, wasteful relic of an economy long past. So I started blogging again. One year later I joined Twitter. I "microblogged." I gained one hundred followers, then one thousand, then ten thousand. I ignored the e-mails that offered pay for my posts to promote brands and products, to write on other platforms I'd never heard of. Even when my posts earned the attention of editors who paid me for other work, I still gave most of it away for free. I licensed as much as I could under Creative Commons. I reported on long, dreadfully boring city council meetings for free, I ran into clouds of tear gas at police riots for free, I drew silly and very popular cartoons for free. Or at least that's what I thought I did.

The gift economy didn't give back. Every post I made was on a platform I did not own. My access was free, and my labor was free, but I was investing primarily in someone else's business. Sometimes this transaction was even more overt. Other journalists used my posts to pad their own stories, or embedded them as a series of posts in order to make one story altogether—one for which they were paid and I was not. They asked me to help them with other stories, ones for which they were paid and I was not. There was no expectation of reciprocity, of equity or community. As the media industry contracted, this became its gift economy. After all, I gave away so much for free—why didn't I expect that they would want to take even more?

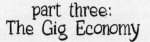

part three:
The Gig Economy

Twelve years earlier, when I was eleven, my father gave me the most salient career advice of my life: "Never have a boss." This seems easier said than done, under most circumstances. Of course, he was my first boss—later that summer I pulled weeds in our front yard at his direction, tallying my totals and my hours in a composition book turned elementary ledger. Baby's first spreadsheet.

Two years later, I was coloring my father's illustrations in Photoshop, laying down flats with a mouse in between AIM conversations with boys. Five years after that, I did the bookkeeping for his small business, logging $10 and $20 checks from small newspapers, magazines, and websites across the world that paid a fraction of what they used to for art. But they paid.

For the next twelve years, I existed at the whims of this economy. I did not have a boss—I had many bosses. My work was a series of discrete, one-off arrangements made far beyond the realm of labor laws and minimum wages. I juggled, I spun plates, I skipped across small rocks in a deep, fast river, slippery and just big enough for one step until I could reach the next. I tried not to slip and drown.

I succeeded—which is to say, I sustained. With the exception of two brief and ill-fated forays into full-time employment, I made a living as a freelance journalist and illustrator for a decade, working from contract to contract for upward of two dozen companies each year. I learned new skills to make myself more indispensable and nimble. I produced some very good work, and some I'd care not to recall. I discovered which editors were allies and which were snakes, sometimes too late. I burned bridges spectacularly and without regret. I have been so privileged and so terrified.

When I recount this modest success, I am met with disbelief. How exactly did I skip across that river? Not very carefully, in fact—I ran as fast as I could.

part four:
The Guild Economy

There's nothing to catch you in the gig economy—it's just you and the water. After five years of freelancing, I was spending more and more time looking down and wondering what would happen if I slipped. I began reaching out to friends and colleagues also working piecemeal. They were supportive but territorial. They were slipping too. We all put on a strange public face—at once successful and satisfied with our work, but also ever hungry for more, for better. We hid from each other, too. We still do.

Two years later, I was arrested while reporting on spec for a magazine that would soon fire its entire editorial staff in a fit of rebranding and cheaper labor costs. I finished the piece after I returned home from jail. I made about $6 per hour, if you don't count the time I spent in a cell. Writers with jobs asked if I really hadn't sought this out—what an opportunity for self-promotion, for my personal brand. They trusted institutions and bosses, so I was a natural target for suspicion. Did I really try to get away? I really did. They didn't believe me.

But other journalists without jobs had seen the insides of those jail cells as well as those office cubicles. We started long e-mail chains and chat rooms, back channels for rate sharing, contract negotiation, and legal advice—all online. The tool that had facilitated so much economic confusion for legacy media—that eased theft, expedited great masses of layoffs, and promoted free labor—that tool in turn helped us to independently publish new, brave kinds of work, to find one another, and to begin to make sense of what could come next.

part five:
The Big Economy

Today pundits like to say we are living in a knowledge economy—a kind of postindustrial wonderland where skill is highly valued, and effort can be freely expended because work is unnecessary not just to survival, but to prosperity.

The sad secret of this economy is that no one knows what anything is or should be worth. Late capitalism is confusing. It is unprecedented wealth, and prevailing austerity. It is many bosses, and few paychecks. It is incredible means of cheap global communication and a predominant rhetoric of sharing and peers—and a dark and creeping isolation.

The grift economy is the fear, the gift economy is the lie, the gig economy is the reality, and the guild economy is the dream. But the big economy is still a mystery. The technological disruptions that swept us from one economy to the next, that facilitated the means to steal and exploit, are the same ones that prompted us to connect and to share. A job isn't what a job once was—but what was so great about those jobs, anyway?

I still steal, I still give my work away for free, I still charge for it, and I still try to help my comrades as we make our way across the river otherwise alone. In my better moments, I think of how I'll work two years from now, five years from now, ten years from now, and I see writing that never could have been made meeting readers that never could have found it. I see co-ops, direct patronage, and the decline of old bosses. I see collective survival.

But two years from now, five years from now, ten years from now—these aren't things you plan for working piecemeal. You look only at the next rock, and then the next. You help your friends, if you can. You run, but you're careful not to slip.

SECURITY

Roxane Gay

in conversation with Manjula Martin

Manjula Martin: You run an indie press, a lit mag, and a blog. You write books, columns, and essays. You teach. You tweet. How are your time-management skills?

Roxane Gay: I have terrible time-management skills. I don't have kids, which helps quite a lot, and I'm an insomniac, and I live in the middle of nowhere. And I write fast and I just have a relentless work ethic, I guess.

I'm curious about your role in academia. You have this whole other life in which you're a teacher. That's a pretty solid day job.
I love teaching and I love the security of a regular paycheck, and I especially love health insurance.

You've talked publicly about being a rather introverted person. Yet you're always putting yourself out there, both in your writing gigs and physically by traveling and speaking a lot. Why do you push yourself to do so much?
Um, student loans? [Laughs.] Seriously, I don't know. With the speaking engagements, I just pretend I'm someone else—not someone else, but I pretend I'm a braver version of myself and just suck

170

it up and do it. In terms of putting my writing out there, I pretend no one's reading it.

How much student loan debt do you have?
$130,000.

Is that a big consideration for you in terms of your teaching career—working toward eliminating that debt?
It doesn't stress me out. I mean, it keeps me working, but the student loan system is really great, and it doesn't bother me.

What's great about it?
The low interest, the really flexible repayment plans, the options for when you can't repay . . . I mean, I'm fortunate in that I used to work for a student loan company, so I kind of know the ins and outs. And I think, if you know the ins and outs, it's a very negotiable system.

In your case, your degrees did actually get you a teaching job.
I'm glad I have my degrees. They have been invaluable to me. But I'm also very lucky to be able to say that because I have a job. I think that if I didn't have a job, I would have a much different outlook on my student loans.

What do you tell your students when they say, "Oh, I just want to write full-time and quit my day job"?
Oh, you know, I think it's fine. But I try to be real. I try to tell them what they're in for. I try to tell them, *You have to have a backup.* You *have* to have a backup. But I don't want to discourage the dream. I think too many people try to discourage the dream, and that's actually really frustrating because, you know, we can do better by our young people. We shouldn't try to discourage

the dream, but we also have to prepare them for the challenges of being out there.

How much of your income comes from teaching versus writing?
Forty percent of my income comes from teaching, thirty percent from speaking, and about thirty percent from writing.

Do you know around how much money you made last year [2014], including 1099s and everything?
Last year I probably made about $150,000.

You sold your books *Bad Feminist* and *An Untamed State* within a week of each other. Can you talk me through that process?
An Untamed State was on the market for about eighteen months. It took a long time to sell, and I switched agents in the middle. And with my new agent it took about six months [of that eighteen months]. And then *Bad Feminist* sold very quickly; Cal Morgan at Harper Perennial had gotten in touch with me and said he was interested in working with me. And we took it from there.

What were those deals like?
For the novel, I got a $12,500 advance. And for *Bad Feminist*, I got $15,000.

After the positive reception both your books received, did you feel like you had a stronger position in selling *Hunger*, your memoir in progress?
Yeah, I did feel like I had a strong position. But *Bad Feminist* actually hadn't come out yet when I sold *Hunger*. But my agent thought it would be a good idea to sell the book then [before *Bad Feminist* was released], and she was right, and she sold it for $75,000.

That's a pretty okay raise.
Mmhmm.

With so many projects going on all the time, where do you find space to take pleasure in your accomplishments?
I love writing. The act of writing brings me great pleasure.

In addition to working my ass off, I have been lucky and I have been privileged. I try not to lose sight of that. And at the base of it all, I love what I do. I love teaching and reading and writing, and the acts themselves rarely feel like work.

What do you aspire to [do] next in your career?
I would like to win a Pulitzer. But more importantly, I would like to write something worthy of a Pulitzer.

That is a very concrete goal!
I have very concrete goals.

MONETIZATION

Choire Sicha

M ost people who end up working as writers haven't gotten there due to a sense of unending careerism—at least not in the traditional and most New York sense of *work as a shortcut to wealth*. Oh sure, somewhere a young writer quite hilariously is thinking *I will write my way to fame and fortune!* but absolutely most writers don't get here due to *Yes, here is how I will procure one of those really large American houses that always turn out to be impossible to heat properly.*

Quite the opposite. Writers are encouraged to believe they are dispositionally opposed to careers in finance, transactions, or law. They are encouraged to self-mythologize as artsy and/or loner and/or incompetent folk. And whether that's native or induced, writer-types tend to withdraw further and further from the world of math and science quite early, some time shortly after Algebra II in high school. I, for example, hated that class so much that I was compelled to take it a second time, which did not go much better.

And so writers cleave off from the real world, where math actually exists. Many of us gleefully profess an incompetence with all kinds of numeric systems, up to and including taxes. If you ever want to see something sad, ask a room full of freelance writers about their tax strategies. It's like asking a pack of baby kittens about space travel.

We did not do this to ourselves at first, to be fair. This is an action of the system. To those who are not invited to join the world of business, the road to commerce is kept hidden. The traditionally all-male, all-white, and extremely publicly heterosexual world of big money is not welcoming to outsiders, which you are, unless you went to *those* schools and/or lived in *those* towns. While some of these worlds have made real change (law most notably, finance less notably), the lack of diversity in commercial real estate, banking at large, computer science, and advertising has been intentional. You're not supposed to get rich with them. Even though many of these fields have, most surprisingly, almost zero barriers to entry, you are encouraged to be afraid to finagle your way in.

You're a writer. You're supposed to flap your hands and make girly gestures when confronted with money or math. You're supposed to give in to the intimidation, to buckle and blush. Particularly, as a writer, you're not supposed to know or even care how advertising works.

There are very few industries where coworkers are set opposed to each other, and yet that opposition is a fundamental tenet of the media industry. The writers get the attention, the ad people get the money, both of those benefits are a bit unwarranted, and there's irritated side-eye all around.

And neither understands the other's job. Absurdity!

The Internet is no longer new; it's old enough to drink legally. Writers whose work is published online should and must understand how websites work in general, as well as how the websites on which they are published work in the specific, so as to not be idiots. This particular pursuit of non-idiocy is sometimes referred to in journalism as "following the money," also known as "understanding the basic economic structure of the industry from which one earns a living, or hopes to." But to even speak to someone in advertising, you will need some background. They speak another language, with coded, dark, and impenetrable phrases.

§

Most websites, infamously, are supported by advertising. Boo, advertising! It's so gross, right? Or . . . is it? What if everything you thought as a writer was backward? What if all the writing on websites was bad, and all the ads were really good? Well, that's literally true at some websites.

Some sites are supported by hybrids of donation, subscription, affiliate marketing, and advertising revenue. It would be nice if writers started out by having a sense of what those things mean.

Donations are when kindhearted people are strangely moved, usually through pity, to give publishers money. Often now people do this through Kickstarter. That's almost always a bad idea, if fun for a season. The money usually runs out long before any kind of stable business can be built.

Subscriptions are when people pay to read a website. (No one knows why people do this! It's pretty rare in America.) But it's related to an important concept. One of the things marketers talk about is the idea of "conversions." One classic example is when someone buys a magazine at a newsstand and enjoys it so much that she fills out the blow-in card to become a subscriber. That's all easier online. For much of the Internet, a conversion is getting someone to give up their e-mail address. For some publications, a Facebook Like or Share will do. The conversion is actually a very useful concept for writers: What about a piece of writing induces a reader to become a regular reader? What about editorial publishing convinces readers to want to consider this place on the web their own? Where, if anywhere, do business and editorial conversions overlap and feed each other?

Affiliate marketing is a formerly shady world that's gone a bit straight. One of the most common examples is Amazon's affiliate marketing program. To use it, you sign up as a vendor at Amazon, and you get a code that you append to any links you make to Amazon. Then, anyone clicking on those links will get tracked as your referral as they traverse Amazon. Any purchase those people make during that visit and in some hours that follow will kick back a percentage to you. Websites like Gawker Media and The Wirecutter make literally millions of dollars from this! Why does Amazon do it? No one knows! But when you hear "affiliate marketing," it basically means product placement, and that the website is getting paid for links. Is it ethical? I . . . have no opinion.

Advertising, well, it comes in many forms. Advertising begins with a "brand"—that's a company, or a company's product, usually—that wants to assert itself in the marketplace. It's something that wants to be loved!!! Somewhere, a goal or web of goals is defined: the advertising is intended to recruit users or stimulate their loyalty, or to move merchandise, or to increase some kind of awareness. To that end, the company's in-house team will create advertising, or, most often, a company's team will hire an agency to do that, working in an unholy alliance. Much of the world's advertising is created by just a handful of very large firms; they devise campaigns that supposedly fulfill those goals, and "calendar" them into seasons. (Advertising involves a lot of nouns being used as verbs, and vice versa. The biz!) They then offer to pay editorial publications money in order to show readers the ads. Often the budget for such campaigns will be allocated across all media: television and radio budgets for instance, and "out of home" budgets (that's like, bus shelters and billboards, but also those horrible elevator TVs and store displays, street teams, and even blimps!), but then way down at the end comes "digital," which means the Internet. Digital is a small, ever-growing slice of the ad budget pie, and it deals in numbers any writer would think of as vast riches but are in fact a paltry amount of money overall.

(I would like to make the disclaimer here that much of what follows loses a bit of nuance. Just as a media buyer talking about journalism would emphasize different facets and omit things writers would find important, so will I surely distort their understanding of this brave industry.)

The digital budgets themselves are broken down into types of advertising.

Display advertising is what we call those very typical web ads, whether they be a simple banner atop a page or a "takeover," dominating the website itself. Those come in some standard(ish) shapes—what are called IAB units, named for the sizes defined by the Interactive Advertising Bureau, whose board of directors includes all kinds of business-side folks from Facebook and Twitter and LinkedIn and NBC and AT&T and the *New York Times*, a *truly* unholy alliance of platforms, content, and advertisers. Many websites also offer custom units, but as you travel the web, most of what you see are the same standard billboards and skyscrapers (not actual buildings; tall skinny ads).

Display advertising is often sold by agencies to publishers in terms that boil down to "the website will show people this ad six million times in July"; the advertising operations people track and ensure that the ad requirements are fulfilled in the course of that "flight." (Fulfillment is their life. A campaign that doesn't meet fulfillment also doesn't get paid.)

There is *video advertising*, with its infamous and annoying pre-roll, so called because it runs prior to the actual content. Yes, we all know it's annoying.

And there is sponsored content, also known as native content or paid posts, and the editorial varieties of this break down into two categories: the more rare of the two is an actual editorial product that is presented by a brand, as refrigerator companies once underwrote radio shows, while the other, more common one is pure sponcon, the sometimes lifelike but often just not quite convincing variety of content that bears the distinct mark of the committee approval system. "Native" just means the ads are coming as close to mimicking the actual content of the site as possible. (That's why a native ad can also be a video.) Think of how the eight-page "come visit Florida" insert in a magazine is supposed to look like the magazine itself. No, the *New Yorker* is not trying to sell you a luxury time-share. Not directly, at least.

It's a myth that sponsored content has to be bad, but it's a myth that ad agencies are trying their hardest to make true.

There's also another, more abstract categorization for advertising: into paid, owned, and earned media. Paid media is a banner ad or a sponsored post or a newsletter sponsorship. It's something a company (or the company's ad agency) bought. Owned media is enacted on products that the brand controls—let's say, the CEO of a company posting his own messaging (verb-as-noun alert!) on Medium or the company Twitter account. But earned media is the dreamy one. You'd never go on the Internet again if you knew how much and how often brands think about earned media. That's when customers or enthusiasts promote a brand of their own volition, whether in a humble blog comment, a strong Yelp review, an editorial write-up, or by giving out e-mail invitations to a product. This is why fandom is such a way of life now: brands are desperate to show earned media results. *20,000 people used our hashtag last night* means someone is getting a promotion.

This, so far, is just the good advertising, the high-end stuff.

These are the ads that some digital "creative" (it's an adjective, but also a type of person!) often actually cares about, and works hard at making good. And these all come to pass by means of direct buys—the brand's agency interacting directly, for the most part, with a publisher.

Down the pipe somewhat come the ad networks. The great era of ad networks likely came to a close in 2015, though they're still chugging away, a few quite successfully. These serve a variety of publishers by selling big campaigns and then fulfilling them across multiple, unaffiliated websites. They generally get fifty percent for their troubles. Obviously it's often not a great deal for anyone in particular—if a cereal company spent $5,000 for a couple of sponsored posts on a mommy blog, and the ad network took $2,500, and the sponsored content writer's fee was $1,000, does that leave enough for the mommy blogger's dignity?—but the system did serve smaller and independent websites . . . until it didn't.

Even with all that, not every ad slot is always going to be sold, so there's a whole world of what is called *remnant advertising*. The vast majority of unsold or unloved ad slots are served for cheap rates by companies like DoubleClick, which is Google. When you see ads following you around the web based on your search history, that's usually low-budget remnant advertising, and it's usually Google. These ads generally pay a small fraction of what a good direct campaign pays—sometimes $1 or $2 CPMs at a quality publisher, or also sometimes pennies.

§

Here we must always pause to explain the CPM concept. Promise: a small child can get it. And if you do, businesspeople will take you somewhat seriously. CPM (Cost Per *Mille*, pardon the French) is a rate metric that just means cost per thousand views. So, a $12 CPM means a web publication gets $12 every time it serves a thousand of those ads. That means you get $120 for 10,000. $1,200 for 100,000. $12,000 for 1,000,000. DO YOU REMEMBER HOW DECIMAL PLACES WORK? $120,000 for 10,000,000. There! You're gold.

Those all add up, of course, into an RPM—that's Revenue Per *Mille*—which is a result of how many ads were served (and/or sometimes how many ads were actually viewed) on a page. It's not rocket science: essentially, six one-dollar ads per page will get you a $6 RPM per page.

From an RPM, you can calculate an eCPM. Do you wish you were dead yet??? HOLD TIGHT. Think of eCPM like the total cost per ad impression, so you can say *Oh, we did a million impressions of those Samsung ads and we made $18,000, so our eCPM on the campaign is $18.* (Don't think about this too long or you'll cry.)

Anyway! Getting those little ad prices from $1 CPM to $1.25 CPM is a big deal. Some people spend most of their days working on this. If you move the RPM from $6 to $7.50, well, if you're serving a million pages, that's the difference between making $6,000 and $7,500. Why wouldn't you?!

That math, if you're struggling, is $1 cost x 6 ads/1,000 views x 1,000,000 pages.

As Internet advertising evolves, success has moved from "people clicking on it" to "people getting served it" and now to "people actually seeing it." Ad servers calculate how long those ads are on-screen; many ad contracts now have conditions, like "Seventy-five percent of the ad must be viewable for two seconds or more." This all falls under the category of viewability.

Viewability is measured, obviously, in time, as well as in on-screenness. Some publishers and platforms already sell ads entirely based on hours viewed, not pages served. This blows up the CPM model quite nicely—and really, who wants to buy an ad that's never seen?

Direct campaigns often go through an RFP process (Request For Proposal!): a very long and weird cultlike document is created by the agency working on behalf of the brand ("seeks to engage single male millennials who love fitness, wine, and capitalism") and potential venues fill out response questionnaires with an intelligence level somewhere between an SAT essay section and a particularly wily CAPTCHA. Then the publishers are like, *Our readers love brands! We promise!* and then the ads get sold and served.

§

It's 2016 as I write this. In just a few short years (or months!), literally all this could sound like ancient junk and nonsense. For one thing, whole new ad formats are being created in distributed publishing. On platforms like Facebook and Snapchat and Medium, where more and more publications are placing editorial content directly, an ad might take any number of hybrid forms. At least there you'll likely see the ads?

For publishers, it feels funny to stand up for advertising, particularly when its abuses have been so remarkable and so always-encroaching. But you get the sites you want to visit, and in the end, no matter how much venture capital they have, they'll get to continue to exist because of ads. There is a libertarian-hued rallying cry popular on the Internet that if publishers deserve to exist then surely readers will pay for them directly. This sounds wonderful, and is sometimes true, but not that often. It would be nice though, particularly because the ones who'll suffer the most in the great consolidation and fallout to come in the world of Internet publishing will be writers.

If you're a writer who works for a decent-sized online publication, there's nothing better you can do for yourself at work than buddy up to a couple of ad sales bros. Most crucially, they know when the ship is sinking long before editors do. At companies floating on a happy bed of venture capital funding, the signs of doom aren't often written on the wall until the wall is being taken down and you are being escorted from the building. But the ad sales bros know what's up; it's their job. They have better stories than editorial people, too—and honestly, they often work longer and harder. Dealing with brands and their values and immense self-regard and endless boring meetings is exhausting. And dealing with ad agencies is harrowing as well. At the end of every ad is a long line of people desperate to not lose their jobs. This means that every decision is a horror show, and trying to create any ad product that is remotely amusing or intelligent is a nightmare.

At any decent-sized publication, the business department will look suspiciously large. Lots of those guys—and they are most often guys—are essentially account managers, a concept with which you are likely familiar from the TV shows. They wait, they hunker, they wine and dine (and strip club and worse), and then, twice a year, when Samsung has a new product, they try to get all the paid media they can out of the company or out of their agency.

Those guys will report to a manager, who ideally helps them strategize on new clients and new agency relationships, and somehow everyone gets reimbursed for the cocaine, or maybe that comes out of pocket, I'm never quite sure how that works, but it's fine, they can cover it.

Even the most basic of ad jobs is a living, and overall it's a good one. Journalists are appalled when they find out how much ad folks make—but then, ad "men" have their fingers on the revenue pipeline, and it's hard to lowball a salesman when he knows what's coming in the door.

NOT A COMPLAINT

Nell Boeschenstein

Almost a decade ago I attended a reading, the impression of which still lingers like the marks of a wire chair on the backs of summer thighs. I didn't go anticipating the impression to be so indelible, although in retrospect I might have: I'd discovered Adam Zagajewski's work in college and become so enamored with it that, wanting to experience the city he loved, chided, and struggled with in verse, I set my mind on living in Kraków after graduation.

It turns out Kraków—being architecturally beautiful and spiritually haunted—is popular with expats and a difficult city in which to find legal employment. I ended up 282 miles away, separated by a major mountain range and an international border, in Bratislava, Slovakia. But that's another story.

This story picks up once the Bratislava chapter reached its inevitable conclusion and deposited me back in my hometown, my heart a little bruised, my plans for the future murky, and all the worldly knowledge I was confident I possessed at twenty-two dissolved into the ether by the time I was twenty-four. In my less melodramatic moments, I recognized I was extraordinarily fortunate: I was educated and had a home to return to. While there were vast swaths of knowledge I lacked, I had at least one fact pinned down: Ever since I'd written something I called a short story in second grade, and first experienced that peculiar rush of gratification it offered, I had known I wanted to be a writer.

What this entailed, however, was beyond me. Knowing what one wants can confound as much as it can direct. The recognition of a point X in the distance means a direction in which to point the compass; and yet, at least for writers, getting to X can be a maze of Hampton Court proportions. The lone guidance is only ever "Write."

But write how?

Not in the sense of "Sit your butt down at your desk," but in the financial sense.

Because my father was a college professor and my mother worked in admissions, I had the vague notion that there were two paths to being a writer: academia and everything else. I knew, too, that higher education was where poets and fiction writers often safely resided, teaching to support themselves and using the relative flexibility of the academic calendar to their creative advantage for colonies, workshops, or time alone. While this was the life those closest to me encouraged, I was resistant. Perhaps it was latent adolescent rebellion. I had no patience with or capacity for theory or jargon. Academia wouldn't do.

As a postgrad full of youthful, dream-following fervor, the "how" had to be answered another way. To bide my time, I finagled my way into an entry-level position in the editorial department of a local alternative newsweekly. I entered event listings into the weekly calendar and wrote a column where readers wrote in asking questions of local mystery to an imaginary gumshoe named Ace Atkins.

One day I was putting events into the calendar when I saw that Adam Zagajewksi—the Polish poet responsible for my detour to Bratislava—was slated to read at the University of Virginia. I rushed to my editor: Could I write it up? Isn't this exciting?

My editor didn't share my enthusiasm, but she indulged it. Two weeks later I was in the second row in the university art gallery, waiting for Zagajewski to read poems in translation. It was the first time I had gone to a poetry reading already familiar with the poet's oeuvre. The effect was like seeing a favorite band, except instead of hoping they'll play specific songs you're hoping he'll read certain poems. He read for a good hour, reading some I knew and some I didn't. He then concluded by saying he would read "Franz Schubert: A Press Conference." This was the poem I had been waiting for, my favorite of favorites. It begins:

> Yes, my life was short, yes, I loved
> felt a light growing, yes, under
> my fingers sparks were born

And ends with the sigh of:

> Yes, I am tired now and no, it's not
> a complaint.

By the time he was done I was in his thrall: unquestioning, worshipful, dizzy. He announced he had maybe twenty minutes to take questions from the audience. The usual struggling crop of pale palms popped up: What was his process? Who does he read? How is Poland different from America with regards to poetry? And then, inevitably: What advice do you have for young writers?

I've forgotten the answers he gave to these pale-palmed questions, save this last, which has stayed with me, nearly verbatim, for going on ten years. He seemed less bored with this question. He cleared his throat with purpose. *Don't be just writers*, he said, and then repeated it: *Don't be just writers. Be firefighters, policemen, teachers, doctors, chemists, electricians, but don't be just writers.* Being writers and only writers, he said, meant you would be stuck in the corral, communing only with the other ponies, when you should be exploring the world beyond the enclosure.

His moral was adamant; I took it to heart.

Because I am afraid of fire, guns, blood, explosions, and loose wires, there was no hope of my becoming a firefighter, police-woman, doctor, chemist, or electrician. And while Zagajewski didn't say so explicitly, it had been clear that the corral full of ponies to which he was referring was academia. It was thus official and de-cided: I would be a journalist.

Let me explain that my understanding at twenty-four of what a journalist did was—again—elementary. In school, I was lit mag, not newspaper. At college, we did not read nonfiction in English classes; we studied fiction and poetry. Journalism classes weren't even offered. When I decided I could be a journalist it was because I saw it simply—and simplistically—as a way to be engaged with language and the world simultaneously and get paid for it. It didn't count as being a writer.

So I decided to be a journalist and I have been, more or less. I have covered murder trials and real estate deals gone bad; I have written society-page captions and 150 words to accompany a full-page spread devoted to a $20,000 bracelet. This last precipitated my first identity crisis and subsequent escape to graduate school for creative writing: I would take time to hone my craft and emerge two years later having hopefully bypassed the necessity of society-page caption writing and plugs for luxury bracelets.

Instead, I emerged four years later, having spent two extra years on a teaching fellowship, trying to break college freshmen of their five-paragraph essay habit. My students ranged from veterans of Iraq and Afghanistan to former ballerinas to single moms to the conventional eighteen-year-old. I loved how, at the beginning of a semester, I faced a class of strangers, but by the end, it was a class of complicated humans.

My friends and family all asked the same question when the subject of "What next?" arose: If I enjoyed teaching, why not look for a teaching job? I told them why: because I wasn't a competitive candidate for a tenure-track position—or even a visiting one—and I couldn't adjunct because of the health insurance issue. Health insurance was big. While in graduate school, I learned I carry a genetic mutation that predisposes me to early-onset breast and ovarian cancer. My chances of getting cancer in my thirties were high—very high. So high I eventually opted for a prophylactic mastectomy. But that does not ensure my health. If diminished in one part of my body, cancer risk persists elsewhere. My ovaries remain for now present and vulnerable. Health insurance was imperative.

In my head, too, Zagajewski's refrain about how the insularity of the academy must be avoided kept repeating: Be firefighters. Be chemists. Be journalists. Do Re Mi Fa Be. Be. Be.

Older, established writers always tell younger writers about the compromises they must make to succeed. You must be willing to be poor, they say. You must make writing your life. You must piece money together in any way that allows room for writing. It doesn't matter what those jobs are so long as they don't sap your creative energy. Wait tables. Walk dogs. Babysit. Make lattes. Figure model. Donate your eggs. Build houses. Bake bread. Freelance at writing. Freelance at anything.

I was no longer in a position to naively agree to the sacrifices a freelance-everything lifestyle required. It is never safe or smart to go with minimal health insurance or—God forbid—none, yet countless aspiring artists do so seemingly without compunction. I can't tell you how many I've met who've copped to this. I also cannot tell you how I envy them.

Even if I had the hustle to piece things together, health insurance was—and is—an impossible compromise. At the time, I was a thirty-one-year-old single woman trying to set up a feasible life that would allow room for cancer and not have it lead to utter financial ruin. When I asked myself, *Is this sustainable?*—with regards to adjuncting or odd jobs—the answer was *No*. It was again decided: I'd return to journalism and, to misquote Cat Stevens, find a job, settle down.

The irony of course was that journalism was hemorrhaging jobs, but I was lucky. I found work, first as a producer of one radio show and then another. The second was what you might call "a plum gig" and rightly so: I was working for *Fresh Air* with Terry Gross, one of the pinnacles of American journalism of the past quarter century.

In one of my interviews, and I remember this clearly, Terry said, *So you want to be a writer?*

Yes, I replied.

You're going to need to figure out a way to pay the bills, she said.

That frank talk was why, when *Fresh Air* offered me the position, I accepted. She was right: I needed to pay bills, and bills were ever mounting. Plus, I'd be working for Terry Gross, and even if the work sapped me of creative energy, the fact would remain that I was in some small way contributing to the monumental collection of voices housed in *Fresh Air*'s archives.

If only satisfaction were so easy and altruistic. While journalism has many salutary aims it is also, partly and by its nature, content production—filling space that needs filling.

At *Fresh Air*, I was producing as many as five thousand words a week. Those words were—by design and as it should be—in service of another voice. As much as I held that voice in esteem, I, myself, was losing what small ability I had to be heard in my own. I was writing for a living, but I wasn't writing. After ten hours in front of a screen, the last thing I wanted to do was head home and log more time at the computer. Nor would it have been healthy to do so. At this point, too, I knew a couple of things about myself beyond my desire to become a writer: frenetically shoveling words into a maw did not energize me but burnt me out, and quickly.

When it came to whatever journalism game I was playing, yes, I was tired, and no, that's not a complaint. I was tired of the Internet and its appetites, and tired of the exacting constraints of the nine-to-five office day. Most importantly, I was tired of trying to be someone I wasn't. Scaling the rock, I'd reached a point where I could no longer find a toehold, and needed to go back down to try and find another way.

It seemed a fortuitous long shot then when a position for a visiting professor of creative writing opened up at a college near my hometown. I threw my name into the hat. For the first time in years I had no ambivalence: I wanted this, and not because I thought I should want it, because some man I admired suggested I want it years ago. I wanted it. Me. Man be damned.

Reader, I got the job. I'm going to be a teacher. I know, too, that I got the job because of the journalism jobs I've had. That tossed-off advice that I took so earnestly to heart and in which I've placed so much stock for so long is well meaning and not uncommon, but it also may be wrong. At least for me.

The attitude that one's insight into the world correlates to, and devotion to one's art is reflected by, a litany of quirky hourly gigs—Christmas elf, erotic video store attendant, fiddler in an old-time string band—is almost so commonplace as to be an occupational joke. This is sacrifice. But what then of immersion, that deep understanding that comes, yes, from one's own study, but also from deep conversation with like-minded souls? What of the healthy (and sometimes unhealthy) competition of one's peers? The exchange of ideas? Conversation, trading books, and recommending articles? Architects talk to architects. Lawyers to lawyers. Why not writers to writers?

But perhaps more than confused, I have been stubborn. I've at last conceded the possibility that teaching doesn't imply a plan to inoculate oneself against the world. It can't. The world comes at you with its decisions and coincidences and past loves and future loves and germs and risks and cancers and deaths and births and weather and seasons and cities and roads and fields and forests beyond the property lines of the ranch no matter what. Insularity is the bane of creativity only so far as we allow it to be.

THE JUMP

Sarah Smarsh

The winter after I quit my tenured professorship, I couldn't afford a haircut. I stood at the mirror with a pair of scissors to my long hair and cried.

What had I done?

When I had resigned a few months earlier, giving up a lifetime of assured income, insurance benefits, research support, and professional belonging to which so many academics aspire, some acquaintances had hinted that I was making a mistake. I'd received cards from friends saying they were worried about me; from colleagues, eyebrows raised in silence. One old pal warned that we weren't in our twenties anymore.

To be fair, I was barely thirty-two. And, thanks to my working-class background, I'd already been in the workforce for almost twenty years. I'd never had the irresponsible twenties some enjoy. If quitting my day job had anything to do with age, it wasn't immaturity but the opposite, the ubiquitous American midlife crisis arriving a decade too soon.

Those who knew me the best fretted the least. A handful of close friends and family nervously supported my unorthodox move, knowing they couldn't rightly question my history of good judgment. That judgment had taken me from a prairie farmhouse to an Ivy League graduate school to a middle-class income in air-conditioned classrooms far from the hand-blistering wheat harvests of my youth. I'd carved a life from being disciplined, even self-denying, in a family that tended toward the impulsive.

So why then the desire to leave, to dismantle what I'd built?

Behind such a monumental decision was a confluence of reasons and events—most of which others couldn't know because I myself was still struggling to articulate them. According to the grapevine, some thought I was running away from, not toward, something. In that way they were wrong. I offered my department, the one party I believed deserved an explanation, the only true reason I fully understood at the time—accurate, if incomplete: my mother's health. Two months after I had received tenure and promotion, my fifty-year-old mom had been diagnosed with a rare, aggressive breast cancer.

The enormity of her prognosis, in the midst of an already auspiciously difficult year, evoked in me that feeling I sometimes get at funerals. You know the one—when you're stunned into clarity, rung by humble reckoning with mortality, a dead body at the front of a precious chapel full of people acting fake. When you look around and ask, *What the hell are we all doing with our lives?*

§

I'd climbed out of hard-soil origins by being intentionally pragmatic, but my nature was a wilder thing. I quit my job to be at my mother's side in another state, yes, but also to heed a more selfish call: the old creative yearnings of a girl who hadn't yet worked herself raw to pay for college, married her high school sweetheart, fought for employment, fixed up houses, planned to have a baby. Before all that, I'd had a different life vision—adventure, travel, and the ultimate Holy Grail: publishing what since childhood I'd quietly thought of as My Book.

I'd never given up those dreams. They had become an amorphous longing, though, as I did what so many of us do in the real world: eke out an authentic enough life that, first and foremost, paid the bills and theoretically allowed me to write My Book in the crevices between other demands. By the time Mom was diagnosed, I'd been chipping away at it for more than a decade. My Book had been a research project when I was an undergrad, my thesis when I was an MFA student. Even then, I hadn't been able to prioritize it while I labored to pay the bills. Soon I found myself in a coveted position with a teaching load of four courses per semester. In such an occupation, a sick mother might be visited over a long weekend, and a book might be written over a summer.

With the sound of my mother's bell tolling from the near future, my usual order of priorities—job first, then my loved ones and my dreams, wherever they might fit in—felt all wrong. I'd woken back up to the beautiful, savage, heart-ripping reality I once knew as a child, in which moments are to be seized because tomorrow never comes. Somehow, not even the promise of lifelong paychecks in a society built around money could lull me back to sleep.

For years I'd behaved as what we might call a "people pleaser"—putting everyone else's needs and feelings above my own. Now, I suddenly had no tolerance for people or actions with even a whiff of bullshit about them. And lo, most academic departments carry more than a whiff. My upbringing as a midwestern farm girl perhaps had honed my sense of smell. In *The Uses of Literacy*, cultural critic Richard Hoggart described the experience of being a "scholarship boy" who is "at the friction point of two cultures": "He has left his class, at least in spirit, by being in certain ways unusual; and he is still unusual in another class." I was a scholarship girl. Hauling lesson plans across a college campus as a professor a mere decade after I'd hauled feed across a cattle pasture was one hell of a friction point.

As chair of my university's diversity initiative, I'd found that academia wasn't the occupational promised land for women, minorities, and other historically marginalized groups that it had been touted as by white men. I'd always felt relatively comfortable as a woman in academia, though. It meant jumping through all the usual unfair hoops, but those hoops I knew existed not just at universities but also behind the bars where I'd poured whiskey for tips. Same shit, different pay grade.

What vexed me more was an otherness of socioeconomic class. I was a woman in a man's world not as a female professor but as a female professor who was the first woman in her family to finish high school.

My blue-collar origins meant the risk I was taking in leaving my job was more foolhardy than even my most cynical critics knew. I had no firm plan about another job, just a handful of creative project leads, a small retirement fund I could cash in if I had to, and a feeling that couldn't wait.

§

When I quit my professorship, it wasn't the first time I'd taken an economic risk that to some might seem outlandish. My undergraduate college tuition was covered by scholarships, and I worked to pay the rent. But after a low-paying stint at a newspaper, in 2003 I got into an Ivy League graduate school. The annual tuition was around $40,000, more than the annual income of anyone in my family. The school offered a small fellowship, and the government would provide up to $18,500 a year in subsidized loans. The rest would have to come from private lenders. I hesitated over the loan documents in my mom's apartment—aching to go to Columbia but wrecked by the repercussions. *You'll regret it if you don't go*, Mom said. Ultimately I agreed. For a kid with my origins, I'd figured, the financial debt was worth the social capital. When it comes to economic risk, what appears reckless to the privileged is often the smartest bet to the poor. By the time I graduated from Columbia and left New York, my bet was upward of ninety grand.

In recent years many have questioned a diploma's value and chastised those who take out big loans to buy one. Most of those critics, I'd wager, never worked a wheat field. Debt burden and being overeducated in an employer's market is psychologically and financially crushing, yes, but an assured lifetime sentence to manual labor can be more crushing—ask my dad, a brilliant thinker who has given me poems written in carpenter's pencil on scraps of two-by-four lumber. Most college graduates who are "under water" financially at least have fish to eat, and though I loathe debt, I indeed would choose it over starving. It takes a toll but buys a chance.

What would justify my student loans, I'd always told myself, would be a book deal that allowed me to pay them off with one big check.

Like those loans, to leave tenure with little cushion to fall back on was a horrible decision on paper. I wasn't delusional on that point and faced a healthy host of reasonable fears: the primitive terrors of starvation and homelessness, the more luxurious concerns of disappointing colleagues and leaving students.

But at my deepest core, I felt the departure was necessary. Spending much of my life in economic poverty—a sort of freedom in that one has little to lose—had afforded me a wealth of self-knowing. The painful requirements of following through on the feeling were, perhaps, less scary to me than they would have been for someone more privileged. I'd gone without before and survived. I figured I could do it again—though I foolishly imagined I wouldn't have to.

The university, for its part, wondered how much money I'd need to stay. This response startled me. I'd never in my life considered manipulating an employer for a raise, let alone leveraging the matter of my mother's health to do so. There was no amount, I said.

They'd hold my position for a year and a half, they said. Grateful, I thought on this, but still the clarity rang through me. I was resigning, I said.

Would I at least sign a letter merely *calling* my departure a leave of absence rather than a resignation, they asked, so as to preserve department funding for my tenure line in a dangerous fiscal climate?

Here I paused. Amid my flush of individualism I still felt protective of and responsible to the writing curriculum I'd helped build. Signing such a letter might behoove that curriculum and my colleagues, on whom my departure placed the burdens of picking up classes and reassigning my many duties. I was leaving one month into a new school year, putting my files in order as best I could for whoever would inherit them. Within a couple of weeks I'd be rambling across the West toward my mother and a host of adventures. Surely I could sign a letter bending language for the sake of a place, people, and mission I held in high regard. Doing so, I realized, would benefit me, too—a way to hedge my bets. If I signed the letter, the job would be waiting for me for a year and a half.

As a child, I liked to reenact a climactic movie scene in which Indiana Jones ducks, runs, and maneuvers through a gauntlet deep inside an ancient temple. He gauges each step to avoid death, only to arrive at a ravine so deep he can't see the bottom. It's far too wide to jump. "Only in the leap from the lion's head will he prove his worth," he reads from a diary of secrets guiding him toward the Holy Grail. "Impossible," he says, sweating. "Nobody can jump this." He's up shit creek at that point, his dad back at the entrance bleeding out next to a cluster of greedy Nazis.

"It's a leap of faith," he says and groans at the metaphorical wink from God. He puts his hand on his heart like he's taking an oath, steadies his breath, stretches one leg into the abyss and sways forward, appearing to the naked eye to be falling to his death. But a stone bridge catches him—invisible by way of optical illusion, it had been there all along. Pretending I was Indy, I used to run and jump along rows of hay bales at the corner of our alfalfa field.

In those years, by necessity I trusted no voice but my own. I believed in myself precisely because so little was expected of me. The knowing that would take me over so many chasms amounted to hearing my highest voice and being true to it.

I considered the matter of the requested letter stating a leave of absence. It amounted to calling what I was doing temporary when the tuning fork inside me said it was permanent. To sign such a letter, I knew, would not be true.

I got the silver, but I'm going for the gold, I had told my mom, who somehow understood. "Silver," to me, was an economically stable life. "Gold," to me, was a fulfilling one.

Mom nodded seriously.

Go for the gold, she said.

I didn't write a letter about a leave of absence. I wrote a letter of resignation. I did not apologize. I was intentionally dismantling every aspect of my constructed identity; killing the darlings of a secure life in order to find the story I needed to live. It all felt terrifying and grand.

§

Months later there I was, standing before a mirror with a pair of scissors, not even ten bucks to spare for a trip to Great Clips. The project leads I'd thought would pan out as income hadn't. Mom had finished surgery, chemotherapy, and radiation with excellent results in Colorado and had decided to move, at least temporarily, to the Kansas town where I still owned a house. None of my reasons for leaving my job had been justified, it seemed. I was a woman crying while cutting her own hair—a familiar image in popular culture denoting madness. Had I in fact lost my mind when I left my job?

Just over a year earlier I had been eating dinner with my husband, putting a tenure application in three-ring binders, paying into a retirement fund with a handsome match by my employer, renovating a dream house perched on a hill in a college town. It was an unhappy marriage, a sometimes inhospitable work environment, and a too-big house that I both paid for and cleaned. In those middle-class discomforts I'd at least been in sync with the rest of society, I realized, feeling like a self-made pariah. Now, at age thirty-two, I had no money, no job, no health insurance, no mate, no plan for a roof once the one I was under sold. There hadn't been a single offer on the house anyway. I'd cashed in my small retirement fund to pay the mortgage, and now my savings was gone. I didn't even own a car, since mine had broken down one morning on the way to campus not long before I resigned, like even *it* thought the job was no longer the right place for me. My grandma was letting me borrow her truck, like she had when I was in high school. She had a limited stash of hard-earned savings and had loaned me money to cover bills. It seemed that I had ruined, not saved, my life.

Familiar generational woes were close by, lapping at my feet like the fire of poverty I'd labored to escape. Dad's house was foreclosed on; he moved into a trailer with his wife, whose painkiller prescription after a car wreck decades prior had led to worse health problems. A sibling confessed to a longtime gambling problem. Mom and her longtime partner back in Colorado were on the outs, but her health insurance was through his employer, and I worried that she couldn't get her own policy with a preexisting condition. My grandma, dismayed by her daughter's cancer and exhausted from caregiving, moved into my place and had emotional and physical breakdowns for which I drove her to emergency rooms.

More than one person said to me, in apparent seriousness, *If I'd had the year you've had, I would kill myself.*

Indeed I was so beleaguered that I sometimes prayed to leave

Earth. Of all my troubles, I'd most underestimated the psychological trauma of relinquishing a professional title that commands respect and proffers identity in a society that values productivity above all else—a trauma likely exacerbated by my having been born, by class and gender, to little respect. As a woman who had worked nearly every day since adolescence for some employer, I'd never had so much time on my hands. I felt lost, crushed by the weight of open space and infinite possibility I'd supposedly longed for. I wouldn't hurt myself, I was sure, but I wasn't opposed to dying in my sleep.

It took a lot to break my spirit. It had never been done. But after that year—the divorce, the cancer, the gossip, the family, the resignation, the return to poverty—I was broken.

So when my former university advertised a search to fill my former position, I did what seemed the only rational thing to do: I tried to get my job back.

A former colleague generously assured me that, while the department legally had to conduct a public search, it was a no-brainer that the gig would be mine if I applied. I wrote a cover letter saying I'd been wrong to leave and sent it, my pride the cost of postage. Like the woman who sells a brooch to buy potatoes in wartime, I cared nothing for pride.

For weeks I awaited word from the search committee, imagining the joys and horrors of returning to gainful employment I'd brazenly walked away from, should I indeed be welcomed back. Then word came:

The search had been canceled.

Amid other budget priorities, the tenure line had been on the chopping block since I vacated it. Funding for the hire hadn't been approved. I couldn't return if only because the job didn't exist anymore. I myself had vaporized it by declining to sign a letter saying that I might come back.

This news was distressing but also, somehow, a relief. The paradoxical turn of events was so preposterous that it was comical. Rather than feeling destroyed by a final blow, I felt renewed.

I remembered that funeral feeling, recalled the sureness with which I had jumped. I had an eerie sense that some hand had known what it was doing when it signed a letter saying exactly what I intended. It was my own hand.

I'd been a sprinter and a long jumper in high school track—good at running fast and taking flying leaps. This one had turned out to be a very long leap, I thought. The leap of a lifetime. It wasn't that I'd landed in ruin. It was that I hadn't landed yet.

In that scary, stomach-turning moment of suspension, I saw, I still had the power to stick my landing. I did so as the only identity that remained after I shed all the others: writer. I was drawn back to the sort of pages I hadn't written since before I earned a living by reporting for newspapers or writing grants for nonprofits. I sat down and did the writing that—by no one's fault but my own—I hadn't been able to do in a life with the wrong husband and eighty students per semester and office dramas and perpetual committees needing tending. I wrote not to pay the bills, as I had for years as a journalist and professor climbing away from the early shames and pains of my life, but to say what I had to express—which, predictably, were those very shames and pains.

In that moment looking in the mirror with the scissors, in the throes of not just poverty but a return to it by my own action, painfully untethered from the solidarity of the rat race and its comfortable trappings, the world questioning my sanity, I wasn't sure I trusted myself. I didn't know what was coming in the next few years: my mother's health declining, months of caregiving and writing at her side, the repair of ailing family connections, the long-dreamed-of book deal, the blissful paying off of debts. I didn't know where I'd land—in a bed next to Mom, three days before she died, telling her that I'd dedicate my book to her.

When troubled by uncertainty, though, I'd remember how I felt when I spoke the hardest, most necessary words: *This marriage is over. This house is for sale. I resign.* I—that woman—had never felt stronger or more clear. She was the one who wouldn't sign a letter even *pretending* she might return to her old job if only to keep the option of going back. She knew that, in my proverbial darkest hour, I would try to turn back. She knew I was setting out on the most difficult, rewarding journey of my life. *I might not trust myself*, I'd think, *but I trust that woman.*

SOMEDAY

SELLING OUT

Austin Kleon

in conversation with Manjula Martin

Manjula Martin: Some writers may have an image of what "*New York Times* best-selling author" means in terms of financial success. But no one's image is very clear. What does it mean for you?

Austin Kleon: People hear "*NYT* bestseller" and they think, *Oh, he's a millionaire or something*, which is just ridiculous, as anyone who's been on that list can tell you.

I don't feel comfortable talking specific figures, but I'll tell you degrees of what each book did for me. My first book, *Newspaper Blackout*, was a poetry collection. At the time, I was a web designer at the University of Texas School of Law, which was a state job. And the book advance was, like, just enough money to put a tiny down payment on a house in an affordable housing development in Austin. Number-wise, we're talkin', like, a used Civic.

And so when we sold *Steal Like an Artist*, I was working as a copywriter. The advance on that book, which wasn't insignificant, was a year's salary at my copywriter job. And *Steal Like an Artist* earned out its advance pretty quickly. It was on the *Times* bestseller list for, like, half a year. So it did great. Then we sold *Show Your Work!*; the money we got for that . . . it was like, okay, I don't have to work for a couple of years.

When you say "we," to whom are you referring?
That's a royal *we*. It's just me. [laughs] But then it is more than me—it's my agent, it's my publisher, my wife. . . .

Why don't you feel comfortable talking specifics about money figures?
It's simply about privacy. Everybody knows so much about everybody—I think actual income in dollars is one of the last things that we *don't* know about each other, and I like it that way, honestly. I can't think of any way that my family or I would benefit from letting other people know the exact amount of money I make.

How much of your total income comes from writing?
I have three income streams: books, speaking gigs, and any art we sell. Interestingly enough, the book money is still more than the speaking money, which is surprising, because those numbers are usually flipped for nonfiction. The art is just a tiny little portion. When we got the *Show Your Work!* money, that was like, okay, if you watch your finances and you keep doing speaking gigs and selling art and putting out a book every couple of years, you can make a go of this. You can do this for a living, as long as the goodwill shall last.

How do you feel about that?
It's terrifying. Look, it's impossible to complain about success without sounding like a complete asshole. But as far as *art* goes—as far as motivating yourself, coming up with ideas . . . After the *Show Your Work!* tour, I came back home and I was burnt out. I think that artistic hunger disappeared for me for a while.

There are things that happen when your passion, when your avocation or calling or whatever you want to call it, becomes your breadwinning. It gets very complicated very quickly, and it can really turn into a drag.

How so?
When you're just a web designer, and you're at your desk and you make these silly poems on your lunch break because you're just passing the time, and you just want to do something creative with yourself, then you throw them online because you're like, *What else am I gonna do with 'em?* . . . that is a different impulse from now, where the minute I post a poem, fifty thousand people see it. And that's just an audience thing.

Money-wise, it would be like being in a band that goes suddenly from "We all play the bar after work" to playing stadiums. It's that kind of shift. What happens when the thing that kept you alive suddenly becomes the thing that literally keeps you alive? The thing that kept you spiritually alive now not only has to keep you spiritually alive, but also has to keep you *financially* alive. Like, literally alive. Like, food in your mouth.

You've spent a lot of time telling people not to quit their day job.
Yeah, and I constantly feel like the biggest hypocrite. But what I quickly realized is, I'm not quitting my day job. I'm swapping one day job for another.

It's probably a lot easier for me because I actually don't consider *Steal Like an Artist* and *Show Your Work!* to be art. I think there's art in them, and I think they're art*ful*, but they are primarily supposed to do something for other people. When I do those books, I know it's a product, I know it's going to be shelved in a certain part of the bookstore. So what I try to do is inject it with as much artfulness and as much of myself and as much honesty as I can. But it never leaves me, the fact that I'm making something that's going to have a barcode on the back of it.

So, how *do* you keep spiritually alive?
There's this weird self-loathing that happens when you promote

yourself too much. (And of course all this is very meta, because I wrote a book about how to promote your work and then I had to go out and promote it.) So the armchair Buddhist in me is always trying to figure out how I can destroy my own ego. How I can talk about the work without making it about me. So there were little tricks on the book tour I would try, like pick five books off the shelf in the bookstore to recommend during the talk. Just to try to emphasize to people, *Hey, it's not just about you, it's about what you love and what you're interested in.*

And it's been incredibly important for me to read a lot. Devouring books, trying to get excited again about this thing that I used to love that then became the work.

All this [success] is so new for me. I don't have all the answers. I can tell you what I'm struggling with, but I can't tell you that I've come out the other end. To be perfectly honest, there isn't a week that goes by that I don't think about getting a proper day job again.

I'm going to venture a guess that when you were younger you didn't envision growing up to be on the *self-help* bestseller list. It's funny, I just bought a first edition of [Nathanael West's novel] *Miss Lonelyhearts* at a bookstore in Austin. It's this really cool New Directions hardback, for like fifty bucks. And that is a book that I've reread since becoming shelved in self-help. Because it's the story of a guy who—the weight of human suffering is causing him to crack, you know? Becoming an advice giver is . . . you know, I get more e-mail than I could ever answer. And a lot of the e-mails are really heartfelt and they're from people who are struggling, and they're trying to make a go of what they want to do, and it can be really crushing.

The word *creativity* only showed up, like, one or two times in my original *Steal Like an Artist* talk. And then we put the word on the cover of the book, and all of a sudden it's an advice book about creativity. And at the time I wasn't sure what exactly it was, but I wasn't sure it was about creativity, either.

Well, creativity is a handily broad and attractive category in terms of marketing and audience.
Absolutely. But it's weird. I have a little bit of baggage about that I guess!

You've written and often ranted about your dislike of the phrase *Do what you love* (which is usually followed by *and the money will follow*). Why do you think that's bad advice?
Because not everyone can do that. There's a selfishness to it. *Do what you love* implies that the only person you're responsible for is yourself, but if you have children or a sick spouse or people to take care of . . .

The other side of that kind of thinking is that it makes people with good day jobs feel like shit, too. And then there's the idea that you *could* make a living doing anything you love. Like, if you love avant-garde poetry . . . I mean, c'mon, man.

Why do you think so many artistic types want to make a living, or think we should be able to make a living, from our art?
I don't know! I think in some ways it's the worst thing to want. I do think that if the economy was better and better jobs were available to people, this desire to make a living off art wouldn't be so big. But certain professions are disappearing entirely. I don't know anyone that's in a profession who feels amazing about the state of that profession.

Except start-up dudes, perhaps?
Right, except start-up dudes. So, unless you have a Ping-Pong table in your office . . . But seriously, even doctors or nurses I talk to

don't feel great about where things are with their professions. The institutions are pushing on us in such a way, and the culture is such a culture of overwork and busyness. If the options were better for people, if we had universal health care, and everyone was paid a living wage, and college was free . . . then I think making money from art wouldn't be such a big deal.

You and I are both in our thirties, and I wonder if the culture of overwork has become accelerated during our lifetime. At a certain stage, I actually *did* work twenty hours a week, and then I did my zines and whatever art I wanted to at night. And I actually wasn't living that much more cheaply in my twenties than I do now. Anecdotally, it's a common experience among artists and writers I know. It used to be you could do your day job and not have it be your entire life.
What job are you gonna get now where you only work forty hours a week and you don't have to take any work home, you don't have to check e-mail on weekends . . . where are those jobs? Because as far as I can tell, everyone's so worried about losing out that we go into this culture of overwork and stress.

I did have those jobs. I got so lucky. I had a librarian job that was twenty hours a week that actually had benefits. My second job out of college was my state job as a web designer, and people went home at five thirty.

Okay, so we live in this culture of overwork now, where a day job doesn't leave much room for writing. So artists and writers are feeling that. But then they learn that they're also expected to promote their work. And they're like, are you kidding me? Now *this* is my job, too?
[Laughs.] Again, I'd say to them: Are you sure you really want to do this? Are you sure you really want this job?

And is that because a person actually can't be successful at being a writer without self-promoting?
Oh man, that's the big question, right? But look, a lot of the people who ask me for advice, they're not just asking about how to be a writer. Because everyone knows that: How to be a writer is: you write all the time, and you read all the time. And you do it for a lifetime, and eventually maybe you'll write something worth reading. The question people are really asking is: How do I become Cheryl Strayed? How do I become J. K. Rowling? How do I become Jonathan Franzen? And that is a whole different question. I'm sorry, I'm dodging your question about self-promotion. . . .

I think you can bring it back around. Go for it.
Okay, it's weird, because this rosy picture is painted of traditional publishing and how it used to be. But if you look at most of the great artists of the twentieth century, they were also amazing marketers. Andy Warhol was a marketing *genius*. The Beatles themselves? You could argue it. Or if they weren't, they had people working for them that were. I mean, Paul McCartney is a self-promotion whiz; he knows what he's doing. So to color all previous artists as not having anything to do with self-promotion is really a disservice that people pay to themselves. Vincent van Gogh had Theo. He wasn't successful, but he had someone sending him money and trying to sell his paintings. There's always some machinery working.

If you're not necessarily interested in having an audience, if you're not interested in making a living off your art, then you don't have to worry about self-promotion. Don't self-promote.

Something I hear a lot is, "I'm not interested in being on social media." Or "I'm not interested in being on the Internet."
Right. Which is like saying "I'm not interested in the printing press."

Sure, but I actually relate to that, because even though I'm on the Internet a lot, it frazzles me.

I relate, too. And that's what I try to do in *Show Your Work!*—get people to quit thinking about self-promotion and start thinking about sharing. How do you share yourself and your passions in a way that's interesting or helpful to others?

Think about you and your writer friends. What do you do when you get together? Well, you probably bitch about how you don't have any money. But after that, you talk about books you love. So when I talk to young writers, I tell them, *You should be keeping a reading log online. And every book you read, post some quote from it or say something about it that's interesting and just, like, become a good citizen.*

When I started out [blogging] I was just trying to shine a light on the stuff I really liked. I wasn't thinking "self-promotion." I mean, in the back of your head, of course, you're thinking, *How can I be part of this?* I remember reading Maud Newton's blog in the very beginning and being very inspired by her. I thought, this is just some woman, and she writes about books, and she writes stories. And she works in law!

What kind of books do you want to write when you grow up?

Oh, that's a great question. I just read Roz Chast's latest memoir. It's so fucking good. It's just so funny and so heartbreaking. I think that's the kind of book I want to write. And I'd like to get a little less bossy. Eventually I'd like to do a book that doesn't tell people what to do!

Look, I do not have it figured out. I feel really good about my output up until this point. It's been my dream to be able to stay at home and have a family and go out to my studio and do whatever I want. But I think the whiplash of it has been so quick that I'm still catching up with it. It's the imposter syndrome thing, where you think someone's gonna knock on the door and take it all back.

So for me it always comes back to the daily practice. Making sure you do that every day no matter what. Do the thing that feeds you, first. Then do the crazy business stuff.

That sounds a little bit like "do you what you love," but I'll let it pass. . . .
I mean, sure, do what you love, but do it on the nights-and-weekends plan.

Well, there's "do what you love," and then there's "love what you do."
Right, and that's the other thing. It's like, now that I am in this gig, how can I become the best? How can I write the best book I can do next? How can I be the best speaker possible? How can I make art that's as good as I can make it? And that's where I find the challenge.

I'm thirty-one, man. I haven't even *done* anything yet. People give her shit a lot, but I thought one of the most honest things I've seen was Elizabeth Gilbert getting up onstage [at a recent TED Talk] and saying, "It's very possible that my best work is behind me." I thought, man, that takes balls. Because that's what everyone is thinking. But for her to say, *Look, maybe there's a different way to think about this. . . .* I thought that was great.

And maybe my big one is behind me, who knows? But I can't do anything about it. You just do the work that's in front of you. Keep going. Oh god, I sound like a self-help author!

A SORT OF FAIRY TALE

Malinda Lo

Publishing is a business based on fiction—and not only the fiction that is packaged between book covers or sold as digital downloads. In order to convince harried, distracted people to set aside hours or even days to read hundreds of pages of non-animated words, we in the publishing business must manufacture an aura of success around a book, a glowing sheen that purrs *I am worth your time.* This aura is conveyed through breathless jacket copy, seductive cover imagery, and blurbs dripping with praise so thick the words seem painted on with honey. This fiction of success is stoked by the fiction of buzz and sustained by the fiction of social media. Plenty of authors who appear to be successful in public are, in private, struggling to get by on dwindling royalty payments, or working an unglamorous day job, or are married to someone with a much more reliable income. That last one is me. For more than a decade I (mostly) supported myself as a freelance writer and novelist. But since I married my wife, who is a lawyer, and we combined our finances, I ceased to be a self-supporting writer.

I estimate that my writing income makes up about ten to fifteen percent of the total household income that my wife and I tabulate at the end of the year. In the eyes of our accountant, my income is an annoying pittance—annoying because I still have to fill out that self-employed Schedule C and pay estimated taxes, despite its relatively small amount. To me, it has been both disappointing and humbling. I grew up absorbing the idea that the size of your salary is a sign of your worth. Having to rely on someone else to pay the bills has forced me to look at my work in a completely different way and given me a perspective I was unable to have until now.

When I tell the story of my career, I often start with "I dropped out of grad school to become a freelance writer." In general terms it's true, but it leaves out many complicating details. For one thing, I had to leave grad school twice to make that dropping out stick. For another thing, I had other jobs besides writing, ranging from working at Williams-Sonoma during the holiday season (I particularly enjoyed the barware section), to staffing a singles' meet-and-greet table at a lesbian burlesque club, to a job that was the equivalent of pushing a button repeatedly for an Internet company you've all heard of but I can't name (I signed a nondisclosure agreement).

I also usually say I didn't do much thinking about what being a "freelance writer" actually meant, because if I had, I probably would have been too scared to try. I had decided to make a living as a writer, so that's what I set out to do, ignoring all the voices in my head that told me it was impossible. I had a kind of blind courage fueled by ignorance about writing as a career, and in retrospect, I'm amazed I was able to silence those doubts. There's something to be said for beginner's mind. But while it's true that I didn't think about it directly, I did have unspoken expectations. Though I started off as a freelance writer of nonfiction, I wanted to become a novelist. I expected that once I sold my first novel, the hardest part would be over. I expected I would be able to support myself entirely on my novels' royalties. That was how I defined success: supporting myself from writing novels. I also expected that becoming a successful novelist would be difficult; that was the only expectation that has turned out to be true.

I started as a freelance writer in 2003. Back then, my income came from a variety of sources; the biggest was a consulting company for which I wrote business reports. They were sometimes so tedious that I felt as if my brain had gone on strike, but they paid better than any other jobs I could find. Another of my earliest gigs was writing pop culture features for a tiny website called AfterEllen, launched by one of my college friends from her home office. AfterEllen aimed to be the *Entertainment Weekly* for lesbians and bisexual women, but in 2003 it was only a small collection of essays about lesbians in pop culture that few people read. I wrote the site's first article about Ellen DeGeneres, whom the site is named after (but is unaffiliated with). Given my credits at AfterEllen, I was able to move into writing for other gay and lesbian media outlets. I wrote encyclopedia entries about lesbian films that would soon be rendered obsolete by Wikipedia; book and music reviews for very small LGBT newspapers and magazines; and eventually turned those reviews into regular columns.

As is often the case, being a full-time freelance writer meant I also supplemented my writing income with non-writing side jobs, and with financial help from my parents and friends. Although my parents had been extremely leery of me dropping out of graduate school (it was Stanford, where I had been pursuing a PhD in cultural anthropology), they nonetheless didn't want me to starve. My friends helped me out with loans, emotional support, food, useful gifts (one friend gave me a salad spinner, which was like a miracle to me), and jobs (see AfterEllen). In aggregate, all these small sources of income allowed me to pay my rent, buy groceries, and carve out the time to write a novel.

While I thought of my freelance gigs as work, plain and simple, my first novel was never a job; it was a dream. But at the beginning, it was a dream I fit in around my other deadlines. The idea had been haunting me for years: a retelling of Cinderella, a book I had always wanted to read because I grew up on Robin McKinley's beautiful retellings of other fairy tales. I started my Cinderella before I left grad school and worked on it off and on during my early years as a freelance writer. I finished the first draft sometime in 2004 and sent it to my friend Lesly for some feedback. Lesly told me that the Cinderella character, Ash, didn't have much chemistry with Prince Charming. In fact, Ash seemed to be much more interested in one of the book's other female characters.

This shocked me at first. I hadn't set out to write a lesbian Cinderella, but when I reread that first draft, I could easily see that Lesly was right. At that time, I was a lesbian living in San Francisco, surrounded by gay culture and writing about it for a variety of publications. It made sense that my retelling of Cinderella would go in this direction. However, at first I didn't want to turn my novel, now called *Ash*, into a lesbian Cinderella. I expected that would make the book unpublishable. I had never heard of any mainstream publisher interested in such a story, and I didn't want to doom my career as a novelist before it even started.

But the idea wouldn't let go of me. I may have thought a lesbian Cinderella sounded bizarre, but it also excited me. This was a story I needed so much that I wrote it subconsciously; it had to come out. Over the next few years, I set aside time to rewrite the novel from scratch.

By this time, my freelance gigs had turned into steady editorial jobs. I became an associate editor at a lesbian magazine, and then I became managing editor at AfterEllen. That website, which had started out so small, had grown into the biggest site online covering lesbians and bisexual women, and in 2006 it was acquired by MTV. I had never imagined it was possible to be an entertainment reporter focusing on lesbians in the media, but that's what I was doing. It was full-time and then some, involving regular travel to conferences, festivals, and Hollywood, where I interviewed actors and producers in the entertainment industry. I still wasn't a professional novelist, but for the first time in my life I had a writing job with a comfortable salary. I had a savings account. I could even afford to buy a new salad spinner if I wanted to, but I continued to use the one my friend had given me. It was immensely satisfying to be able to tell people I met at parties, "I'm a writer," and not feel like I was fudging the truth.

Meanwhile, at the end of every breakneck week at AfterEllen, I shut myself in my bedroom and reworked the story of Cinderella into a tale that included people like me. Over Christmas 2006, alone in my apartment during a self-imposed holiday writing retreat, I finished a presentable draft of the novel. In January 2007, I sent it to eight literary agents, whom I found through *The Writer's Market* and AgentQuery.com. Eleven months later, one of those initial eight agents offered to represent me and *Ash*.

By the time 2007 was over, I was on top of the world. Not only had I found a literary agent, but I had also just met the woman I was going to marry. Both of these events intertwined into a dream of a year when, in early 2008, my literary agent sent *Ash* out to publishers. Within weeks, we had received five offers to publish the book: my impossible lesbian retelling of Cinderella was not so impossible after all. For two years beginning with the signing of my contract to publish *Ash*, I was able to make my living from my fiction. My early expectation that my income would come entirely from royalties wasn't exactly right; it came from my advance on royalties, plus a nest egg of savings I'd worked hard (at AfterEllen) to build. But those were just details. I wasn't rich, but I had done it: I was a successful novelist. I quit my day job. And I got engaged.

After my two years of *Ash*-related income trickled to a close, I did continue to earn income from writing fiction. I sold more novels; I wrote short stories for anthologies; my agent sold foreign and audio rights; and because of *Ash*'s critical success, I began to get paid speaking and teaching invitations. Nonetheless, these combined sources of income were not what supported me; my wife and her job did. My income, while certainly more than I made in my early years as a freelance writer, simply did not compare to the steady paychecks of a corporate lawyer. I was relieved to no longer be so worried about money, but I also felt disconcertingly unmoored by my new financial freedom. I knew I was in a privileged position that many writers would envy, so why did it feel less like a fairy tale and more like a shoe that didn't quite fit? Now I didn't have to hustle as much as I had in earlier years, but to my surprise, I missed some of that hustle.

The fact is, financial necessity can be extremely clarifying. When your goal is to make enough money to pay the rent, writing loses a lot of its artistic mystique and becomes something much more mundane: a job. Thinking of writing as a job made the countless uncertainties that come with being a writer manageable. It gave me a rubric by which to measure my success. But without financial need, I found it difficult to continue thinking of writing as my job. And if I didn't need to write for money, why was I writing?

For most of my life I'd kept the truth of my deep-seated desire to write at arm's length, partly out of self-defense (if I didn't look at it too closely, it couldn't scare me), and partly out of pragmatism (my art had to pay the rent, so I had to favor what the market would buy over any deeper personal vision). But now I was free to look my artistic goals in the eye. Let me tell you, art alone can be a terrifying beast. It demands naked honesty, an intimate appraisal of my desires. It's much easier to allow financial need to direct what I write.

In our capitalist society the worth of a novel or any piece of art is in many ways incalculable, ever shifting, a fiction just like success. Of course, publishing is a business. Royalty statements exist, and publishers have equations that purport to calculate whether enough profit was made. Every writer who wants to be published in the mainstream must account for this reality. (Those in self-publishing have different realities to deal with.) Before I married my wife, this was the only reality I could see. It was a reality with clear boundaries and expectations, and though it was limited in scope, those limits could be comforting.

I may not be a "successful" writer in the terms I once imagined, but I have been given a more precious gift: the ability to decouple my writing from financial necessity. I still recognize the so-called realities of mainstream publishing, but now I have the freedom to not be completely limited by them. I can think of my writing as art rather than simply a means to pay the rent. This freedom has turned my world upside down. It has been soul shaking in what it asks of me. But beneath my fear, I have rediscovered what drove me to write *Ash* despite my early, market-based doubts about the viability of a lesbian Cinderella. My subconscious urge to write people like me—queer, Asian, female—into stories that traditionally excluded us has been the bedrock beneath everything I write, and now I can honor it consciously.

When my wife and I combined households, I discarded the salad spinner my friend had given me because my wife's salad spinner was more technologically advanced. Recently, this salad spinner's handle broke, snapping in half in the middle of cleaning a bunch of kale. Part of me, accustomed to making do with what I have, wants to keep using it. If I cling to the nub that's left, the basket spins more securely than it used to, so maybe the handle even works a little better this way. But hanging on to a broken salad spinner is refusing to admit that things change.

When I started writing *Ash*, my novel was a dream that I fit into the margins of my life. Today my dream is front and center, but living the dream isn't the happy ending I once imagined. The truth is, my dream has changed; it has become clearer to me, and also more challenging. Coming to terms with this change goes hand in hand with shifting my perspective on success, art, and money. There has never been a simple relationship between these things, but now I am better positioned to negotiate a balance among them. I imagine that Cinderella—or, at least, my Ash—faced a similar tension after her happily ever after began. Your story doesn't end when your dreams come true; it changes.

GROWING UP

Nick Hornby

in conversation with Manjula Martin

Manjula Martin: When you were a child, what did you want to be when you grew up?

Nick Hornby: I don't really remember wanting to be anything until I wanted to be a writer, sometime in my late teens. That was my first serious ambition.

What do you want to be *now*?
Ha! I think I'm more or less happy with my professional lot. I'm fifty-seven and fear it's too late for a new career. Plus I'm incapable of doing anything else.

What kind of an economic environment did you grow up in?
It was . . . schizophrenic. I was brought up by my mum—single parent, a secretary in a pharmaceutical firm. There wasn't a lot of money around. My dad, though, was doing well. He lived in the South of France and then Connecticut as he rose through the managerial ranks. So during the holidays I had glimpses of another kind of life.

I guess the most truthful answer is that my mother, my sister, and I lived in straitened lower-middle-class circumstances, with the occasional flight from reality.

I think in my early life I was suspicious of my father's newfound prosperity and disapproved of it. He liked nice clothes, nice restaurants, nice wine, so I made it my business not to. This shaped a lot of my tastes, as you can imagine. He used to take me to football [soccer], but I always preferred to stand behind the goal rather than sit in the good seats in the stands, so in the end I preferred going without him.

When I first started earning, I wanted enough for my food and rent, the pub, cigarettes, music, and football. That was it. I had no financial needs beyond these, and they could be met by more or less any full-time job. I trained as a teacher and taught—first kids, and then English to foreign students. I had no objections to earning large sums of money, but I did have objections to the kinds of things I'd have to do to earn them, and the kind of people I'd be working alongside. I think my family thought I wasn't ambitious, but actually I was hugely ambitious, because I wanted to make some kind of mark with my writing.

In my midthirties, my first son, Danny, was diagnosed with a profound disability—he has severe autism—and that changed an awful lot of things.

We'll come back to the topic of Danny. But first, why did you want so badly to make a mark? Some may say that artists should just have a day job and leave it at that—that our economy and society just aren't set up to value artistic work. What made you think differently?
It's an argument, I suppose, the one that says artists should have a day job and do their art in the evenings or at weekends. But at the moment it's purely theoretical. Lots of artistic work is very highly valued in the marketplace, and I could see that many artists I admired seemed to be making a living, and I wanted to make my living that way too. And I have, and I know lots of other people that have too.

My work is important to me, and I have never written for the money. But I do understand I'm working in a marketplace, and I have to produce stuff that people actually want to read or watch. That's not the same thing as writing commercially.

Earlier I asked about what you wanted to be when you grew up because, to me, a lot of your work seems concerned with the concept of growing up—and, in your earlier work, specifically men growing up. Are the responsibilities of being an adult something you've struggled with yourself?
First of all, I should say that I think a career in the arts does retard maturity, whoever you are and however old you think you are. The impulse to create is a healthy one, but the decision to try and make a living from your creative endeavors, probably less so. Strip everything away and you find the equivalent of an over-indulged kid—*Look at me! Listen to me! I'm special! I have something to say! And you have to pay me for it!*

The process of growing up involves accepting that we're not as special as we thought we were (or as mummy and daddy thought we were). But artists have to keep that feeling alive. So I must have that in me.

My adult responsibilities have been much more onerous than I had anticipated, and I suppose that because of them I started looking at my peer group with a moralist's eye. If my characters had trouble growing up, it's because I'd had to grow up fast, although probably belatedly. The guy in *About a Boy* was in a diametrically opposite place to me when I wrote that book.

How were the film deals for your books made?
They were all very different. A guy made a small piece about *Fever Pitch* for a nightly arts show on the BBC. This seemed incredible enough to me, but he then said he wanted to make a feature from

the book, and he wanted me to adapt it. His ambition and his confidence were staggering. But he had no money, or access to money, and he didn't know much about how to make a feature, so we set off on this long road together. It wasn't paved with gold. We found someone who wanted to produce, and the three of us—a first-time director, a first-time producer, and a first-time screenwriter—hustled. Eventually we persuaded Film4 in England to develop and then make it.

High Fidelity came about in the more conventional way—an option offer after publication. And with *About a Boy*, I hadn't actually finished the book, but someone from my US publishers gave it to someone who worked at a film company, and this insane bidding war started. It ended with a seven-figure sum. Things changed for me literally during the course of an evening.

Did you feel like you struck it rich?
Of course it all depends on how you define *rich*. Certainly the money I made wouldn't have been enough to last me for the rest of my life. But I made much, much more than I'd been anticipating. It began with the paperback of *Fever Pitch*, which spent six months on the bestseller list, and then *High Fidelity* did about the same. *About a Boy* was the life-changer. The advances had been going up anyway, and then the film sale made me feel as though I was going to be able to do things I hadn't anticipated being able to do—live without a mortgage, for example.

So I started earning well in the mid-'90s, and it's stayed that way. I don't have to worry about money. The point of the money for me was that it enabled me to take care of my family and myself through writing; I was never trying to hit an amount that enabled me to quit work. And I don't have expensive tastes. Maybe if the money had started to come in when I was in my midtwenties, I might have blown it on fast cars and so on. But my tastes were set by my midthirties, and also Danny—and my divorce from his mum—has put certain boundaries on my lifestyle. I can't go and live abroad, for example, not without uprooting two families. I have two kids from my second marriage; Danny's mum has remarried and she has two stepsons—we have this complicated infrastructure that means we stay close, in the same part of North London that I've lived in for twenty-five years or so.

I actually don't think it's possible to make that kind of money anymore. Publishing has changed. I got in just before the gate shut behind me. The slow disappearance of independent bookstores, the influence of supermarkets, e-books—we more or less give books away now, and it's much harder for non-genre books to achieve mainstream success. It still happens, but more rarely. For most of the six months that *Fever Pitch* was in the nonfiction bestseller list, it was number two in the chart. It's hard to imagine that now.

You mentioned your son's autism diagnosis as a turning point in your outlook on money. How so?
My son was diagnosed properly in 1996, and the film money for *About a Boy* came in 1997. So just when it was beginning to sink in that Danny would always need looking after, for the whole of his life and not just until he was twenty-five or thirty, money came along that made it a lot less frightening to contemplate the enormity of this.

I was able to make a decent donation to the school that Danny's mother and I were trying to set up. There were five autistic kids whose parents couldn't find the education they were looking for, and these five kids became the basis for this new school. We had no premises, no nothing, really. Now there is a proper school with its own building, for eighty kids. Danny isn't there anymore, but the school will be there forever. I also gave Danny's school the film rights to *How to Be Good*—sadly, the one movie that never got made. But it was optioned and re-optioned, and the school did well out of it. Sometimes, when we're lucky, writers get paid several times over for the same piece of work.

How did your relationship with Dave Eggers change your perspective on your career?

When I met Dave I could see he had a very unconventional approach to money. Back then, he ploughed a lot back into McSweeney's and 826 [his publishing company and charity organization], and that mind-set seemed . . . well, challenging. Most people are very cautious with charitable donations, even if they earn a lot and give a lot. If you earn ten million a year, why not give six million away? Or nine? I don't earn ten million a year, by the way, and I don't give nine-tenths of what I do earn away. But Dave made me rethink what was possible or advisable; hence the decision to give away the *How to Be Good* rights. It sounds like a noble gesture, but it really wasn't. I'd been paid very well for the book, in the UK, the United States, Germany, and lots of other European countries. Giving that money away didn't affect my life, or my family's life.

Dave also made me rethink my job. He's a publisher, and he has founded several nonprofits—only a part of his life is a recognizable writer's life. Watching him loosened me up. I was on a schedule—two years writing, one year of promotion, pretty much. I didn't want to do that for the rest of my life—hence the screenplays, the *Believer* columns, the album with Ben Folds, etc. Some of these things paid, some didn't, but it was all interesting.

FAQ: HOW TO BUY A HOME

Mallory Ortberg

The best reason for a writerly person to buy a house is probably "because you particularly wish it." There may be other worthwhile reasons, but none come readily to mind. I will not attempt to talk you into buying a house if you are having a perfectly good time renting; no one should yoke a mortgage around their neck because they feel guilty about not acting enough like the Greatest Generation. I purchased a home in 2015 myself, despite being both a millennial and a writer, and would like to take this opportunity to endorse the home-buying process heartily and with only a few reservations. I have assembled a ha'penny's worth of questions a writer might ask during the home-buying process and answered them as gorgeously as possible.

The enpurchasement of a home, you have no doubt heard, strengthens the dollar both at home and abroad while striking fear into the hearts of America's enemies, eliminates student loans and credit card debt, counteracts moral turpitude, brightens the complexion, and gladdens the eye. It also sticks it to every building manager who ever refused to return your security deposit even after you scrubbed the baseboards and provided documentation that the scuff marks in the front hallway were there when you moved in.

Having accomplished this task in under six months with a minimum of anxiety, fewer than fifty e-mails, and a relatively comprehensible closing process during which I received a complimentary cup of coffee, I now wish to share with you the lessons I learned along the way. (The best financial advice I can ever give anyone, I think—if you take nothing else from my story, I hope you will remember this—is that whenever you are offered a free beverage, *take it*. How often in life is one presented with a drink without a bill? Informational interviews, AA meetings, some car dealerships, church, and *nowhere*. Whenever someone asks "Can I get you a drink?" say "Coffee would be great," or the name of whatever drink you think would be great just then. They're offering because they want to! You're really not putting anyone out, you know, if you say yes to that fizzy water, and that way even if things don't pan out during the meeting, at least you're one La Croix can the richer for it. Life is stern and life is earnest and free drinks aren't proffered every day. Take the coffee and ask if they have any real cream, not just the powdered Coffee-mate.)

But you're a writer. How ever did you get enough money to buy a WHOLE HOUSE?

Anyone with a certain amount of money and the ability to sign documents can buy a house, probably. Which is to say: get some money. If you live in Manhattan, you are going to need to assemble a vast pile of money. If you live in Eastern California, the vastness of the pile will be less. If you don't have at least a certain pile of money, you're not going to be able to get a house, at least not for a while. Acquire a pile of money through a combination of wages and savings—writing jobs, non-writing jobs, shrewd investments, generous and eccentric aunts, owning a company that pays you to write jokes about paintings in the public domain. If you believe personal finance blogs, the act of not buying a daily cup of coffee should enrich you enough to buy a home in about thirty years or so. I'll wait.

Mallory Ortberg

What do I need to know in order to buy a home?

The first thing to bear in mind, of course, is that, despite the moaning about unforeseen costs and unexpected headaches one so often hears from homebuyers both incipient and fully ripe, being able to buy a home is a very lucky thing! You are about to stake out your very own claim on a corner of creation—a plot of something that belongs to you and to your name and to the people who may someday bear your name. You will be able to buy signs that say things like PLEASE PICK UP AFTER YOUR DOG—HOUSE ELVES DON'T LIVE HERE and SMILE! YOU'RE ON CAMERA and humorous mats for feet-wiping that introduce visitors to the fact that *this* house, is in fact, a *nut*house, and that while being crazy may not be a requirement for living here, it certainly helps. You will be able to begin sentences with "As a homeowner . . ." possibly while placing your thumbs through your suspenders. You will have the chance to build a lovely life in whatever direction you please. A vast new world is opening up for you!

You are still participating in the decadent, deeply compromised system of late-stage capitalism, which is less than ideal for many of us, but that cannot presently be helped.

But isn't owning a home the worst kind of headache? Aren't I dooming myself to a life of home repairs and grumbling at dinner with friends?

The most important thing to remember, I think, is that even though you are buying a home, it is not necessary to become the kind of person who deprecates their own *unqualified good fortune* by saying things like, "It's such a hassle! What a headache, home-buying, now that you can't call your landlord to tuck you in at night and kiss your bills away! Good luck when your foundation slides off and your roof turns into a single mushroom, your house will be as a millstone round your neck, a constant tribulation and sorrow!" It is not inevitable that, whenever you happen to ascend a rung on the financial ladder, you must also increase your number of complaints.

What are the hidden costs of buying a house?
Ask anyone you know who has recently bought a home what the process is like, and you will almost invariably hear not "Well, I feel really excited to be building equity, and it's wonderful to have a house that I can call my very own, and I'm enormously proud of the years I spent building good credit and setting aside money for a down payment," but, "Oh, you won't believe the hidden costs, the exploding sewer lines, the Tax Extractors who beat me nightly, this is tenfold worse than renting, my house brings me no pleasure and will serve only as my grave." There is, I think, a general tendency among the middle class and its various aspirants to smooth over any possible class anxiety by showily complaining about any good fortune. If someone has bought a nice new car, they are likely to offset any suggestion of bragging with "You wouldn't *believe* the insurance rates, though." If someone has bought a house while the rest of their friends struggle to make rent, or moves to a fancier neighborhood, they may seek to keep everyone from feeling jealous with "The walls leak gravy! I'm up all night sanding the fridge! Please don't think that I think I'm doing better than you."

It is for this same reason that ninety-eight percent of wealthy people refuse to acknowledge that they are rich, and will insist upon using "comfortable" or "we're doing okay" instead. (Your mileage may vary. Perhaps everyone you know is a delightful braggart who takes great joy in proclaiming good fortune when they encounter it.) But there is no reason to pretend good fortune isn't good fortune. If you find it, be grateful! If it is possible for you to dispense it to others, do so, and do that with a right goodwill! If you haven't any, I'm sorry and hope things turn around soon!

There are so many different ways of being a writer and having money that my advice is almost impossible to apply to the majority of us. There is such an enormous difference between being the kind of writer who has a steady full-time job and minimal debt and no student loans versus the kind of writer who goes without health insurance and can't make rent and all the varieties of writer in between that generalities here are impossible. But it is important to acknowledge the distinction between being *broke* and being *poor.* If you are in the position to put down a down payment on a home, however modest, you are probably doing better than ninety percent of writers, perhaps better than ninety percent of people! *Allow yourself to experience gratitude for this.*

Okay, but how much money do I actually need? Ballpark.
I don't know that my mentioning numbers will be especially helpful to you on your journey. I live in a particularly expensive city in a particularly expensive state; I have often heard that one should spend no more than thirty percent of their monthly income on rent, and it has never failed to draw a grim, world-weary chuckle from me. Residents of the San Francisco Bay Area are routinely locked out of their homes by platinum-skinned dragons if they cannot produce their own weight in rubies, so any number I might suggest as a reasonable down payment might cause a practical-minded resident of, say, Oklahoma to weep blood. It is more helpful, instead, to suggest choosing a mortgage before choosing a house. This way you will not run the risk of falling in love with a house you cannot afford, something I was cautioned against repeatedly as I looked for a home to buy. *Do not allow yourself to love. Fill your heart with pitch and lime and vinegar, close it off from all things.* This was quite good advice! There are thousands of homes, probably, that I could have been enormously happy in, and that would have been sensible choices for me. I had a specific price range in mind, a bright and

sympathetic Realtor who knew what I wanted, and a fresh Google Document labeled "DIFFERENT HOUSES PROS AND CONS." I came prepared. I was excited, because I knew it was a joy and a privilege to be in the position to buy my own house; I was patient, because I have an exceedingly docile temperament, and I was capable of signing checks once I found a house that met the majority of my criteria, and that someone richer than me didn't want more.

But what if someone richer than me makes an offer on the same house? I *love* this house. So much. It must be mine.

There is nothing to be done when someone with more money wants the same house as you. They will offer more money, and they will be accepted, and you will have to find someplace else. Hold everything loosely, for someday Death will take everything out of your hands.

Should I have the house inspected?

Of course; be reasonable. They don't even let you buy a house without inspecting it first, I don't think. Make sure it has, you know, floors and whatnot.

Should I hire a lawyer?

I cannot say! I didn't, and I don't believe I was cheated for it. But I may not know.

Should I look at comparable houses and find out whether or not the home I wish to buy is under- or overvalued?

Sure! Also, at some point, you're going to have to pay taxes on the house. They'll send you a note to remind you, just be sure to write it down so you don't forget in the excitement of it all.

I bought a house! Now what do I do?

Live in your house and enjoy it! People much stupider than you, with far worse financial habits and less attractive hairstyles, have bought houses and lived to tell about it. The fridge might not work at first, and you might not realize where the water heater is, and maybe you'll never make back your initial investment if you decide to sell eight years from now when the market has collapsed, but you'll fill the house with televisions and snacks and pets and eventually you'll put a whole life in it.

DIVERSITY IS NOT ENOUGH: RACE, POWER, PUBLISHING

Daniel José Older

"Cuando el EZLN logre lo que busca, entonces ya no será necesario el EZLN, por eso decimos que luchamos por desaparecer."

"When the Zapatista Army of National Liberation achieves what it seeks, it will cease to be necessary, and so we say that we fight in order to disappear."

—Subcomandante Marcos, EZLN, February 2001

A young writer that I mentor reached out to me recently. "None of these agents look like me," she said, "and they don't represent anyone that looks like me." She was wrapping up a final draft of her first novel and I'd told her to research literary agencies to get a feel for what's out there. "What if they don't get what I'm doing?"

I thought back over the many interactions I'd had with agents—all but two of them white—before I landed with mine. The ones that said they loved my writing but didn't connect with the character, the ones that didn't think my book would be marketable even though it was already accepted at a major publishing house. Thought about the ones that wanted me to delete moments when a character of color gets mean looks from white people because "that doesn't happen anymore" and the white magazine editor who lectured me on how I'd gotten my own culture wrong. My friends all have the same stories of whitewashed covers and constant sparring with the many micro- and mega-aggressions of the publishing industry.

"I don't know," I said. Useless words, but it was all I had in that moment. I don't. There are so many paths to success, so many meanings of the concept, and race and power complicate the equation infinitely. It's not enough for writers of color to learn craft; we need to navigate the impossible waters of an unwelcoming industry. I flailed for words that would prepare her for all that lay ahead; none came.

In the *New York Times* in 2014, children's book illustrator Christopher Myers wrote about "Th[e] apartheid of literature—in which characters of color are limited to the townships of occasional historical books that concern themselves with the legacies of civil rights and slavery but are never given a pass card to traverse the lands of adventure, curiosity, imagination, or personal growth."

In the same edition of the newspaper, Myers's father, author Walter Dean Myers, wrote about growing up a bibliophile in Harlem, falling out of love with books when they offered up no characters he could relate to, and the revelation of reading *Sonny's Blues* by James Baldwin: "I was lifted by it, for it took place in Harlem, and it was a story concerned with black people like those I knew. By humanizing the people who were like me, Baldwin's story also humanized me. The story gave me a permission that I didn't know I needed, the permission to write about my own landscape, my own map."

These two essays perfectly frame the emotional and social debacle of publishing and diversity today. They begin with this stat: "Of 3,200 children's books published in 2013, just 93 were about black people, according to a study by the Cooperative Children's Book Center at the University of Wisconsin." The wide world of literature in general, and by no coincidence, the publishing industry itself suffers from similarly disastrous numbers.

When Christopher Myers asked his uncomfortable questions about the apartheid in children's lit, the industry hid behind The Market. The publishing industry, people often say as if it's a gigantic revelation, needs to make money and as such, it responds to The Market, and people don't buy books about characters of color. This is updated marketing code for "you people don't read," and it's used to justify any number of inexcusable problems in literature. "The Market is so comfortably intangible," Myers writes, "that no one is worried I will go knocking down any doors. The Market, I am told, just doesn't demand this kind of book . . . because white kids won't buy a book with a black kid on the cover—or so The Market says, despite millions of music albums that are sold in just that way."

By blaming an intangible force, the publishing industry absolves itself of any responsibility, when in fact it is very much in the business of manipulating The Market to its ends. "Those conversations happen without acknowledging that there's a huge disparity in how books are marketed and publicized," Sarah McCarry tells me. McCarry worked in publishing on and off for a decade, most recently at a New York literary agency. "That money and attention overwhelmingly goes to what the industry has already decided is 'marketable'—heterosexual narratives featuring white characters. A book has very little chance of doing well if there's no marketing push behind it."

Lee & Low Books convened a panel in 2013 and asked agents what they could do to help shift the troubling lack of diversity in publishing. "I think the change is going to have to come from within those who are affected," one agent responded, "just like any underrepresented group in any profession. But since the return on the investment for the author is so low, I don't know how many people of color are going to have the desire to climb the mountain to publication that every new author faces, or have the luxury of dedicating the time it takes to master the craft."

Another agent, when asked why less than one percent of her submissions were from people of color, captured what seems to be the publishing industry's general attitude in just ten words: "This seems like a question for an author to answer."

This is the language of privilege—the audacity of standing at the top of a mountain you made on the backs of others and then yelling at people for being at the bottom. If it's not the intangible Market that's to blame, it's the writers of color, who maybe don't have what it takes and don't submit enough anyway. Read the subtextual coding here—the agent first places the onus of change on the folks with the least institutional power to effect it, then suggests we probably won't be able to find the time (i.e., we're lazy) to master the craft.

Of course, we have climbed many mountains, and mastery of craft is not a luxury for writers of color, it is a necessity. But many of our gifts and challenges won't be seen or recognized within a white cultural context. Nuances of code-switching, racial micro-aggressions, the emotional reality of surviving white supremacy, self-translation—these are all layers of the nonwhite experience that rarely make it into mainstream literature, even when the characters look like us.

The disproportionally white publishing industry matters because agents and editors stand between writers and readers. Anika Noni Rose put it perfectly in *Vanity Fair*: "There are so many writers of color out there, and often what they get when they bring their books to their editors, they say, 'We don't relate to the character.' Well it's not for you to relate to! And why can't you expand yourself so you can relate to the humanity of a character as opposed to the color of what they are?"

So we are wary. The publishing industry looks a lot like one of these bestselling teenage dystopias: white and full of people destroying one another to survive.

But let's go back to this: "It's not for you to relate to!" Write that in the sky. And it's true—often, as writers of color, to portray our stories in all their vibrant authenticity, in all their difficult truth, means we're not writing for editors and agents, we're writing past them. We're writing for us, for each other. And it's not just a question of characters of color; it's not a numbers game. It's about voice, about narrative flow. Because of who we are and what we've lived, our stories often contain implicit critiques of white supremacy, critiques that we know stand little chance of surviving the gauntlet of the majority-white publishing industry. We see diverse futures, laden with the tangled past of oppression, and we re-envision models of empowerment and survival. But only a few of us make it through. There is a filter and the filter is white culture.

Ultimately, editors and agents hold exactly the same amount of responsibility that writers do in making literature more diverse. The difference is, editors and agents have inordinately more power and access in the industry than writers do. As Arthur A. Levine's executive editor, Cheryl Klein, said: "It's important to have advocates at every stage, from editing to marketing, from librarians to authors, so it's an industry-wide effort." Klein cofounded the Children's Book Council Diversity Committee, a group of editors "dedicated to increasing the diversity of voices and experiences contributing to children's and young adult literature." And that's what I'm talking about.

The question industry professionals need to ask themselves is: How can I use my position to help create a literary world that is diverse, equitable, and doesn't just represent the same segment of society it always has since its inception? What concrete actions can I take to make actual change and move beyond the tired conversation we've been having for decades?

"As I discovered who I was, a black teenager in a white-dominated world," Walter Dean Myers writes, "I saw that these characters, these lives, were not mine. I didn't want to become the 'black' representative, or some shining example of diversity. What I wanted, needed really, was to become an integral and valued part of the mosaic that I saw around me."

And the "shining example" Myers speaks of is exactly what the industry responds with when we raise the question of diversity. No one is demanding more tokens though. We're talking about systemic upheaval.

Here's where the critique is met with deafening silence.

In 2014 CNN published an article on diversity in young adult literature that asked, "Where's the Mexican Katniss?" In the *Hunger Games* novels, Katniss isn't white, so let's also ask: Where are the publishing industry players who will take a stand to make sure literary characters of color become big-screen characters of color? And let's go back even further. Octavia Butler gave us Lauren Olamina in 1993. Nalo Hopkinson gave us Ti-Jeanne in 1998 and Tan-Tan in 2000. Where were the mass-marketing resources, multimillion-dollar ad campaigns and spin machines when *Parable of the Sower, Brown Girl in the Ring*, and (my favorite) *Midnight Robber* dropped?

Nancy Larrick begins her essay, "The All-White World of Children's Books," with essentially the same question: "Why are they always *white* children?" That was written in 1965. The CNN article refuses to make a cohesive statement about race and publishing that isn't tempered with phrases like "Some writers feel." It ends with the hope that a nonexistent contest with five winners could be "the beginning of real change in young adult fiction." The 1965 article, on the other hand, concludes with a reminder to editors that "what is good for the Ku Klux Klan is not necessarily good for America—or for the book business. White supremacy in children's literature,"

Larrick writes, "will be abolished when authors, editors, publishers, and booksellers decide that they need not submit to bigots."

"What happens," my student asked me, "if none of them want a book about a black girl and I never find an agent?"

Writing—becoming a writer—is the greatest thing that's ever happened to me, and the only thing comparable is seeing that love of craft blossom in someone else. But navigating the complexities of an industry that still hasn't dealt with its own institutional racism is a struggle I wouldn't wish on anyone.

I closed my eyes, tossed up a tiny prayer, almost without meaning to—that she'd find good people like I have; people that would cultivate her voice instead of mangling or silencing it. I'd had this conversation before, years ago, when I was starting out and I didn't know what lay ahead. My mentors shook their heads, and, I imagine, sent up their own tiny prayers. The faces they made probably looked much like mine as I said, *You just have to find the right folks.* I cringed when I said it—tepid words for such a devastating labyrinth.

Diversity is not enough.

We're right to push for diversity, we have to, but it is only step one of a long journey. Lack of racial diversity is a symptom. The underlying illness is institutional racism. It walks hand in hand with sexism, cissexism, homophobia, and classism. To go beyond this same conversation we keep having, again and again, beyond tokens and quick fixes, requires us to look the illness in the face and destroy it. This is work for white people and people of color to do, sometimes together, sometimes apart. It's work for writers, agents, editors, artists, fans, executives, interns, directors, and publicists. It's work for reviewers, educators, and administrators. It means taking courageous, real-world steps, not just changing mission statements or submissions guidelines.

Maybe the word hasn't been invented yet—that thing beyond

diversity. We often define movements by what they're against, but the final goal is greater than the powers it dismantles, deeper than any statistic. It's something like equity—a commitment to harvesting a narrative language so broad it has no face, no name.

We can love a thing and still critique it. In fact, that's the only way to really love a thing. Let's be critical lovers and loving critics and open ourselves to the truth about where we are and where we've been. Instead of holding tight to the same old, failed patriarchies, let's walk a new road, speak new languages. Today, let's imagine a literature, a literary world, that carries this struggle for equity in its very essence, so that tomorrow it can cease to be necessary, and disappear.

WORTH

Jennifer Weiner

The first time my father filed for bankruptcy was in 1988, two years after he'd left my mother and the four of us with the words *I don't want you to think of me as a father. Think of me as more of an uncle.*

We got the message. He didn't want to be a husband. He did not want to be a father, either. He was lighting out for the territories, to have adventures, to have fun.

I never got to have a childhood, we'd all heard him complain. He'd been pushed to excel since he was old enough to read and help his Canadian mother study for the citizenship exam. Growing up, he'd always known that not only would he be the first in his family to attend college, he'd be expected get an advanced degree and be a professional, a doctor or a lawyer, thus securing his spot in respectable upper-middle-class America. My father's parents, my mother's parents, everyone in that generation of Jews knew that almost anything of worth could be taken from you—your home, your jewelry, your possessions, everything you owned—but no one could ever steal an education.

My father's father wanted his son to be both educated and respectable, not being entirely respectable himself. A jovial, enormous man—he'd weigh more than three hundred pounds when he died at fifty-three—he was bright enough to have been accepted to law school right out of high school. But there was a depression, and two younger sisters still at home, so Abe worked construction and eventually became a contractor instead. The story my father told was that people would ask his dad over to look at their houses, their theoretical additions, their enlarged kitchens and en-suite bathrooms, and he'd show up with a sledgehammer. They'd tell him what they wanted. *Great!* he'd say. *We can start right now!* He'd hoist the sledgehammer over his shoulder and slam it down, shattering a bathtub, a countertop, a sink, or a tiled floor. *They'd always sign the contract*, my dad would say, chuckling in admiration. My father's glee at such unorthodox tactics should have been a clue to how he felt about work and money: Honesty and integrity don't matter as much as getting away with something you shouldn't; as pulling one over on the people who aren't as smart as you.

My father did what was expected. He graduated from Wayne State University School of Medicine in 1967. He and my mom got married in 1968, in the big wedding her family insisted on. They had two daughters in Louisiana, on the army base where he was stationed, and two sons in Connecticut, where they moved so he could finish his training, and where they decided to settle. He went into private practice as a child psychiatrist and my mom, Fran, stayed home with the kids. In 1986, we lived in a four-bedroom house in a pretty suburb with quiet streets, expansive lawns, and excellent public schools, with an Audi sedan in the garage and a swimming pool out back. My father wasn't handsome—his face was dominated by his nose, his curly black beard covered in pale, pockmarked skin—but he was elegant in his tailored suits and heavy silk ties, accessorized with a slim leather briefcase and, eventually, the should-have-been-a-warning bright red sports car. The six of us lived like our friends and neighbors and classmates: ski vacations in the winter, sleepaway camps in the summer, trips to Florida over spring break. College was a given. *You just get in*, my father would say, watching in approval as I double-checked my problem sets or wrote my English papers. *You get in, and I'll take care of the rest.*

By the summer of 1988, my father was gone. He was a collage made up of red-bordered envelopes and our own conversations and guesses. We didn't see him, didn't even know where he was living, but we could trace his movements through the mail that kept coming to our house—the trips he'd taken with other women, the restaurants where they'd dined, the hotels where they'd slept. *Thank you for staying* and *please come again* postcards arrived from Saratoga and New Mexico, New York City and Cape Cod. He wasn't paying his alimony or child support. Small stuff—clothes, groceries, gifts for birthday parties—went on my mother's credit card. Big things meant panic. When our refrigerator broke, my mom had to ask her mom for money to replace it. He had the life he'd wanted, the fun he'd missed, travel and glamour and a rotating cast of women. We got the bills. It was as if he'd hefted his own sledgehammer and sent it smashing down, but instead of shattering a countertop or a tile floor, what he broke was our life; the illusion that we were a happy, normal family, the idea that he'd loved us or valued us enough to stick around.

§

The letters came first, in flimsy envelopes with plastic windows for the address. They came from unfamiliar zip codes, and they read as if someone had translated them from English into some obscure language with a spiky and difficult grammar, and then translated them back again.

"*Your obligations to this creditor are seriously delinquent.*"

"*This letter will serve as formal demand for payment of amounts owed to my client.*"

"Please be advised," they would begin. *"We are confident that you would like to resolve this matter now,"* they would conclude.

As things progressed, the tone would become at first passive-aggressive, then simply aggressive:

"Frankly, we would like to know if you intend to pay this," wrote American Express Travel. *"If your answer is 'yes,' please fill in the space below, and we will both feel better. But do it now! Courtesy costs so little; means so much."*

Later, the niceties would be abandoned, and the letters would be written in shouty caps-lock:

YOUR FAILURE TO RESPOND TO OUR PREVIOUS RE-QUESTS HAS CONSTRAINED US TO REFER YOUR AC-COUNT TO OUR LEGAL DEPARTMENT FOR REVIEW. IF IT IS DETERMINED THAT YOU ARE A CANDIDATE FOR LEGAL PROCEDURES TO RECOVER THE AMOUNT DUE, YOU MAY BE REQUIRED TO PAY ALL COLLEC-TION COSTS TOGETHER WITH ANY INTEREST, AS ALLOWED BY CONTRACT OR LAW. TO AVOID THIS UNPLEASANT OCCURANCE, UPON RECEIPT OF THIS NOTICE, PLEASE CONTACT THIS OFFICE TOLL-FREE.

My father owed money to American Express and Citibank and Barclays, to the mechanic that cared for his cars and the garage that housed them, to a storage facility and to the car-phone company and a half-dozen department stores. He had lawyers representing him in the bankruptcy proceedings. Eventually, those lawyers would add their own pleas for remuneration to the pile.

The letters didn't work. They couldn't—my father wasn't there to receive them; and we didn't know where to send them. By the summer, the phone calls began, starting at seven in the morning and ending at ten or even eleven o'clock at night. Every phone in the house would ring—the white plastic landline bolted to the wall in the kitchen above the desk where my mom paid the bills, the cordless phone that we'd keep out by the pool, and the one in their bedroom, next to her side of the bed.

"Let me speak to your father," the voice on the other end of the line would say, or "Is Doctor Weener there?" mispronouncing our last name, turning it into a smutty-sounding joke. Sometimes the voices belonged to men, sometimes to women, but that tone—nagging, exhausted, bossy, aggrieved—was always the same.

"He isn't here," I—or my brother Joe, or Jake, or my sister, Molly, would say. "He doesn't live here anymore."

Over and over and over again—*We don't know where he is, he doesn't live here anymore.* Each of us must have said it a hundred times that summer.

The collection agents never believed us. "I know he's there," the voice would say. Or, "Put him on the phone, or "I'm going to call your neighbors." There'd be a pause, a rustle, as the agent found a name. "I'm going to call the Kilmartins and ask if his car's in the driveway." The Kilmartins lived to the south of us and rarely even said hello; the Efkins, an older couple with no kids, lived to the north and were friendly. The creditors' failure to pronounce 'Efkin' correctly was one of the many things we tried to laugh about that summer. "Eefkin!" my brother Joe would repeat, shaking his head. "Eefkin!" They were dummies, we thought, not clever enough to get an easy last name right or figure out where our father was and how to get him to do what he'd promised to do. Then again, neither were we.

He's not here, we would say. *No, we don't have another number. No, we don't know where he is.*

You're lying, one of the agents said to my brother, who was eleven at the time.

Didn't anyone teach you that it's wrong to lie? Joe hung up the phone and, tight-lipped, white-faced, walked out of the family room, up the stairs, into his bedroom, and locked his door. He didn't leave for eighteen hours, not even after we knocked and told him not to worry, that he hadn't done anything wrong, that this would all, somehow, be fine.

§

As a lifelong reader, I was used to escaping into stories, where there was an internal logic, where actions had explanations, where things made sense. That summer, I was rarely without a book in my hand. Sometimes, I'd try to imagine what the collectors' stories might be. Maybe to them the world was full of people who ran up bills they had no intention of paying; people who laughed when the phone rang, women and children who would say *He's not here* while winking at a man who was there, bare-chested in the kitchen, maybe tilting a beer bottle to his mouth, laughing smugly at what he'd gotten away with.

No, no, I don't want to talk to you, a male collector yelled at me when I answered the phone. *Put your father on the phone.*

We'd spent years by then knowing our father didn't want to be our parent. That summer, we heard daily from people who told us we had nothing, that we were worth nothing—to them or him or anyone. No matter where you go from there, what you do with your life, what you get, what success you achieve, it is hard to unhear that; hard not to believe it, hard not to find yourself—or, at least, hard for me not to find myself—nodding in agreement when someone says that you're worthless. Throughout the course of my career I have been told by critics and by the literary establishment that my work is trivial and meaningless; dumb, numbing comfort food for silly, frivolous women; empty calories at best, poison at worst; something noxious and toxic and actively injurious to the body of literature. When I hear it, it never sounds like new information, doesn't carry the sting and slap of a fresh insult. It is, instead, the reopening of an old, deep wound; confirmation of a judgment rendered long ago, now motioned and seconded and voted into law.

When I'm awake and thinking, moving around in the world, writing, being a mother, handling the hundreds of tiny details of my life, I don't buy it. I can scoff and roll my eyes, consider the double standards and gender stereotypes that go into those assessments, and weigh them against the voices of the girls and women who've thanked me for my work, who've told me that my books mean something to them. They don't think my work is worthless, I tell myself. They're glad I'm here.

In the daytime, I believe myself. Some nights, though, when it's late and the darkness of old worries presses down, it's another story.

§

Thanks to the Women's Studies course I'd taken the spring of my freshman year at Princeton, I came home that summer determined to reject the gendered norms of the workplace. No traditionally female, pink-collar-ghetto work for me; no nannying or waitressing or answering some man's phone. Instead I got a job at a landscaping company, a move that I hoped would both destabilize the patriarchy and possibly result in noticeable weight loss and a killer tan by September. From seven in the morning until four in the afternoon, in a bright yellow T-shirt, khaki pants, a green-and-yellow baseball cap, and steel-toed work boots, I pushed a giant mower across the wide lawns of the companies whose offices lined the Berlin Turnpike. I drove the truck, filled the mowers' tanks with gas, and gulped quarts of Gatorade as the temperature rose past ninety every afternoon. My hands blistered from spending hours wrapped around the vibrating metal handle of the mower. I got very tan but not appreciably thinner. And I saved every paycheck, forty hours a week times seven dollars an hour, knowing I'd need the money to pay for extras at school—books, shoes, and clothes.

Molly scooped ice cream at Friendly's on Route 44. (This was ironic, given that my sister was then, and remains, only selectively Friendly.) That summer, she served up some truly disturbing Cone Head sundaes to the children of happier families, whose dinners weren't interrupted by the blast of the telephone, the beep and hiss of the answering machine. Jake worked at a country club, carrying golf bags, making small talk with the fathers of his friends who belonged there. *How's your dad?* they'd ask, and Jake, the most socially adroit of the four of us, would just say, *He's fine.*

My mother, a teacher, had the summer off. She swam. When she was home, she was in the water, churning out endless laps of the crawl, back and forth like a metronome, a mile every day. You couldn't hear the phone under water. Even if you could, you'd never have to be the one to answer.

When September came, I couldn't go back to school fast enough. My boyfriend—the older guy I'd fallen for the summer before my senior year of high school and clung to as my family fell apart— drove me to campus and I stood in line to collect the keys to my dorm room. When I got to the front of the line, the woman peered at the ledger in front of her then looked up at me. She conducted a whispered conversation with her supervisor before directing me to the bursar's office. I had to ask for directions. I'd never been there before. The office turned out to be all the way at the other end of campus and I walked uphill, along the slate paths, listening to my classmates call greetings to one another, exchanging hugs and in-formation about their summers. *Oh, we were in the Hamptons . . . Italy, with my mom . . . San Francisco, and then New York.* My hands were still calloused from mowing lawns. I kept them in my pockets and presented myself to a smiling woman behind a desk, who directed me upstairs to an unsmiling man in an office, who told me that I wouldn't be allowed to sign up for classes because no one had sent a check for my tuition.

Do you know how to reach your father? I remember him asking. His office, in an ivy-covered building, had glowing, honey-colored floors and spindly wooden chairs with the university's crest embossed in gold on the headrests. It was, of course, a polite version of the question I'd been getting all summer. I shook my head, reciting my lines. *We don't have another number for him. We don't know where he lives.* I wondered if I could go home, get my landscaping job back, mow lawns until summer was over, rake leaves until it got cold, then learn how to run a snow blower and a plow. I'd get friends to send me the curriculum and the reading lists; I'd be an autodidact, and write my first novel before I turned twenty-five, and wouldn't my dad—not to mention Princeton—be sorry then?

I'd never thought much about money before that summer. Growing up, I'd never even seen a bill with a red border and a LAST NOTICE stamp on the front. Money—for vacations, a pair of used skis or hockey skates from Play It Again Sports, pets and vets and doctors' bills—had always been there, the way there was water when you turned on a tap; light when you flicked a switch. Even if my parents wouldn't pay for the designer clothes I coveted as a teenager, I knew that they could. I'd thought as little about my financial future as I did about my financial present. That fall—maybe even that moment, in the bursar's office—was when I decided that I was going to be rich. Somehow I would earn myself a big, giant pile of money. I didn't want things; didn't imagine myself draped in diamonds or opening the door of my mansion to the camera crews of *Lifestyles of the Rich and Famous.* I wanted security. I wanted to never be pulled out of another line, or receive a single overdue notice in the mail, or feel that sense of dread when the telephone rang. I wanted to never have to worry, to never feel attacked or insecure or worthless, and I believed—foolishly, incorrectly, with a heartbreakingly youthful naivete—that having money meant I never would.

It's true what they say about Ivy League schools: getting in is the hardest part. You have to work hard to get thrown out, even if you're flunking, or a drug addict, or you've had a nervous break-down, or you're broke. My mother explained to the financial aid officers that my father had promised to pay my tuition. They were sympathetic but unmoved as they pointed out that both parents had signed my enrollment forms. They helped us take out private loans, which were all I qualified for. On paper, I was still a doctor's daughter, comfortably middle-class, a girl with a father who should easily be able to fund her degree.

My plan, for as long as I'd had one, had been to go to graduate school. Just as my father had once stepped into the fantasy life his parents had imagined for him, I was ready to step into the life my parents had dreamt for me, and that life included getting a PhD and teaching and publishing papers. It seemed like a good fit for someone who was smart but absentminded; someone who, in her parents' opinion, wasn't entirely suited for the real world. (The story my mother still loves to tell is how I'd read books on the bus on the way to camp, read on the bus on the way home from camp, even read while *boarding* the bus in either direction, and that I once came home missing my shoes. *But she never lost her book!* was the triumphant punch line.)

For the rest of my time at Princeton, it felt like I was stuck in that same head-down, hands-in-my-pocket hurry, like I was rac-ing through campus toward the finish line of my degree. I had a part-time job waitressing at one of Princeton's eating clubs; when a local orchard hired help for a Columbus Day weekend festival, I worked every hour they'd give me. Every spring, after classes ended,

I worked at Princeton's reunions. Two weeks of work could net you a few thousand dollars, enough to permit a six-week unpaid internship. The next summer, I took a train to Washington, DC, where I'd be working for the Fund for the Feminist Majority.

The problem was, my internship started before my check arrived. After three days in DC I was down to my last five bucks. I'd bought bread and peanut butter, but when that ran out I didn't know what I was going to do. I called my mom and asked if she could loan me a hundred dollars, just until my check came in.

She turned me down. "Ask your boss for an advance on your paycheck," she instructed.

Struggling not to panic, I said, "It's an unpaid internship. There is no paycheck."

Fran was serene. "I'm sure if you tell your boss what's going on she'd be able to lend you some money."

Of course I was too embarrassed to ask my boss, a formidable former head of the National Organization for Women, for a loan. Instead, I found a CVS that accepted the for-emergencies-only credit card. I bought cold cuts and canned soup, got a paying, part-time job, and turned down invitations to the movies and museums that weekend because I didn't want to use up a fare on my Metro pass.

Years later, when I asked my mom, in a tone I tried not to make too accusatory, why she couldn't have just sent me some money—even twenty dollars!—she replied that she probably didn't even have twenty bucks to spare. I think, of course, that if it were one of my daughters asking for money, I would have found a way, even as I recognize that what my mother gave me, instead of money, was the gift of resiliency, of knowing that, whatever went wrong, I could count on myself to find a way out.

I graduated from Princeton with highest honors, took the GRE, and got into some excellent schools, both in PhD programs for English and MFAs for writing. I didn't go to graduate school. I went to work instead, for a small newspaper in central Pennsylvania, where I earned $16,000 a year (*You're kidding me*, Fran said, in a flat, incredulous tone, when I told her my salary.). I wanted to get out of the classroom and on with life. I wanted to write, to put my stuff out in the world. I wanted more readers, and a broader platform than academia would allow.

The other reason? I didn't want to take out more loans. Those phone calls had marked me, more deeply than I knew, and I wanted to be making money, even very little, instead of borrowing any more. I burned at the very idea of being in debt. I wanted to get out from under, to be able to help my brothers and my sister. I wanted that great big fat pile of money. Stupid money. Fuck-you money. Fuck-you-DAD money.

§

You don't become a writer to get rich. Still, people got rich doing it. By the late '90s, when I was approaching my thirtieth birthday, I could recite a list of every one of my contemporaries who'd landed the fabled six-figure deal for a novel, every man and woman my age who'd sold a screenplay or a novel or been hired to write for *Saturday Night Live*. I knew it was possible to do the thing I loved the best and get paid, a lot, if you were good at it, if you wrote something wonderful, something that people wanted to read.

All through my twenties, as my mom dragged my dad to court every six or eight months, trying to get him to pay her what he owed, as my sister and brothers struggled through college and then into jobs of their own, I gave myself deadlines. By twenty-five, I wanted a job at a national newspaper. I wanted a column by the time I was twenty-eight, and, by the time I was thirty, I wanted to have my own six-figure deal. Luckily, I went through a bad breakup when I was twenty-eight. I moped for six months, and when I couldn't cry about it anymore, when the sharpness of the pain had dulled to a constant ache of misery, I decided, *This is my story.* The girl who was a lot like me, the guy who was a lot like Satan, the happy ending I never thought I'd have, which included—wait for it—selling a screenplay for a great, big, stupid, fuck-you pile of money. Books like *The Secret*, with the idea that you tell the universe precisely what you want and thus the universe delivers it to you, hadn't yet come into vogue, but I wonder now whether there wasn't something like that at work. I wrote a novel about what I wanted, and then my wish came true . . . But, of course, answered prayers often turn out to be both a blessing and a curse.

You can't always get what you want. In my case, what I got was a kind of fairy-tale bargain, the one where the good fairies gather around a baby's cradle and hand out beauty and kindness and grace and wit, and then the bad fairy says, *But, oh, BTW, you will prick your finger on a spindle and critics will revile you and say you're a terrible writer and also a terrible, self-centered, cruel person; you will have all the money you could ever want, but absolutely no respect. You will never have to worry about paying your bills, but you will hear, at least once a week and sometimes daily, that your work is a cancer on the body of literature. You will have a big, beautiful home in a city you love, full of light, with art on the walls and jewel-colored carpets on the mahogany floors, you will have fresh flowers and eight-hundred-dollar dresses and new cars to drive and a cleaning lady five days a week, but big-name critics will call your work "subliterary," and big-deal writers will sneer at the notion that your books deserve even a smidgen of attention in the* New York Times. *You will be courted by charities and politicians and even your alma mater, all those telephoned requests careful to emphasize how much your gift would matter, how much your support would be worth . . . but when your college asks alumni to come speak or teach writing classes, it will never ask writers like you.*

Would I have taken the deal, knowing what it meant? In the

business of being an author, is it better to be broke but respectable than it is to be rich but dismissed? *And why does it even matter?* I've been asked, more than once—usually by one of the writers on the broke-but-respectable side of things, unpublished or underpublished or underappreciated, well-reviewed but not well-read, one who can't imagine that it's anything other than heaven on the other side of the fence. *You've got money. What could be wrong? Who cares what people are saying? Just laugh all the way to the bank!*

I can't answer them. Shouldn't money be enough? Shouldn't I be able to enjoy what I have, the things I can buy, the summerhouse in Cape Cod, the trips I've taken with my family? Shouldn't I believe the women who love my books as much as I believe the writers and critics who despise them or haven't read them, or despise them without having read them because none of the *right people* say they should? If it's true that, in addition to "subliterary," "worthless," and "delusional," I hear *You changed my life, you helped me when I was in a dark place, you made me feel like I wasn't alone, like there was hope for me, like I mattered, like I could be loved, too*, then shouldn't that matter even more than money in the bank, even more than knowing that my daughters will never be turned away from a class-registration line, never denied their dorm-room keys, never be told that there's something they need that they can't have?

History ought to give me some context. Women's work has always been devalued, seen as less than. "Commercial." *She asks for what she doesn't deserve*, says the privileged white man, who gets both sales and respect—as if privileged white men haven't always been the ones to make those judgments, and those judgments haven't always been in their favor. *Disposable*, say the critics, as if they can see into the future, and know what will be read and what will be ignored, as if they, and not future readers, get to decide *This means something, still. This is worth something to me.*

I know all this. Still, the compliments and the accolades always fade into the background, the praise evaporated almost as soon as it's been uttered. The bad reviews and criticism echo; they linger like scars or like brands. I hear them, over and over, in voices that sound like my father, or like God.

Every time someone says, *You have nothing that matters, you've done nothing that we want,* a piece of me nods in agreement, because they're only affirming what my father taught me, what his creditors confirmed, and it's easier to believe something you already know than it is to try and make yourself believe something new. Even now, when it's summer, when it's the end of the day, when the air smells like grass cuttings and chlorine, when I see the early-evening shadows stretch across the floor, or a certain configuration of trees or slant of sun or when I hear the cough and rumble of a lawn mower being yanked to life, I remember the words that the house used to whisper in D. H. Lawrence's short story, "The Rocking-Horse Winner": "There must be more money! There must be more money!"

In that story, a boy whose parents were living beyond their means rides a rocking horse until it gives him the names of the real live horses that will win races. By betting on the winners, he makes his parents rich—or, at least, he makes them enough to get by, before his final ride, when the rocking horse tells him the name of a fourteen-to-one winner, and the boy dies.

There must be more money, I'll think, and then I'll come back to myself and remember that, actually, I've got enough money, and that no one, no matter what their opinion of my work, can take it away. But every *worthless* is a confirmation of what I was taught so long ago; what I struggle to unbelieve; and I think that the phone will never stop ringing, that it will always be ringing, and that it's never me the caller will want.

LIKE A FISH IN A TWEED SUIT

Jonathan Franzen

in conversation with Manjula Martin

Manjula Martin: What was your first book deal like?

Jonathan Franzen: You know, it was a saner publishing world back then. Nowadays I think *The Twenty-Seventh City* would have gotten a six-figure advance just because, whatever its merits are in hindsight, it was considered an impressive first novel. But when you're spending half a million dollars on a hot first novel, well, that's twenty-four $20,000 advances you're not giving to twenty-four other people.

So you're not a fan of the practice of publishers giving huge advances to authors?
What would be the argument for it?

That the publishing industry needs stars, basically. And the "hot" novels will make enough money to enable the publishing of the rest. Which I'm not saying I agree with, but . . .
The way it used to be is that Farrar, Straus and Giroux made *The Twenty-Seventh City* its lead title in the fall of 1988, and they did that having invested only $20,000 in it. And then I earned good royalties beyond my advance.

That's an earnable advance. That's like seven thousand copies and you've earned out. So between that and some foreign sales I had enough to not worry about money for a couple of years. My then wife and I eventually graduated to a $450 a month apartment. And, you know, she baked our bread; we shopped at the cheapest supermarkets and drank jug wine and Rolling Rock.

Classic.
Yeah, totally classic. But it works. And once you do that for long enough, you just get used to it. I spent quite a bit of the '90s living like the characters in Colson Whitehead's *John Henry Days*, subsisting on food from book parties. I should add that another problem with big advances is that if you don't come close to earning out, your stock goes way down with the next book. I took quite a bit more money for my second novel, *Strong Motion*, because the first book had done well. Then *Strong Motion* did not do well, and the relatively small advance I got for the first two hundred pages of *The Corrections* reflected that. I earned out my advance for *The Corrections* in literally the first week of publication.

At what point did you realize you didn't have to drink the jug wine anymore?
Probably the week *The Corrections* hit number one on the bestseller list. At some point I realized I was going to be picking up restaurant and bar tabs for the foreseeable future. But even then, you know, I lived for another year and a half in a six-hundred-square-foot apartment with [my partner] Kathy.

How did it feel? Was there a moment when you knew "I am successful"?
It's difficult to sort out because so much happened in the fall of 2001. Obviously nationally, but I also got in hot water with Oprah in a hurry, and almost to a man the entire literary community

of America turned against me. So I wasn't entirely clocking the success part.

I was never in writing for the money anyway. My ambition, starting in 1982, was to write critically acclaimed novels, and after publishing a couple of them, I figured, I might not be making a living but I could get a teaching job with a light load at a good school. The money really only mattered all along as a token of fame, a token of recognition. The main thing I was clocking in the fall of 2001 was, *Hey, I had a feeling this novel might do this, and it's doing it.* I could finally relax. A little bit. I didn't have so much to prove. Maybe as important as anything was the sense of being read.

How did you learn about the business side of publishing?
I got some basic pointers in the years when I subscribed to *Poets & Writers* magazine. The rest I've picked up from discussions with my agent and trading notes with my writer friends.

I think the literary novelist who makes money is like a fish in a tweed suit. Flannery O'Connor talks about the fiction writer's concern being "a poverty fundamental to mankind." You lose touch with that impoverishment at your own risk. Edith Wharton stands out as one of the rare really happening novelists who had a fair amount of money.

Not many serious novels end up at number one. Some finely executed, entertaining ones do end up there, along with a lot of really terrible ones.

Define "serious novel."
Read the first five pages. Count clichés. If you find one, the buzzer goes off: It's not a serious novel. A serious novelist notices clichés and eliminates them. The serious novelist doesn't write "quiet as a mouse" or paint the world in clichéd moral terms. You could almost just substitute the adjective "cliché-free" for "serious."

I too have this perception of a literary novelist who makes money, who is both critically and popularly acclaimed, as a unique thing, a rarity—perhaps more of a unicorn than a fish. There's a feeling of resignation among a lot of emerging writers I know, a suspicion that the sort of success you have enjoyed might be impossible because the prospect of publishing as a functional economic industry might be over. Are you the last unicorn?

There are a lot of cliché-free writers, and there are still dozens who make a very good living at it. Alice Munro is a number one bestseller in Canada. Ian McEwan had a string of hits, and so did Cormac McCarthy, belatedly. I'm not the only one.

But are you the *last* one?

Are there people who are twenty years old today who have some hope of that? That depends on the larger economics of book publishing. People will not stop reading books. But I think there's no question that people are reading fewer books than they did thirty years ago—how not, with all the good cable shows and electronic distractions?

The result is that life has gotten much harder for the so-called midlist writer, because people reach for the star writers when their reading time is limited, and when conventional media coverage of novels is shrinking. I think e-books may actually be helping to offset these trends, because they present a lower barrier of investment— it's so easy to try something new, and if you don't like it you can just delete it. The publishers and bookstores, of course, are worried that e-books will take over completely. But the early adopters have already adopted, and the number of e-books as a percentage of all books sold seems to be plateauing.

Let's say the economics hold up more or less as they are now. I don't see any reason to think that the particular kind of literary writer who's dedicated to entertaining as well as to writing without cliché would not continue to have a shot at finding a commercial-sized audience. And the possibility of that larger audience is important, it's part of what kept me in the game long enough to write *The Corrections*. I was probably more ambitious and more competitive than the average writer starting out, and I couldn't help feeling disappointed by the size of the audience I found for my first two books, especially *Strong Motion*.

With regards to ambition, you mentioned a driving motivation early on in your career was being read—fame, recognition.
That's an ego thing that I will cop to but not want to place too much emphasis on.

I think it's legit, though, because I think everyone has that. Most writers want to be famous.
I rationalize my competitive and ego-driven wish for fame as being something that is also good for the novel.

In what way?
When *USA Today* does its annual tiresome "What is life in the culture now?" spread and they list ten TV shows and fifteen websites and five Twitter feeds and a couple of music acts, and there's not a single fiction writer on the list? That is bad for the novel. It's bad for the community of the novel. I mean, writers are horribly envious and so nobody likes stars, we always feel like it's a zero-sum game and whatever stardom somebody else has is being taken directly from us, so we hate the stars. But we also need them. Because the possibility of some level of stardom is what will continue to attract new writers to the game. If you're a linguistically talented twenty-two-year-old, there's a list of things

you can be: you can work in Hollywood, you can be a blogger, etc. And if being a novelist equates to some quaint thing like being a Morris dancer, who's going to choose this? You need the excitement that comes with some people actually being in the public eye.

Do you find being in the public eye exciting? In your interview with the *Paris Review* you spoke about having a fantasy, when you were younger, of being followed around by a camera. Do you remember this?
Yeah, yeah. Turns out to be not so fun. [Laughs.]

But it's also sort of your job now.
Yes, I've appointed myself as one of the spokesmen and public advocates for the cliché-free novel.

As such, you get a lot of what I'll call blowback. Do you make an effort to insulate yourself?
Totally. I haven't googled myself since the fall of 2001. Because I don't experience the blowback firsthand, and rarely even second-hand, I mostly encounter it when I'm trying to find something related to bird-watching on Google. This little headline, "World's Most Annoying Birdwatcher," referring to me, pops up. So that's there to remind me what's out there. But at this point I'd worry more if I weren't being hated. Who said it's the writer's job to be liked by everybody?

That seems to happen pretty consistently with you. The literary world tends to react strongly to things you say in public. It seems beyond being about you as a writer and more about you as . . .
As a psychological object?

Yes, I was going to say a symbol. A symbol of the literary establishment, perhaps. It is consistently fascinating to me how strongly other writers react to you. Since you don't read your press, are you aware of that?

Well, people project things onto people who happen to be visible.

Yes, but do you consider it?

The great thing about the Oprah affair was that all the hatred was right out there. I had about three weeks of enjoying the success I'd always wanted, and then the fire hose of hatred came. [Laughs.]

And when you survive a thing like that, you realize, you know, that it's all just words and it's not going to hurt me. So if anything, I hold back less now. Earlier in my life I might have been afraid to say some of these things, because I didn't want to be disliked. But it's like, boy, is that horse already out of that barn for me.

Right. Like, whatever.

Whatever. Really. Whatever. Which is, I think, what every politician goes through. By the time you get to be even just a state legislator, you've already survived a bunch of vicious campaigns against you. You've learned that, you know, that's just part of the game.

It's interesting that you compare yourself to a politician, because part of being in the position to have everybody talking about you in the first place means you already have power—you're coming from a place of power.

The only power that matters to me—and it matters a lot—is the power of writing. If the writing is weak, everything else is bullshit. But, yeah, sure, people want the famous writer to endorse this and appear at that and support this cause and comment on that current event. It's a kind of power, I guess, but only in a fairly narrow little world. For me, the important thing to do with power is to try to stand up for those who have less of it. My pet projects have to do with threatened migratory birds, illegal hunting of migratory birds—animals that by definition have no voice in the public discussion. I also do my best to promote cliché-free writing by younger writers. I have, my whole career, tried to bring public attention to women writers who belong in the canon and who've been undervalued. People may see me as the man, but I don't feel like I'm working for the man.

Earlier you mentioned Edith Wharton's wealth as a rare privilege for a literary writer to have. But there are other kinds of privilege than money. Consider the VIDA Count, which tallies how many writers of each gender are published in major literary magazines each year, or the debate around lack of reviews of books by writers of color in outlets like the *New York Times*. Can you understand, then, how some writers might look at you and your power and see someone who looks suspiciously like "the man"?
Well, I am a male animal, and there's nothing I can do about that. I can't stop writing and disappear just because someone chooses to project onto me her grievance with a million years of sexist human history. I can only do what I've always done, which is try to be gender-balanced in the books I recommend, the authors I write criticism about, the characters I put into my novels. I wince as much as anyone else does when I read the table of contents of *Harper's* or the *New York Times Book Review* and see mostly male names. The point where I draw the line is when politics starts dictating literary judgments. I don't think we should call pedestrian writing great, or vice versa, just because it makes someone feel better.

I guess I do find it ironic that I'm considered "the man," given

Jonathan Franzen

what I'm doing with my so-called power. What about all the white guys who are using their power to support large multinational corporations, or $50 billion Silicon Valley enterprises, or the Republican Party? Go take on those guys.

Okay, let's talk about those guys. What do you *really* think of Twitter?
[Laughs] I have a particular animus to the social-media world because I feel as if the kinds of writers I care about are just temperamentally not very good at that. Hard to see Kafka tweeting, hard to see Charlotte Bronte self-promoting. If we don't maintain other avenues for establishing a literary reputation and finding some kind of readership—things like traditional publishers and reviewing, where the writer could just be a writer and not have to wear the flak hat, the salesman hat, the editor hat, the publisher hat—if we don't maintain those, then we hand over the literary world to the personality types who are, I would say, less suited for the kind of work I care about.

It could be that my model of literature is simply outmoded, but I feel closer to Joyce with his "silence, exile and cunning." I worry that the ease and incessancy of communication through electronic media short-circuits the process whereby you go into deep isolation with yourself, you withdraw from the world so as to be able to hear the world better and know yourself better, and you produce something unique which you send out into the world and let communicate in a non-discursive way for you.

The author Gabriel Roth—whose novel *The Unknowns* I would certainly call cliché-free—has said he loves Twitter because it's basically a formal way to play with language. It's text.
A great artist can make great work out of anything, even Play-Doh. It doesn't mean Play-Doh is an expressive medium for the ages.

But isn't it possible to structure an online discourse that enables the creation of literature, even for cliché-free or introverted writers?

It's not like I'm militantly opposed to discursive interactive communication. It's fine, it's great. But there's a tipping point you reach where you can't get away from the electronic community, where you become almost physically dependent on it. And that, I persist in thinking, is not compatible with my notion of where terrific literature comes from.

Are you worried because people can't get away from electronic media, or because we may not want to?

I think the model of the new technology is addiction. You're sort of asking, "You can't quit cigarettes, or you just don't want to?"

For me and cigarettes, the answer was actually a bit from column A and a bit from column B. What about journalism, though? You're a journalist as well as a novelist, and journalism as a form is well suited to the electronic space.

It is and it isn't. Where's the pay model? I have many reasons to resent this new electronic world, and one of the big ones is that the people whose job it is to report responsibly are getting kicked out of work, downsized, reduced to half time, having their pay slashed, by this bloodsucking monster squid the Internet. All these blogs—they all need information. Where's the information coming from? Who is paying for the information? The Silicon Valley visionaries say, *Oh, well, we'll crowdsource it*. Yeah, give me a fucking break. As if you therefore don't need people whose job it is to have a beat, to work contacts for years, to understand a subject thoroughly, to put things in context, to be able to distinguish meaningful information from nonsense . . . it's just not doable. And nobody is talking about what happens when the Internet kills journalism.

267

In my experience a lot of people are talking about that. On the Internet.
Good.

But nobody seems to have the answer.
Well, I've got an answer. [Laughs.]

I'm listening.
Um, pay the fucking journalists! Obviously I have a vested interest in this, as someone who lives off royalties, but I think we should put an end to the expectation that stuff be free. I think we're unfortunately at sort of a middle point right now where you have a few blue-chip journalism sources like the *New York Times* and the *New Yorker* that can get away with paywalls. So even there, as in publishing, you have the reasonably well-paid stars and then the unpaid non-stars.

In calling the Internet a "bloodsucking monster squid," I assume you're referring to journalist Matt Taibbi's takedown of Goldman Sachs and the company's role in economic crises. In *The Kraus Project,* you speak with vitriol of "the Internet's accelerating pauperization of freelance writers." How do you make the connection between the tech corporations that have become global economic powers and the economic environment for writers, particularly freelancers and non-stars?
I think the tech corporations are like the nineteenth-century coal magnates, and the freelance writers are like the people slaving in the mines, the only difference being that the tech corporations can't stop congratulating themselves on how they've liberated everybody. I think the Internet should be really strictly regulated, the way the airwaves used to be. If an entire region of the country had its main industry suddenly lose ninety percent of its paying jobs because of

the predatory practices of a different region's industry, you might, if you were the government, step in and say, *We can't actually let this entire region starve. We're going to subsidize prices; we're going to redistribute some income.* Why should Apple shareholders be getting rich while working journalists are getting fired? This is an unjust situation, and the libertarians in Silicon Valley are either moral idiots or liars. They know they're getting away with shit they shouldn't get away with, and all they've got is this idea of libertarianism. That, and the mantra of making the world a better place.

Plus all the money.
Plus all the money. But who knows? It's still early days. It's a scrimmage. Let's see how the game plays out.

THE IF OF IT:
LUNATIC INDEPENDENCE
IN NINE EASY STEPS

Laura Goode

STEP 1: ARROGANCE

Any working artist knows that believing you can make a living through art requires a hubristic, narcissistic, delusional faith that the rules don't apply to you. Steady, reliable monthly income? That shit is for suckers. IRA, W-2, 401(k)? What the fuck do those acronyms even mean?! Your plan is to make art so beautiful that someone will inevitably want to buy it. You can't be bothered with basic logic. The world awaits your dream.

No, but really: It does take a certain kind of arrogance to put art at the forefront of your life. To say, *This is what I do. This is my priority. Everything else is adjacent, in service to this.* This also takes a certain denial of adult realities, as well as the humility to, say, bartend in shitholes, as I did throughout my early twenties. The tension between such arrogance and such humility is why most people who are artists at twenty-two aren't at forty-two.

STEP 2: ACCOMPLICES

One afternoon sometime in 2009, Meera, my college friend and frequent collaborator in lunatic art-making, and I were sitting on her patio, drinking beers, talking about movies.

I've always kind of wanted to write a story about a girl trying to lose her virginity, but in her twenties, Meera said. *There are no movies about girls losing their virginity. Would you ever want to do that?*

Um, we should definitely do that, I said. *Like, right now.*

A year and many conversations later, Meera and I found ourselves on Venice Beach, scribbling an outline of a screenplay in my notebook. Probably everyone around us was doing the same thing, but this did not compromise the wonder of the moment.

STEP 3: LONG, PAINFUL ADJUSTMENT OF EXPECTATIONS

During most of the two years that Meera and I spent writing *Farah Goes Bang*, I was making money from freelance work, Craigslisted household items, and unemployment checks, and she was in film school. This fact—that neither of us had full-time job commitments—allowed us to write. We were broke but not destitute.

We wrote the first draft, just over a hundred pages, in three weeks. Writing had never felt like this, as dialogic, as combustive. We holed up in coffee shops, in her sister's house, in my house, writing all the time: *You take the scene where she sees the hot guy and the squirt gun in the convenience store. I'll take the scene where she shoots the gun.*

Preliminary research revealed no studio would acquire or produce a screenplay about three diverse women trying to discover America and themselves through politics and sex. And no one was going to just cough up a million dollars so two girls who had never written or made a feature film could play around with learning how to make one themselves. Private investors tend to balk, with good reason, at the film industry, and with less good reason, at filmmakers with breasts.

If we wanted our screenplay to become an actual movie, it became clear that we were going to have to grovel for every dollar ourselves. So we started thinking about how our script could be produced cheaply. We mined our creativity for a story that could be shot for $100,000 or less. We cut the priciest elements—an elaborate wedding, a motorized gazebo, a Bollywood dance sequence—and, eventually, we had the story we had always meant to tell: a travelogue of one's twenties, composed of authentic relationships, wild idealism, and purposeful poverty. Those, after all, were our only assets.

STEP 4: BUSKING ON THE INTERNET

We launched a Kickstarter campaign for $75,000. We're members of the Facebook generation. Other people had done this. Why couldn't we?

I obsessed together a thirty-day strategy for the campaign. We collected six thousand e-mail addresses. I sent so many Facebook messages that Facebook thought I was a spambot and threatened to shut down my account. "I want this more than I've ever wanted anything," I wrote to people over and over again.

During the campaign's last two weeks, I was e-mailing/Facebook-messaging/tweeting upward of five hundred times a day. I refreshed our Kickstarter page every minute. And all the while, we were planning a production: auditioning actors, negotiating with agents, hiring our crew, organizing our equipment. I began to lose my mind a little bit.

I was driving across the San Francisco–Oakland Bay Bridge when I refreshed the Kickstarter page (PSA: Don't crowdfund and drive) and saw that we were about to hit our $75,000 goal. People had started to donate more and more rapidly, hoping that theirs would be the donation that put us over the top. I pounded the steering wheel, grinning. We were making a motherfucking movie.

We'd raised $81,160 in total. I turned off my phone, crawled into bed, and slept peacefully for four hours.

My rest period was short-lived. I said good-bye to my husband for two months and got on the 5 South: just another blonde with a carful of dreams, heading for Los Angeles to make a movie.

STEP 5: MANIPULATING OTHERS

It's best to know supremely talented people before you embark on a flight of fancy like this, and if you're prepared to exploit every talent and connection they have, well, then you might just have the balls it takes to write and produce your own independent film.

Meera and I assembled a five-spoked producer/director wheel we later came to call the Charm Squad: myself, Meera, and our other producers, Danielle, Liz, and Fish. Here, assembled, was a crew of competent, confident young women who didn't look bad either, and short of actual handjobbing, we worked this advantage to the hilt. We were endearing, we had next to no money, and if we could use our likeability to get a cheaper rate on the next day's location, who were we not to take it?

The best and definitely most fun route to thrifty art-making lies in talented, persuasive people. Fish and Danielle sweet-talked a gas station in Oxnard into letting us change their sign to 2004 gas prices, and its lovely owner, Moe, threw in free beef jerky and played a bit role for us to boot. Liz temporarily evicted her three roommates so we could shoot at her apartment. I offered cold sodas and friendly small talk to passing cops in the hopes of distracting them from our unpermitted shooting location. Danielle, Fish, Meera, and I all nobly drank at a dive bar until we convinced its owner to let us shoot there.

In the spirit of the story, we built a mobile and modular production, inexperienced but committed, young but gutsy. Though the FGB road trip spanned eight script states, we shot seven in LA and the eighth on my family's property in Wisconsin. Though

Laura Goode

a road-trip movie about canvassing door-to-door for a candidate necessitates a cast of dozens, we signed a SAG ultra-low-budget contract, structured almost all the supporting roles into one-day shoots, and persuaded our incredible cast members to work for $100 a day. We found other young, hungry, and impatient film-makers to collaborate on the production, supplementing their meager salaries with the promise of a once-in-a-lifetime opportunity. See Step 1.

STEP 6: SURMOUNTING BASIC NEEDS

Film production runs on two primary resources: human and material. I was tasked with overextending both. Under the extreme conditions of production—eighteen-hour days, extended sleep deprivation, punishing LA summer heat, intravenous Diet Coke use, chain-smoking—you see a lot of quirks, talents, and Achilles' heels come out in people. For example, Fish's standard Starbucks order is seven espresso shots over ice topped off with soy milk in a venti cup; bringing her one is like throwing bacon to a dog. Danielle goes weak in the presence of cupcakes; our director of photography, Paul, existed solely on gummy bears for five weeks straight. For me, being a producer was all about learning how to throw people just enough bacon bits of affection, indulgence, and encouragement that I could keep asking them to do the unthinkable.

Then there are the material resources. Here is a list of ridiculous things that happened on our set because we had no money:

- The whole company having to vacate a parking lot and find a replacement parking lot because (a) there was a kid smoking crack ten feet away from us, (b) we needed to call the cops because he was acting threatening toward us and our camera equipment, and (c) we needed to leave before the cops arrived because we had no permit to be shooting there.

- My stealing a FIREWORKS FOR SALE sign from the side of a country highway in Wisconsin so we wouldn't have to schlep everyone thirty miles away to shoot at the fireworks store.
- All of us calling in every single fucking favor we could pull out of our hats: Can you be an extra at 6:00 A.M. on Friday morning? Can we shoot at your parents' house? Can you donate your pre-2004 cell phone?
- Meera and I not getting paid anything, ever, up to the date of this publication, for writing, directing, producing, editing, or promoting the film.

I feel compelled here to state the obvious: There is nothing about making an independent film that is sustainable financially or physically. Anyone possessed of logic or reason would wisely run in the opposite direction. See Step 1.

STEP 7: SITTING ALONE IN A DARK ROOM WITH YOUR BRILLIANCE

About an hour after giving birth to my eight-pound, fourteen-ounce son without the aid of an epidural, the hospital heroin they'd hooked up to my arm after he was out had kicked in, the doctor had finished stitching me up, and she told me I could take my legs out of the stirrups they'd been straining in for the last three hours of pushing. Finishing production felt like finally taking my legs out of those motherfucking stirrups.

Thankfully, my son arrived in one piece. A film does not. Our task was far from finished: We had something like eighty hours of footage to sift into a ninety-minute movie, and we had to come up with more money to do it. The good news was that it wasn't my job to edit the film.

The bad news was that we needed another $75,000 to fund post-production.

So while Meera slashed together rough cuts for the major festival deadlines (Sundance, September; SXSW, October; Tribeca, November) in a dark, hot editing bay, I e-mailed everyone I could think of in our personal and professional networks, looking for money. I went to lame networking events. I worked every impressive person I knew for introductions to other impressive people. I hustled about $30,000 from investors, and we parceled out the rest of our post-production costs (color correction, musical scoring, sound editing, licensing) as slowly as possible on yet more wings and promises, buying me a few more months to raise the remaining $45,000.

By the New Year things were getting scary. I'd ginned up another $15,000, but we wouldn't be able to finish the film if I couldn't find anyone to invest the last $30,000.

Then, one otherwise ordinary day in late February, we got into the Tribeca Film Festival. Finally, a lifeline. An affirmation. We joy-cried.

Suddenly, our phones were ringing off the hook. Sales agents and investors we'd been trying to reach for months were calling us. I raised the $30,000 I'd been chasing for six months in three weeks. I remember very little about this period, so filled was it with meetings and calls and errands, but I do remember lolling in and out of consciousness while watching *Extreme Couponing* on Netflix during a forty-eight-hour marathon sound-editing session. How apropos: We were the extreme couponers of independent film.

STEP 8: MADDENING LACK OF RESOLUTION

We premiered at Tribeca to a sold-out audience and respectable reviews. We had a raging after-party where my dad held court in the VIP lounge of a Chelsea club until 1:00 A.M. At a Tribeca brunch for women in film, where we met Mira Sorvino, Glenn Close, Anna Wintour, Sandra Bernhard, and various other lady luminaries, Meera was awarded the first Nora Ephron Prize for excellence in writing and directing by a woman. The $25,000 that came with the Nora allowed us, blessedly, to retire all the remaining debt we had from making the film: credit cards, outstanding payments, a replacement for Meera's ailing computer. We left Tribeca with a suitcase full of great press, connections, and hope of finding distribution for the film.

And then.

The deafening silence. The phone, not ringing. That ghostly echo you hear the moment after the phone stops ringing, your ears remembering how, once, it rang.

We rode out the not-ringing for a year after Tribeca, realizing, again, that no one was going to deliver us from our own independence: that just as we had risen to the task of writing, producing, editing, and premiering the film ourselves, so were we now tasked with distributing it through our own clout and resources. We pulled up our big-girl pants and partnered with Seed&Spark, the first 360-degree independent crowdfunding and distribution company for microbudget filmmakers, to release the film on iTunes, Amazon, Google Play, Vimeo, and S&S in April 2015. And then, one day, there it was: our film in the permanent imprint of the Internet, five years of dreaming in one discrete link. It didn't make us famous. It didn't make us rich. But it was ours. No one would deliver us from our own independence, so instead we stood up and claimed it.

I'm still the cocky, hubristic dreamer I was when Meera and I sat on Venice Beach and outlined the story we most needed to tell. But I'm still far from living comfortably on the fruits of my labor. I'd be lying if I said I wasn't a little more world-weary now. There isn't always—almost ever—a million dollars waiting at the end of the very best thing you ever did.

STEP 9: THE IF OF IT

I like to read poetry to my son. I'm particularly fond of "If—" by Rudyard Kipling. Jed's still just a baby and doesn't understand why I always break down crying in the middle of this poem:

> *If you can make one heap of all your winnings*
> *And risk it on one turn of pitch-and-toss,*
> *And lose, and start again at your beginnings*
> *And never breathe a word about your loss;*
> *If you can force your heart and nerve and sinew*
> *To serve your turn long after they are gone,*
> *And so hold on when there is nothing in you*
> *Except the Will which says to them: "Hold on!"*

If I choke up a little reading these lines to my sweet, bewildered baby, it's not because they make me bitter, or sad, or regretful. It's because they fill me with such joy and gratitude that Meera and I dug up the grit to live them; it's because we'll never have to wonder what might have happened if we had risked everything to tell the story we most needed to tell.

The if of it is beautiful. All the gravitas, the risk's reward, the odyssey lies in the if. Answering the if is where the work gets done. I lived the if, and I live it still, continuing the hustle, dreaming the next dream, passing it on to my son. I'll never be sorry.

CONTRIBUTORS

Nell Boeschenstein teaches creative writing at Sweet Briar College in Virginia. She is a former producer for *Fresh Air* hosted by Terry Gross and *BackStory with the American History Guys*. Her writing has appeared in *The Rumpus*, *This Recording*, the *Guardian*, and elsewhere. "Not a Complaint" copyright © 2013 by Nell Boeschenstein. This piece originally appeared online in *Scratch*.

Sari Botton is a writer and editor living in upstate New York. She edited the award-winning anthology *Goodbye to All That: Writers on Loving and Leaving New York*, for Seal Press, and its *New York Times* best-selling follow-up, *Never Can Say Goodbye: Writers on Their Unshakable Love for New York*, for Touchstone Books/Simon & Schuster. Botton is a columnist for *The Rumpus* and Longreads, and her writing has appeared in the *New York Times*, the *Village Voice*, *New York* magazine, *Harper's BAZAAR*, *W*, *Women's Wear Daily*, *Billboard*, the *New York Daily News*, *Drinking Diaries*, *This Recording*, and other publications. She is a partner in TMI Project, a nonprofit that empowers at-risk and marginalized teens and adults through workshops in memoir writing and live storytelling. "Ghost Stories" copyright © 2014 by Sari Botton. This piece originally appeared online in *Scratch*.

Susie Cagle has written and drawn for the *New York Times*, the *Guardian*, ProPublica, and many others. She loves to talk about money. "Economies 101" copyright © 2017 by Susie Cagle.

Alexander Chee is the author of the novels *Edinburgh* and *The Queen of the Night*. He is a contributing editor to the *New Republic*, a critic at large for the *Los Angeles Times*, and an editor at large for the *Virginia Quarterly Review*. He lives in New York City. "The Wizard" copyright © 2017 by Alexander Chee.

Colin Dickey is the author of, most recently, *Ghostland*, a cultural history of haunted places in America. He is also the author of *Cranioklepty: Grave Robbing and the Search for Genius*, and *Afterlives of the Saints: Stories from the Ends of Faith*. He is the coeditor (with Nicole Antebi and Robby Herbst)

279

of *Failure! Experiments in Social and Aesthetic Practices* and (with Joanna Ebenstein) *The Morbid Anatomy Anthology.* His work has also appeared in *Cabinet, The Believer, LA Review of Books*, and he is a regular contributor to *Lapham's Quarterly.* "The Mercenary Muse" copyright © 2017 by Colin Dickey.

Julia Fierro is the author of the novels *Cutting Teeth* (St. Martin's Press, 2014) and the forthcoming *The Gypsy Moth Summer* (St. Martin's Press, 2017). A graduate of the Iowa Writers' Workshop, Julia's work has been published in *The Millions, Poets & Writers, Flavorwire, BuzzFeed, Glamour, TimeOut New York, Psychology Today*, and other publications. She founded The Sackett Street Writers' Workshop in 2002, and it has since become a creative home to over three thousand writers. Sackett Street was named a "Best NYC Writing Workshop" by the *Village Voice, TimeOut New York*, and *Brooklyn* magazine, and a "Best MFA-Alternative" by *Poets & Writers* and the *L Magazine*. Julia lives in Brooklyn and Los Angeles with her husband and their two children. "Owning This" copyright © 2017 by Julia Fierro.

Jonathan Franzen is the author of *Purity* and four other novels, most recently *The Corrections* and *Freedom*, and five works of nonfiction and translation, including *Farther Away* and *The Kraus Project*, all published by Farrar, Straus and Giroux. He is a member of the American Academy of Arts and Letters, the German Akademie der Künste, and the French Ordre des Arts et des Lettres. A version of this interview originally appeared online in *Scratch.*

Roxane Gay is the author of the books *Ayiti, An Untamed State, Bad Feminist*, and *Difficult Women.* Her writing has appeared or is forthcoming in *Best American Mystery Stories 2014, Best American Short Stories 2012, Best Sex Writing 2012, A Public Space, McSweeney's, Tin House* magazine, *Oxford American, American Short Fiction, West Branch, Virginia Quarterly Review, NOON*, the *New York Times Book Review, Bookforum, Time*, the *Los Angeles Times*, the *Nation, The Rumpus, Salon*, and many others. A version of this interview originally appeared online in *Scratch.*

Laura Goode is the cowriter and producer of the feature film *Farah Goes Bang*, which premiered at the Tribeca Film Festival in 2013, as well as the author of the novel *Sister Mischief* (Candlewick Press, 2011). Her essays, poems, and fiction have appeared in numerous publications and anthologies, and she writes the Antiheroines column for *BRIGHT IDEAS* magazine, where she is a contributing editor. She lives in San Francisco. "The If of It: Lunatic Independence in Nine Easy Steps" copyright © 2015 by Laura Goode. A prior version of this piece originally appeared online in 2015 in *Scratch* as "Betting on If."

Emily Gould is the author of *Friendship*, a novel; and *And The Heart Says Whatever*, an essay collection. With Ruth Curry she co-operates Emily Books, a subscription-based feminist publishing project. "Unlikeable" copyright © 2017 by Emily Gould.

Harmony Holiday, poet and choreographer, is the author of *Negro League Baseball* (Fence Books, 2011), winner of the Motherwell Poetry Prize; *Go Find Your Father/A Famous Blues* (Ricochet, 2015), and *Hollywood Forever* (Fence Books, 2016). Holiday curates the Afrosonics archive of Jazz Poetics and audio culture as well as a fantastic blog, *nonstophome*. She teaches at Otis College in Los Angeles and has a BA from the University of California, Berkeley and an MFA from Columbia University. She runs a boutique production house devoted to the crossing between archiving, improvisation, myth, and black music. "Love for Sale" copyright © 2017 by Harmony Holiday.

Nick Hornby is the author of seven internationally best-selling novels (*Funny Girl, High Fidelity, About a Boy, How to Be Good, A Long Way Down, Slam*, and *Juliet, Naked*) and several works of nonfiction including *Fever Pitch, Songbook*, and *Ten Years in the Tub*. He has written screenplay adaptions of Lynn Barber's *An Education* and Colm Tóibín's *Brooklyn*, both of which were nominated for Academy Awards, and Cheryl Strayed's *Wild*. He lives in London. A version of this interview originally appeared online in *Scratch*.

Leslie Jamison was born in Washington, DC, and grew up in Los Angeles. She has worked as a baker, an office temp, an innkeeper, a tutor, and a medical actor. A graduate of Harvard College and the Iowa Writers' Workshop, she is currently finishing a doctoral dissertation at Yale. She is the best-selling author of *The Empathy Exams*, and her work has appeared in *Harper's, Oxford American, A Public Space, Virginia Quarterly Review*, and *The Believer*. She currently resides in Brooklyn, New York. "Against 'Vs.'" copyright © 2014, 2017 by Leslie Jamison. A different version of this piece was originally published online in 2014 in the *New Republic* as "Which Creates Better Writers: An MFA Program, or NYC?"

Contributors

Porochista Khakpour was born in Tehran, raised in Los Angeles, and lives in New York City. She is the author of a forthcoming memoir (Harper Perennial, 2017) and the novels *The Last Illusion* (Bloomsbury, 2014)—a 2014 "Best Book of the Year" according to NPR, *Kirkus Reviews*, Buzzfeed, PopMatters, Electric Literature, and more—and *Sons and Other Flammable Objects* (Grove, 2007)—the 2007 California Book Award winner in "First Fiction," one of the *Chicago Tribune*'s "Fall's Best," and a *New York Times* "Editor's Choice." Her writing has appeared in or is forthcoming in *Harper's*, the *New York Times*, the *Los Angeles Times*, the *Wall Street Journal*, Al Jazeera America, *Bookforum*, *Slate*, *Salon*, *Spin*, the *Daily Beast*, *Elle*, and many other publications around the world. She is currently writer in residence at Bard College. "Portrait of the Artist as a Debut Novelist" copyright © 2008 by Porochista Khakpour. A different version of this piece was published in 2008 in *Canteen*.

Austin Kleon is the *New York Times* best-selling author of three illustrated books: *Steal Like An Artist*, *Newspaper Blackout*, and *Show Your Work!* His latest release is *The Steal Like An Artist Journal: A Notebook For Creative Kleptomaniacs*. His work has been translated into over twenty languages and featured on NPR's *Morning Edition*, *PBS NewsHour*, and in the *New York Times* and the *Wall Street Journal*. *New York* magazine called his work "brilliant," the *Atlantic* called him "positively one of the most interesting people on the Internet," and the *New Yorker* said his poems "resurrect the newspaper when everybody else is declaring it dead." He speaks about creativity in the digital age for organizations such as Pixar, Google, SXSW, TEDx, and the *Economist*. He grew up in the cornfields of Ohio, and now he lives in Austin, Texas, with his wife and sons. Visit him online at www.austinkleon.com. A version of this interview originally appeared online in *Scratch*.

Kiese Laymon is a black southern writer, born and raised in Jackson, Mississippi. He is the author of the novel *Long Division* and a collection of essays, *How to Slowly Kill Yourself and Others in America*. Laymon has written essays and stories for numerous publications including *Esquire*, *ESPN the Magazine*, *Oxford American*, *Colorlines*, NPR, *Gawker*, Truthout, Longman's *Hip Hop Reader*, *The Best American Nonrequired Reading*, *Guernica*, *Mythium*, and *Politics and Culture*. His memoir, *Heavy*, and a novel called *And So On* are forthcoming from Scribner. "You Are the Second Person" copyright © 2013 by Kiese Laymon. Originally published in 2013 in *How to Slowly Kill Yourself and Others in America*.

J. Robert Lennon is the author of two story collections, *Pieces for the Left Hand* and *See You in Paradise*, and seven novels, including *Mailman, Familiar*, and *Happyland*. He holds an MFA from the University of Montana, and has published short fiction in the *New Yorker, Harper's, Playboy, Granta*, the *Paris Review, Electric Literature*, and elsewhere. He has been anthologized in *Best American Short Stories, Best American Nonrequired Reading*, and *The O. Henry Prize Stories*, and his story "The Rememberer" inspired the detective series *Unforgettable*. He cohosts the podcast *Lunch Box*, with poet Ed Skoog. His book reviews have appeared in the *New York Times Book Review*, the *Guardian*, the *Globe and Mail*, and the *London Review of Books*. He lives in Ithaca, New York, where he teaches writing at Cornell University. "Write to Suffer, Publish to Starve" copyright © 2017 by J. Robert Lennon.

Yiyun Li grew up in Beijing and came to the United States in 1996. She is the author of *A Thousand Years of Good Prayers; The Vagrants; Gold Boy, Emerald Girl*; and *Kinder Than Solitude*. She is the recipient of the Frank O'Connor International Short Story Award, the PEN/Hemingway Award, the Whiting Writers' Award, and the Guardian First Book Award. In 2007, *Granta* named her one of the best American novelists under thirty-five. Her work has appeared in the *New Yorker, A Public Space, The Best American Short Stories*, and *The O. Henry Prize Stories*, among others. She teaches writing at the University of California, Davis, and lives in Oakland, California, with her husband and their two sons. A version of this interview originally appeared online in *Scratch*.

Malinda Lo is the author of the young adult novels *Ash, Huntress, Adaptation*, and *Inheritance*. *Ash* was a finalist for the William C. Morris YA Debut Award, the Andre Norton Award for YA Science Fiction and Fantasy, the Mythopoeic Fantasy Award, and was a *Kirkus* Best Book for Children and Teens. She has been a three-time finalist for the Lambda Literary Award. Malinda's nonfiction has been published by the *New York Times Book Review*, NPR, the *Huffington Post, The Toast*, the *Horn Book*, and *AfterEllen*. She lives in Massachusetts with her partner. Her website is www.malindalo.com. "A Sort of Fairy Tale" copyright © 2017 by Malinda Lo.

Cari Luna is the author of *The Revolution of Every Day*, which won the 2015 Oregon Book Award for Fiction. Her writing has appeared in *Salon, Jacobin, Electric Literature, The Rumpus, PANK*, and elsewhere. She lives in Portland, Oregon. "Five Years in the Wilderness" copyright © 2015 by Cari Luna. This piece originally appeared online in *Scratch*.

Contributors

Nina MacLaughlin lives in Cambridge, Massachusetts, where she works as a writer and a carpenter. Her first book, *Hammer Head: The Making of a Carpenter*, was published in 2015 by W. W. Norton. "With Compliments" copyright © 2017 by Nina MacLaughlin.

Rachael Maddux is a writer and editor whose work has appeared in *Oxford American, Guernica, Matter, Best American Travel Writing 2015*, and elsewhere. She lives in Atlanta. "On Staying Hungry" copyright © 2014, 2017 by Rachael Maddux. A different version of this piece originally appeared online in 2014 in *Scratch* as "Hunger."

Manjula Martin is the founder of *Who Pays Writers?* and *Scratch* magazine. She is the managing editor of *Zoetrope: All-Story*. Her writing has appeared in the *Virginia Quarterly Review* online, *Pacific Standard, Aeon, Hazlitt, The Millions*, The Billfold, and *The Rumpus*, and she wrote The Dough, a series about creative professionals and money, for *The Toast*. She has also been a bookseller, waitress, receptionist, personal assistant, sign installer, and copywriter. "The Best Work in Literature" copyright © 2013 by Manjula Martin. Originally published online in 2013 in the *Virginia Quarterly Review*.

Kate McKean is a literary agent in Brooklyn, New York. She earned her master's in fiction writing at the University of Southern Mississippi. "The Insider" copyright © 2017 by Kate McKean.

Caille Millner is the author of a memoir, *The Golden Road: Notes on My Gentrification*, which won the Barnes & Noble Emerging Writers Award and was listed as one of the *San Francisco Chronicle*'s Notable Books of the Year. Her fiction has appeared in *Zyzzyva* and *Joyland*. Her nonfiction has appeared in the *Los Angeles Review of Books* and *A New Literary History of America* (Harvard University Press). She lives in San Francisco. This interview originally appeared online in *Scratch*.

Meaghan O'Connell is a columnist for *New York* magazine's The Cut and her book of essays, *And Now We Have Everything*, is forthcoming from Little, Brown. "Sad Birth Lady™" copyright © 2017 by Meaghan O'Connell.

Daniel José Older is the author of the Bone Street Rumba urban fantasy series from Penguin's Roc Books and the young adult novel *Shadowshaper* (Scholastic, 2015), which was shortlisted for the Kirkus Prize in Young Readers' Literature. He coedited the Locus- and World Fantasy–nominated anthology *Long Hidden: Speculative Fiction from the Margins of History*. You can find Older's thoughts on writing, read dispatches from his decade-long career as an NYC paramedic, and hear his music at ghoststar.net/ and @djolder on Twitter and YouTube. "Diversity is Not Enough" copyright © 2014 by Daniel José Older. Originally published online in 2014 on Buzzfeed.

Susan Orlean has been a staff writer at the *New Yorker* since 1992. She is the author of seven books, including *Rin Tin Tin, Saturday Night*, and *The Orchid Thief*, which was made into the Academy Award–winning film *Adaptation*. She lives with her family and her animals in Los Angeles and may be reached at SusanOrlean.com and Twitter.com/SusanOrlean. This interview originally appeared online in *Scratch*.

Mallory Ortberg is the cofounder of the *Toast* and the author of *Texts From Jane Eyre*. "FAQ: How to Buy a Home" copyright © 2017 by Mallory Ortberg.

Richard Rodriguez is the author of the autobiographies *Hunger of Memory, Days of Obligation: An Argument with My Mexican Father* (1992), and *Brown: The Last Discovery of America* (2002). He is an editor at Pacific News Service and a contributing editor for *Harper's Magazine, U.S. News & World Report*, and the Sunday Opinion section of the *Los Angeles Times*. He has published numerous articles in the *New York Times*, the *Wall Street Journal*, the *American Scholar, Time, Mother Jones*, and the *New Republic*. Rodriguez received a 1997 George Foster Peabody Award for his *NewsHour Essays on American Life*. He lives in San Francisco. This interview originally appeared online in *Scratch*.

Choire Sicha is cofounder of the *Awl*. A two-time editor of *Gawker*, he has written for the *New York Times* and the *Los Angeles Times* as well as a suspiciously large number of magazines exactly one time. He lives in Brooklyn. "Monetization" copyright © 2017 by Choire Sicha.

Sarah Smarsh's writing on the American working class, public policy, and socioeconomic boundaries has appeared in the *New Yorker* and *Harper's* online, the *Guardian, The Believer, Guernica, Vela, Creative Nonfiction*, the *Texas Observer*, and others. Her essay "Poor Teeth," for *Aeon*, was selected as notable in *The Best American Essays 2015*. A former grant writer and development director for social service agencies serving low-income families, Smarsh chaired campus diversity initiatives as a writing professor and now

Contributors

advises I'm First, a national organization championing first-generation college students. Her book *In the Red*, on the American poor and her upbringing in rural Kansas, will be published by Scribner in 2017. She lives in Kansas and Texas. "The Jump" copyright © 2017 by Sarah Smarsh.

Cheryl Strayed is the author of the international best seller *Wild: From Lost to Found on the Pacific Crest Trail*, which was the first selection for Oprah's Book Club 2.0 and became an Oscar-nominated film starring Reese Witherspoon; *Tiny Beautiful Things: Advice on Love and Life from Dear Sugar*; the novel *Torch*; and *Brave Enough*, a book of quotes. Her writing has appeared in *The Best American Essays*, the *New York Times Magazine, The Rumpus,* the *Washington Post Magazine, Vogue,* the *Missouri Review, Creative Nonfiction,* the *Sun,* and elsewhere. She lives in Portland, Oregon. A version of this interview originally appeared online in *Scratch.*

Jennifer Weiner is the #1 *New York Times* best-selling author of twelve books. With over twelve million copies in print in thirty-six countries, her books have spent a combined total of more than five years on the *New York Times* bestseller list. Weiner published her debut novel, *Good in Bed*, in 2001. She went on to write *In Her Shoes* (2002), which was made into a major motion picture starring Cameron Diaz, Toni Collette, and Shirley MacLaine; *Little Earthquakes* (2004); *Goodnight Nobody* (2005); the short story collection *The Guy Not Taken* (2006); *Certain Girls* (2008); *Best Friends Forever* (2009); *Fly Away Home* (2010); *Then Came You* (2011); *The Next Best Thing* (2012); *All Fall Down* (2014), *Who Do You Love* (2015), and the essay collection *Hungry Heart: Adventures in Life, Love, and Writing* (2016). Weiner grew up in Connecticut and graduated with a degree in English literature from Princeton University. She worked as a newspaper reporter in central Pennsylvania, Kentucky, and Philadelphia, where she wrote a series of popular columns for the *Philadelphia Inquirer.* She is a contributing opinion writer for the *New York Times Sunday Review.* "Worth" copyright © 2016 by Jennifer Weiner. Originally published in 2016 in *Hungry Heart* by Jennifer Weiner.

ACKNOWLEDGMENTS

Thanks are foremost due to this book's contributors, who by now have probably said yes to me one or two more times than any writer should say yes to any low-paying gig. I am filled with infinite gratitude and respect for all the writers and readers who have been a part of *Scratch* magazine and *Who Pays Writers?* over the past five years.

Profound thanks go to the pros who helped make this idea into an actual book—Kate McKean, Millicent Bennett, and Julianna Haubner, and everyone on Team *Scratch* at Simon & Schuster. Thanks to the members of the Blood Moon writing group, who always reminded me that writing is more important than publishing: Katie Coyle, Brandon Petry, Melissa Graeber, Arianna Stern, Kate Garklavs, Melissa Chandler, Phillip Britton, Justin Bagby, and the Royal Baby. For space and time, The San Francisco Writers Grotto and the Mechanics Institute Library have been invaluable. Thanks to Kathy Chetkovich, Blake Eskin, Lydia Kiesling, Caille Millner, and Ted Weinstein for guidance, gossip, and coffee dates.

I'm grateful to Michael Ray and Francis Coppola for giving me the best day job ever. Sean Strub taught me everything I know about publishing twenty years ago, even though I probably didn't realize it at the time. And to my parents, Mary Kay, Orin, and Stephanie, who taught me to read and write and think: Thanks, fam.

To Max: Thank you for the Year of the Book, and for all the other years too.